50 YEARS

lonely

DEVON &
CORNWALL

Dartmoor,
Exmoor &
North Devon
p99

Exeter &
East Devon
p47

North Cornwall &
Bodmin Moor
p161

South & East
Cornwall
p131

Plymouth &
South Devon
p67

West Cornwall &
the Isles of Scilly
p187

Oliver Berry, Emily Luxton

CONTENTS

Wimbleball Lake, Exmoor (p114)

Toolkit

Storybook

St Agnes (p168)

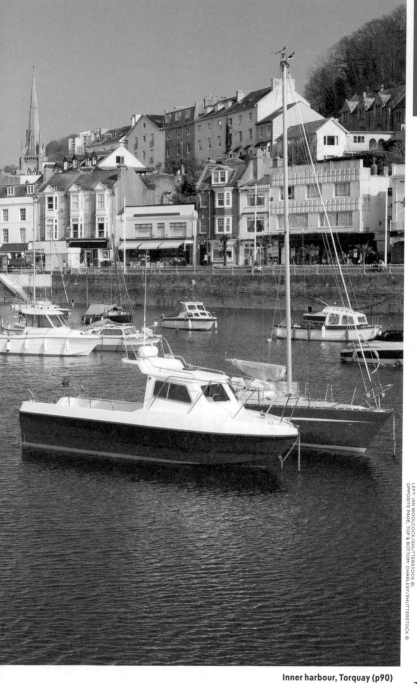

Inner harbour, Torquay (p90)

IAN WOOLCOCK/SHUTTERSTOCK ©

Gwithian and Godrevy (p196)

DEVON & CORNWALL
THE JOURNEY BEGINS HERE

I've spent 20 years wandering around the world, but no matter how long I'm away or how far I travel, somehow I always end up shipwrecked back where I started – in Cornwall, my home county. I know the southwest better than anywhere else on the planet, but I still find surprises every time I walk out of my door. That's the beauty of this place: there always seems to be another cliff to walk, an unknown cove to climb down to, a new tidal pool to paddle in or pub in which to sink a pint. Whether it's walking Dartmoor's tors, cycling on Exmoor, watching the waves over Mount's Bay or getting completely lost on Scilly, it's a land of endless adventure. And though everyone reckons summer's the best time, it's winter I prefer: when the winds whip up, the fog rolls in and the sea gets restless, that's when you get a glimpse of the region's granite soul.

Oliver Berry

@olivertomberry

My favourite experience is walking the wild stretch of coast from Botallack to Zennor. It doesn't get more epic than this: mine stacks, monuments, coves, cliffs, caves, and a cracking pub to end the day.

WHO GOES WHERE

Our second writer and expert chooses the place that,
for them, defines Devon & Cornwall

At first glance, there is a harshness to Dartmoor's landscapes that some might think hard to love. But there's something about these wide, windswept moors – such as Combestone Tor (p110, pictured above) – with their scrub grass shorn to stubble by free-roaming sheep. There is wild beauty, and a whispered promise of adventure: you feel it amid the tangles of shivering purple heather and in the soft silence of the moss-carpeted woodlands. I've travelled the globe, but that untamed land still thrills me like nowhere else.

Emily Luxton

@em_luxton

Emily is a writer and travel blogger focusing on solo female travel and adventure.

0 — 50 km
0 — 25 miles

ATLANTIC
OCEAN

Lundy Island
Spot puffins, wild ponies and seals (p125)

Lundy Island

Gwithian and Godrevy Towans
Epic beach walks among the dunes at sunset (p168)

St Ives
Polish up your painting skills (p192)

Boscastle
Tintagel
Port Isaac
Polzeath
Padstow
Wadebridge
Bodmin
Bodmin Moor

Geevor
Brave the darkness of an old tin mine (p199)

Newquay

Perranporth
St Austell

Portreath
Truro

Penzance
The southwest's most stunning swimming pool (p201)

St Ives
Hayle
Redruth
Falmouth

Penzance
Helston

Land's End
Mousehole
Porthleven
The Lizard

Mullion

Isles of Scilly

St Michael's Mount
Pilgrimage to an iconic island abbey (p205)

Eden Project
Jungle plants and space-age greenhouses (p157)

Falmouth
Sea shanties, sail boats and a maritime museum (p136)

WALES

CARDIFF ✪

Severn Estuary

Bristol ◉

Dartmoor National Park
Hike tors and trails in wild landscapes (p104)

Weston-super-Mare

Bristol Channel

Bridgwater Bay

Burnham-on-Sea

Wells

Ilfracombe ●

Lynmouth ○

Porlock ○

○Dunster

Croyde ○

Exmoor National Park

Exford ○

Bridgwater ●

Glastonbury

Barnstaple Bay

Barnstaple ●

Clovelly ○

Bideford ●

Taw

Dulverton ○

ENGLAND

Yeovil ●

Heartland Peninsula

● Tiverton

● Chard

● Bude

○ Crediton

● Bridport

Tamar

Okehampton ●

Dartmoor National Park

Chagford ○

Exeter ◉

○ Beer

Lyme Bay

Lydford ○

Moretonhampstead ○

Sidmouth ●

Branscombe

Tavistock ●

Widecombe-in-the-Moor ○

Teignmouth ●

● Exmouth

Start Bay

Princetown ●

● Ashburton

● Liskeard

Totnes ○

● Torquay

Greenway
Visit Agatha Christie's summer home (p80)

● Plymouth

● Brixham

○ Looe

Bigbury-on-Sea ○

Dartmouth

Polperro

Hope Cove ○

Salcombe

Plymouth
Get lost in a multimillion-pound museum (p72)

Totnes
Ecofriendly town with a superb local food scene (p85)

English Channel

Taunton ◉

7

COAST & COVES

Hidden coves, wooded inlets, sandy harbours, epic bays: the southwest has a beach to suit all moods. Around the coastline of Devon and Cornwall, you'll find everything from busy, bucket-and-spade resorts to secret spots known only to a chosen few. Some are easy to reach; others take time, dedication and a hike along the coast path (with a decent map in hand) to discover. Just don't forget to pack the fins and snorkel.

Safe Swimming

The official lifeguard season runs from May to September, but only larger, busier beaches are guarded. Swim between the flags and beware of rip tides.

Cliff Walks

Many beaches can only be reached via the South West Coast Path, a stunning circuit of the entire Devon and Cornwall coastline: the views are worth every step.

Weather Watch

Check the weather before choosing your beach: sometimes, when it's blowing a hoolie on the north coast, there might not be a breath of wind in the south.

BEST BEACH EXPERIENCES

Walk for golden miles along **Gwithian and Godrevy Towans** ❶ from the Hayle Estuary to Godrevy Lighthouse. Grassy dunes, rock pools, surf, seals and more. (p168)

Hike down the steep cliffside to the Lizard's loveliest beach, **Kynance Cove** ❷ Look out for choughs on the surrounding cliffs. (p143)

Escape the outside world altogether on **Hell Bay** ❸, Bryher's most magnificent beach. (p211)

Catch the sea tractor across **Bantham Beach** ❹ to Burgh Island and its landmark art deco hotel. (p89)

Wander through the dunes at **Saunton Sands** ❺ and nearby Braunton Burrows, a nature reserve with the UK's biggest sand piles. (p126)

LEFT: ALLAN BAXTER/GETTY IMAGES ©; RIGHT: SCORSBY/SHUTTERSTOCK, RUTH ASHMORE/SHUTTERSTOCK ©

St Michael's Mount (p205)

HISTORY LESSONS

From clifftop fortresses to soaring cathedrals, Devon and Cornwall are heaven for history buffs. This corner of Britain has been inhabited since pre-Christian times, and you'll have the opportunity to experience every era as you explore: Neolithic, Bronze Age, Roman, Viking, medieval, Georgian, Victorian and more.

Heritage Organisations

Membership of English Heritage comes in very handy here: you'll get free admission to many sites. Overseas visitors can buy a nine- or 16-day pass.

Ancient Past

If you're a fan of stone circles, you'll find scores of them here, mostly dotted around Dartmoor, Bodmin Moor and Penwith.

BEST HISTORY EXPERIENCES

Cross the tidal causeway to **St Michael's Mount ❶**, Cornwall's dramatic island abbey and the star of a million postcards. (p205)

Climb the tower of **Exeter Cathedral ❷**, which was built by the Normans, for incredible panoramic city views. (p53)

Brave the gravity-defying new bridge and explore the cliffs at **Tintagel Castle ❸**, King Arthur's fabled birthplace. (p178)

Time-travel into Britain's prehistoric past at **Chysauster ❹**, one of the country's best-preserved Iron Age villages. (p198)

Visit the former home of swashbuckling Sir Francis Drake at **Buckland Abbey ❺**, then head out along Drake's Trail. (p77)

PARTY ON

County shows, food fairs, music festivals, pagan parties: Devon and Cornwall definitely know how to let their hair down. No matter what time of year you visit, chances are there'll be a lively festival or event where you can party like a local.

County Shows

Devon and Cornwall both host their own summer county shows, showcasing the best local food and drink, top producers and, of course, a parade of prize-winning animals.

Ditch the Car

Avoid trying to navigate through the crowds on festival days: it's far less stressful to catch a train, hop on a bus or take your bike instead.

Book Ahead

For the most popular events, accommodation can be booked up months ahead, so it's always worth reserving as early as you can.

BEST FESTIVAL EXPERIENCES

Join the party at Padstow's **May Day ❶**, a raucous knees-up that's said to date back to pagan times. (p175)

Put on your best pirate voice and and belt out a tune at the **Falmouth International Sea Shanty Festival ❷**. (p135)

See ships of all shapes and sizes during the **Dartmouth Royal Regatta ❸**, one of the southwest's biggest sailing celebrations. (p84)

Watch crews from around the world compete at the **World Pilot Gig Championships ❹** on St Mary's in the Isles of Scilly. (p209)

Look to the skies during the **British Fireworks Championships ❺**, which light up Plymouth for two nights in mid-August. (p72)

THE GREAT OUTDOORS

With miles and miles of unspoiled coast and countryside, getting out and about in the great outdoors is guaranteed to be a highlight of your trip in the southwest. Surf, SUP, cycle, climb, hike or forage for wild food – the choice of outdoor adventures is endless. If you fancy trying a few different outdoor experiences, look out for one of the region's many multi-activity centres.

Public Transport

Using local trains, buses and bikes enables you to avoid parking headaches and clogged-up summer roads – and it's obviously greener, too.

Tide Times

If you're exploring the coast, stay aware of the tide: it's always worth picking up a local 'tide times' booklet to be safe.

Cover Up

When spending a lot of time outdoors, remember to slather on some suncream: the summer sun can be fierce, even on overcast days.

BEST OUTDOOR EXPERIENCES

Cycle the **Tarka Trail ❶**, a cross-Dartmoor route running for 30 miles between Braunton and Barnstaple, partly via a disused railway. (p127)

Surf in Newquay and **Croyde ❷**, the southwest's surfing hotspots, or seek out quieter beaches to find more peaceful waves. (p126)

Take a dip in the **Jubilee Pool ❸**, Penzance's wonderful art-deco lido. Plymouth has one of its own, too – the Tinside Lido. (p201)

Kayak on the **Fowey River ❹** in search of local wildlife: herons, kingfishers, egrets, cormorants and more. (p154)

Go wild at **Adrenalin Quarry ❺**, offering all kinds of crazy outdoor pursuits – from cliff jumping to zip lining and axe-throwing. (p158)

Greenhouses, Lost Gardens of Heligan (p157)

HOW GREEN IS MY GARDEN?

The southwest's balmy climate and numerous sheltered coastal valleys give it a definite edge when it comes to green-fingered ventures. Many species of trees and plants survive here that would wither anywhere else in the UK – and landscapers have taken full advantage, planting some of the nation's most spectacular gardens.

Spring's the Thing

To see the southwest's gardens at their best, come in early spring, when rhododendrons, azaleas and magnolias are in full bloom. It's also bluebell season.

Online Advice

Great Gardens of Cornwall (greatgardensofcornwall. co.uk) publishes a free map detailing 13 of the county's landmark gardens.

BEST GARDEN EXPERIENCES

Travel the world in the biomes of the **Eden Project ❶** – there are giant plants from across the globe here. (p157)

Walk over a jungle rope bridge in the **Lost Gardens of Heligan ❷**, then see what's growing in the walled kitchen garden. (p157)

Get muddled up in the ornamental maze at **Glendurgan ❸**, perhaps the most impressive of the garden estates around Falmouth. (p140)

Experience Scilly's unforgettable garden hideaway at **Tresco Abbey Garden ❹**, blooming with subtropical species. (p210)

Get inspired at **RHS Rosemoor ❺** – the show garden has veg patches, flower meadows, cottage gardens, woodland and a nationally important rose collection. (p128)

LEFT: ALICE-D/SHUTTERSTOCK ©; RIGHT: PETE STUART/SHUTTERSTOCK ©, JEAN-PHILIPPE OFFORD/ALAMY ©

EATING LIKE A LOCAL

Whether it's savouring a cream tea, tucking into fish and chips or trying a traditional Cornish pasty, the southwest is a picnic hamper filled with foodie delights. Pick up crabs off the boats in Newlyn or Brixham, try fresh oysters in Falmouth or pack a picnic and head for the beach.

Anyone for Tea?

The correct way to eat a cream tea is a hotly contested issue: in Devon it's cream then jam on your scone, but in Cornwall it's jam then cream.

Foodie Festivals

Many towns host food-themed events year-round: the biggest ones are Porthleven Food Festival (April), Falmouth Oyster Festival (September) and Dartmouth Food Festival (October).

Fine Wines

There are several renowned vineyards dotted around the southwest – there's even one on the Isles of Scilly.

BEST FOOD EXPERIENCES

Stop by **Ann's Pasties ①** near Lizard village – it's said to be Cornwall's best pasty-maker, though the competition is fierce. (p145)

Book well ahead for sustainable homegrown grub at **Riverford Field Kitchen ②**, a famous organic farm just outside Totnes. (p85)

Pick your own fruit and veg or settle in for a slap-up Sunday roast at **Trevaskis Farm ③**, a working farm near Gwithian. (p199)

Head down to the wilds of west Penwith to try the unusual flavours of ice cream at the award-winning **Moomaid of Zennor ④**. (p196)

Buy your crabs, lobster and fish straight off the boats from **Newlyn ⑤** fishmongers. (p203)

THE WILD WEST

Whether you're an animal lover or a birdwatcher, you'll find plenty of wildlife-spotting experiences in Devon and Cornwall to keep you occupied. Hop aboard an organised boat trip, go rock-pooling at low tide, or slip on a pair of fins and a snorkel – and make sure you always have a decent pair of binoculars to hand.

Basking Sharks

The world's second-largest fish (after the whale shark), these gentle giants are regular summer visitors to the southwest's shores.

Grey Seals

It's pretty easy to spot seals – they often haul themselves onto the rocks or chill out on offshore islands.

Choughs

The red-billed, red-footed Cornish chough was once a rare sight, but is gradually making a comeback.

BEST WILDLIFE EXPERIENCES

Deep-dive without getting wet at the **National Marine Aquarium ❶** in Plymouth, where sharks, rays and tropical fish fill the tanks. (p72)

Spot basking sharks, dolphins and seabirds on a wildlife boat trip from St Ives or **Falmouth ❷**. (p139)

Take a trip out to National Trust–owned **Lundy Island ❸** to see puffins and red squirrels. (p125)

Visit the honking residents at the **Cornish Seal Sanctuary ❹** near Gweek, a rehabilitation centre for orphaned and rescued seals. (p144)

Swim with seals, delve into rock pools or catch a boat to your very own deserted island on the **Isles of Scilly ❺**. (p213)

17

Kitchen at Lanhydrock (p185)

GREAT ESTATES

Country houses litter the countryside, a reminder of the days when Devon and Cornwall were the playground of the landed gentry. These days, many of them are owned by the National Trust. Remember to leave plenty of time to explore the grounds: often, they're even more spectacular than what's on show inside.

Trust Us

Membership of the National Trust lasts a year and gains you free admission. There is a seven- or 14-day Touring Pass for overseas visitors.

Free Time

Some estates, such as Trelissick near Truro and Penrose Estate near Porthleven, enable you to walk their trails for free (though you'll probably have to pay for parking).

BEST COUNTRY HOUSE EXPERIENCES

Step into *Upstairs, Downstairs* England at **Lanhydrock** ❶, and wander around cavernous kitchens, antique-filled rooms and a huge great hall. (p185)

Pretend you're Hercule Poirot at **Greenway** ❷, Agatha Christie's summer retreat on the banks of the River Dart. (p80)

Feel like you're in *Alice in Wonderland* among the outlandish topiary of **Antony House** ❸, on Cornwall's Rame Peninsula. (p159)

Relive the Jazz Age at **Coleton Fishacre** ❹, a south Devon house that shimmers with art-deco style and has gardens to match. (p87)

Admire a fabulous collection of horse-drawn carriages at **Arlington Court** ❺, a wonderful slice of life from the Regency era. (p128)

AGE OF INDUSTRY

A couple of centuries ago, the southwest was far from the peaceful landscape we see today – it was one of the beating hearts of Britain's Industrial Revolution. The hills and valleys of Devon and Cornwall once resounded with mine stacks, mineral trains and pump engines, and tall ships sailed here from the far corners of the empire.

Unesco Protected

Large areas of Devon and Cornwall form part of a Unesco World Heritage Site: the Cornwall and Devon Mining Landscape (cornishmining.org.uk).

Clay Country

At St Austell, you can cycle around a strange lunar landscape of spoil hills and mica pools now known collectively as the Clay Trails.

Safeguarding Historic Sites

Cornwall Heritage Trust safeguards 13 of the county's most important monuments and historic sites, including the landmark Treffry Viaduct near Luxulyan (cornwallheritagetrust.org).

BEST MINING EXPERIENCES

Delve into the darkness of **Geevor** ❶, the only Cornish tin mine where you can actually venture underground. (p199)

Walk the cliffs around **Botallack** ❷ to see some of the most picturesque mining landscapes in the region. (p199)

Cycle the **Great Flat Lode Trail** ❸, the rich seam of minerals that runs right along Cornwall's spine. Expect mine stacks aplenty. (p167)

See the **Levant Mine & Beam Engine** ❹ in full steam: it's one of the world's only working examples of a beam engine. (p199)

Wander along the quays of **Charlestown** ❺, a historic china-clay port that's often used these days as a filming location. (p155)

19

FAR FROM THE MADDING CROWD

With two national parks and a wealth of nature reserves and protected areas of coastline, Devon and Cornwall are brimming with wild places where, with a bit of luck, you'll be able to leave the summer crowds far behind. These remote areas feel a world away from the coastal honeypots – they are for people who prefer to experience nature in the raw.

Leave No Trace

Wild camping is only legal on Dartmoor (p112). Make sure you pack out all your rubbish, don't feed the gulls and definitely leave the barbecue at home.

Stargazing

Since 2011, Exmoor has been a designated Dark Sky Reserve. Stargazing safaris and night-time walks are offered by the National Park Authority.

Route Finding

It's worth having a decent map when you're exploring: the Ordnance Survey publishes a range of 1:25,000 Explorer maps, or you can download its excellent app.

LEFT: HENRY TRICKEY/SHUTTERSTOCK ©. BEN BIRCHALL/PA IMAGES VIA GETTY IMAGES ©. RIGHT: HELEN HOTSON/SHUTTERSTOCK ©

BEST CROWD-FREE EXPERIENCES

Strap on your boots and hit the **South West Coast Path ❶**, which runs for more than 450 miles around the Devon and Cornwall coastline. (p119)

Hike between strange granite outcrops, bike old railway trails, explore ancient woodland and uncover the forgotten past of **Dartmoor ❷**. (p104)

Lose the crowds on **Exmoor ❸**, combining craggy coast, steep valleys and impossibly green countryside. (p114)

Delve into slate caverns, picnic by crashing waterfalls and conquer Cornwall's highest hill, Brown Willy, on **Bodmin Moor ❹**. (p183)

Forage the cliffs and hedge-rows around **St Ives ❺** and other parts of Cornwall with a wild-food expert, then head home for a wild feast. (p195)

LEFT: TOM MEAKER/SHUTTERSTOCK ©; RIGHT: RON ELLIS/SHUTTERSTOCK ©; A G BAXTER/SHUTTERSTOCK ©

National Maritime Museum (p138)

MARVELLOUS MUSEUMS

You can't understand this corner of Britain unless you get to grips with its complicated, fascinating and often conflicted past. There are many excellent museums to visit, ideal for a rainy day (contrary to the brochures, it doesn't shine all the time in the southwest, you know).

BEST MUSEUM EXPERIENCES

View the astounding collection of vessels at the **National Maritime Museum ❶**, and get a fine view over Falmouth Harbour from the Lookout tower. (p138)

Tune in to the unlikely story of globe-spanning telecommunications at **PK Porthcurno ❷**. (p202)

Marvel at the eclectic, imaginative exhibits on show at **The Box ❸**, Plymouth's multimillion-pound new museum. (p74)

Search for treasure at the **Shipwreck Treasure Museum ❹** in Charlestown, where a quirky collection of artefacts reclaimed from local wrecks is on display. (p155)

Winter Blues

Double-check opening times if you're planning on visiting in winter: many museums close early outside summer.

Book Ahead

At many places you can buy your tickets online in advance, enabling you to dodge the summer queues.

Get spooked at the **Museum of Witchcraft and Magic ❺** in Boscastle, which has a frankly disturbing collection of witchy relics. (p180)

ART LESSONS

Is it the rugged landscape? The coastal scenery? The special quality of the light? Whatever it is, the southwest has long been a magnet for artists and sculptors, and there are some first-rate art institutions to visit here – along with scores of little galleries where local artists ply their wares.

BEST ART EXPERIENCES

Learn all about the history of Cornish art and the St Ives School at **Tate St Ives ❶**, the award-winning gallery overlooking Porthmeor Beach. (p192)

Brush up on your own art skills at the **St Ives School of Painting** (p194) or the **Newlyn School of Art ❷**. (p201)

Spot imaginative artworks among the foliage at **Broomhill Sculpture Gardens ❸** (p128) near Barnstaple, and **Tremenheere Sculpture Gardens** (p204), near Penzance.

View canvases by Stanhope Forbes and other members of the Newlyn School at **Penlee House Gallery & Museum ❹** in Penzance. (p204)

Visit the **Jackson Foundation Gallery ❺**, local landscape artist Kurt Jackson's impressive eco-orientated art gallery in St Just. (p196)

Shapes in Stone

The abstract sculptures of Barbara Hepworth can be seen in many places around St Ives, including her own studio and garden.

Still Like Statues

Devon is home to two controversial female sculptures: Damien Hirst's *Verity* (pictured above), beside Ilfracombe Harbour and Joseph Hillier's *Messenger,* outside Plymouth's Theatre Royal.

Stay Informed

Cornwall 365 is a great place to get the year-round low-down on events, exhibitions, festivals and other cultural happenings around the county (cornwall365.com).

REGIONS

Find the places that tick all your boxes.

North Cornwall & Bodmin Moor

COASTS & CLIFFTOPS

The north coast is classic Cornwall: big beaches, big cliffs and even bigger views. It's home to many of the county's most celebrated stretches of sand and popular beach towns, but don't expect to have much of it to yourself in summer.

p161

West Cornwall & the Isles of Scilly

LAST-STOP BRITAIN

The wild west feels like its own country: a land of craggy cliffs, weird stone monuments, secret coves and enough art galleries to fill an entire holiday. The British mainland runs out of road at Land's End, while, far out to sea, the Isles of Scilly beckon to island adventurers.

p187

North Cornwall & Bodmin Moor
p161

West Cornwall & the Isles of Scilly
p187

South & East Cornwall
p131

South & East Cornwall

CORNWALL'S GENTLER SIDE

The south coast makes a pastoral contrast to the showy north – this is a place for sleepy road-tripping, country bike rides and long beach days. That's not to say it doesn't have its wild side, though: countless ships have come to grief on the Lizard's ink-black cliffs.

p131

Dartmoor, Exmoor & North Devon

SHORES AND MORES

Devon on the edge: rocky tors and stark skies on Dartmoor, big cliffs and sandy beaches on Exmoor, fishing villages and surfable waves along the north Devon coast. Join in the tourist fun in Ilfracombe, Croyde or Clovelly, or leave the summer crowds behind on the wild moors.

p99

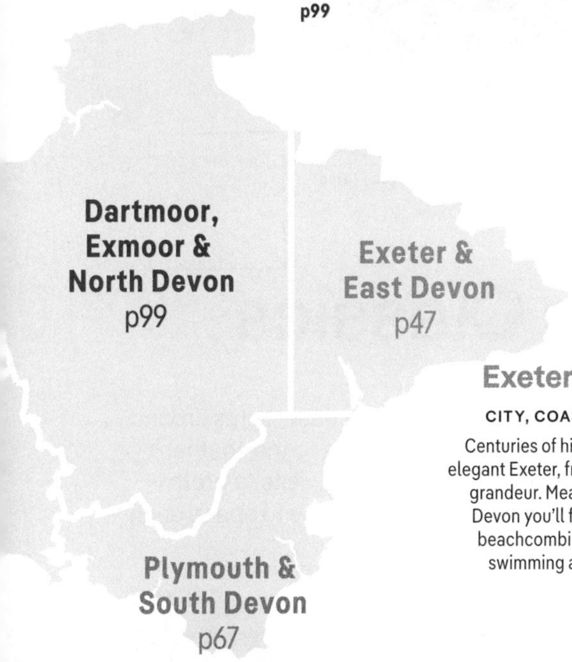

Dartmoor, Exmoor & North Devon
p99

Exeter & East Devon
p47

Exeter & East Devon

CITY, COAST AND COUNTRYSIDE

Centuries of history await on the streets of elegant Exeter, from ancient Rome to Georgian grandeur. Meanwhile, on the east flank of Devon you'll find yourself fossil-hunting, beachcombing, coast walking and wild swimming along the Jurassic Coast.

p47

Plymouth & South Devon
p67

Plymouth & South Devon

PORTS, RIVERS AND RIVIERAS

Holiday times are here. Paddle in the surf, bring out the windbreak, visit charming seaside towns and sail up the stately River Dart. And when you want a break from the countryside, head for big-city Plymouth for maritime history and a world-class aquarium.

p67

Newquay (p166)

ITINERARIES

Cornish Classics

Allow: 7 days   **Distance:** 112 miles

This week-long adventure takes in the must-see sights around Cornwall, from the rocky north coast across to the southern harbour town of Falmouth, then out west for visits to pretty Penzance and arty St Ives. With a bit more time to spare, each area makes a good base for local day trips.

① TINTAGEL ⏱ 1 DAY

Start by exploring Cornwall's most atmospheric castle, **Tintagel** (p178), where the mythical hero King Arthur is said to have been conceived. A striking new bridge has been built to link the two parts of the clifftop castle.

🔁 Detour: Spin along the coast to the pretty harbour of Boscastle, followed by Port Isaac, a seafood hotspot and the home of chef Nathan Outlaw. ⏱ 5 hours

② PADSTOW ⏱ 1 DAY

Day two revolves around the super-popular harbour town of **Padstow** (p172), where celeb chef Rick Stein has kicked off a foodie revolution. There are loads of top restaurants to try, and you can catch a ferry over to Daymer Bay, or go cycling around Padstow's sandy Seven Bays.

🚗 30-minute drive

③ NEWQUAY & THE NORTH COAST ⏱ 2 DAYS

For the most spectacular stretches of sand, Cornwall's north coast is impossible to top. A whole string of beaches and coves can be visited on the way to surfing central **Newquay** (p166), followed by visits to the sea-smacked cliffs around St Agnes and the golden sands of Perranporth.

🚗 1-hour drive

🚗 45-minute drive

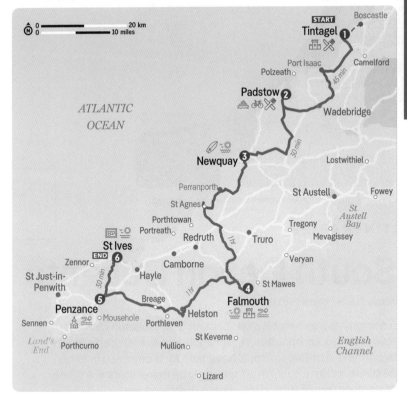

④ FALMOUTH ⏱ 1 DAY

Cut across the peninsula to the lovely old harbour of **Falmouth** (p136) , a handsome town with numerous alleys, shops and a landmark Tudor castle to explore, not to mention a trio of great beaches where you can swim, SUP and sunbathe the day away.

🚗 *1-hour drive*

⑤ PENZANCE ⏱ 1 DAY

Head west for a day in **Penzance** (p201), the last stop on the Great Western Railway. Factor in time for a dip in the art-deco Jubilee Pool, a wander around nearby Newlyn and Mousehole and an afternoon visit to St Michael's Mount – the island abbey that rises like a vision in the middle of Mount's Bay.

🚆 *30-minute ride*

⑥ ST IVES ⏱ 1 DAY

Round the week off with a day in **St Ives** (p192), Cornwall's arty hub. It's awash with galleries, including the unmissable Tate St Ives. It's also a great spot for some more beach time – Porthminster and Porthmeor are nearest to the town, but you'll find more space out on the dunes at Gwithian and Godrevy Towans.

Branscombe Beach, Jurassic Coast (p62)

ITINERARIES

South Devon Delights

Allow: 7 days **Distance:** 123 miles

A shimmy along Devon's scenic south coast takes in classic towns, gorgeous beaches, remote headlands and pretty much everything in between. You'll have time for a day or so in each destination, but it's worth allowing a little more: there are plenty of gardens, beaches and villages to discover here.

❶ JURASSIC COAST ⏱ 2 DAYS

Begin with a bit of fossil-hunting and beach walking on the **Jurassic Coast** (p62), a Unesco World Heritage Site that's characterised by its rust-red cliffs, pebbly beaches and fishing coves. Sidmouth and Beer make good bases; don't miss beautiful Branscombe Beach, a ride on the Seaton Tramway and a spot of paddle-boarding on Ladram Bay.

🚗 *45-minute drive*

❷ EXETER ⏱ 1 DAY

Swing along the coast via Exmouth to **Exeter** (p52), where history seems to lurk around every corner: Roman walls, medieval passageways, Georgian houses and one of Britain's mightiest Gothic cathedrals. Despite being one of Devon's two biggest cities, it's eminently walkable and in many ways still feels like the market town it once was.

🚗 *45-minute drive*

❸ TOTNES ⏱ 1 DAY

Offbeat **Totnes** (p85) has long been known for its alternative, arty, ecofriendly leanings, and it's a town that definitely has a charm all its own. Wander along the main street, browse the quirky shops, walk up to the castle then paddle downriver on the Dart for an evening pint. Sounds to us like a good way to spend a day.

🚗 *30-minute drive*

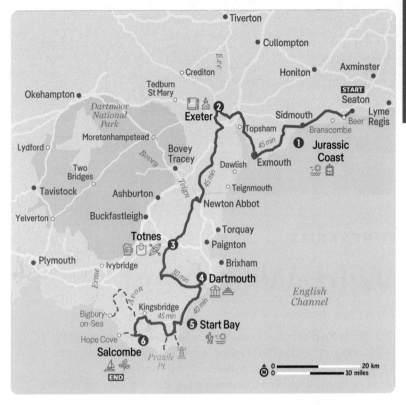

④ DARTMOUTH ⏱1 DAY

Guarding the mouth of the Dart Estuary, **Dartmouth** (p79) is a handsome old harbour that's also home to one of Britain's most prestigious naval colleges. It's a brilliant spot for boat trips along the Dart, and you can combine trips with a heritage steam railway. Visits to the National Trust houses of Greenway and Coleton Fishacre are recommended, too.

🚗 *40-minute drive*

⑤ START BAY ⏱1 DAY

The remote stretch of coastline around **Start Bay** (p84) is a glorious area for secluded coastal walks. The impressive lighthouse at Start Point and the rocky apex of Prawle Point both make ideal targets, and there are a number of little coves along the way to investigate – perfect for a wild swim.

🚗 *45-minute drive*

⑥ SALCOMBE ⏱1 DAY

Head west through the attractive town of Kingsbridge, then loop round via swish **Salcombe** (p86) for a spot of the yachting high life or a visit to the amazing Overbeck's Garden.

🚗 *Detour:* *Swing round via Hope Cove and end the day with a paddle, perhaps on Bantham Beach or Bigbury-on-Sea, where you can catch a ride on a sea tractor to Burgh Island.* ⏱ *3 hours*

Combestone Tor (p110)

ITINERARIES

Wild, Wild West

Allow: 7 days   **Distance:** 230 miles

This trip is for people who want to experience the southwest's wilder side, including the Dartmoor and Exmoor national parks. There are moors, headlands, heaths, crags and coves, so (with a bit of luck) you'll be able to leave the big summer crowds behind.

❶ EXMOOR ⏱ 1 DAY

The national park of **Exmoor** (p114) offers a little something for everyone: coast walks, beach time, country pubs and quaint villages where time hardly seems to tick by from day to day. Visit castles, cycle quiet lanes, explore hills, search out waterfalls: the choice is yours. Follow the coast road for a memorable drive.

🚗 1½-hour drive

❷ DARTMOOR ⏱ 1 DAY

Nowhere offers a finer choice of hikes and bike rides than **Dartmoor** (p104), a windswept landscape defined by rocky granite tors that loom like watchtowers on the horizon. You could spend a month here and not see them all, so choose carefully – Hay Tor and Hound Tor are classics. If you prefer to pedal, try the Granite Way or the Tarka Trail.

🚗 1-hour drive

❸ BODMIN MOOR ⏱ 1 DAY

The main target on moody **Bodmin Moor** (p181) is Brown Willy, the stark peak that marks Cornwall's highest point. But it's not all about hiking here: there are lots of fascinating prehistoric sites to visit, along with slate caverns, pretty villages, crashing waterfalls and pleasant woods.

🚗 1¼-hour drive

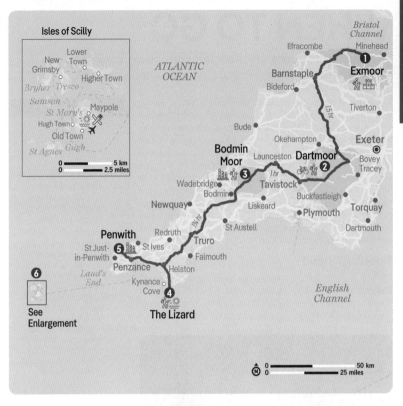

Isles of Scilly

ATLANTIC OCEAN

Bristol Channel

Minehead

Ilfracombe

Exmoor ❶

Barnstaple
Bideford

Tiverton

1.5 hr

Bude

Okehampton

Exeter

Bovey Tracey

Launceston

Dartmoor ❷

Bodmin Moor ❸

Wadebridge
Bodmin

1 hr

Tavistock

Buckfastleigh

Newquay

Liskeard

Plymouth

Torquay

1¼ hr

St Austell

Dartmouth

Penwith

Redruth

St Ives

Truro

Falmouth

St Just-in-Penwith ❺

Penzance

Helston

Land's End

Kynance Cove

The Lizard ❹

English Channel

0 — 50 km
0 — 25 miles

N

See Enlargement ❻

❹ **THE LIZARD** ⏱1 DAY

The jagged coastline of the **Lizard** (p142) has claimed who knows how many ships down the centuries, and nowadays makes a glorious place for blustery cliff walks. The most picturesque trail of all leads down to celebrated Kynance Cove, but there are lots of tiny coves, beaches and quaint villages to discover.

🚗 *1-hour drive*

❺ **PENWITH** ⏱1 DAY

Relatively few visitors take the time to dig into the prehistoric past of **Penwith** (p197), but if you're a fan of old stones, spooky stone circles, burial mounds and local legends, you'll be in seventh heaven here. The Iron Age villages of Chysauster and Carn Euny are well worth exploring.

⛴ *3-hour boat ride*

❻ **ISLES OF SCILLY** ⏱2 DAYS

Whether you fly from Land's End Airport or catch the ferry from Penzance, you'll never forget your first sight of **Scilly** (p207): an archipelago of low-slung islands, scattered like shards over the blue Atlantic. Five are inhabited, but for a really wild experience, head for one of the deserted islands like Samson or Teän.

WHEN **TO GO**

Summer nights, spring greenery, autumn colours or winter drama: the southwest looks good no matter the season.

Not that long ago, Devon and Cornwall's holiday season was all about boom and bust: packed to bursting point for two months in summer, and pretty much deserted the rest of the year. While there's still a huge spike in visitor numbers in July and August, these days the season is much longer, often extending from Easter to October, with an extra seasonal boost around Christmas. It depends a lot on the weather: late spring and early summer are often the most settled times, weather-wise, with another balmy period in early autumn. Ironically, August is often a hit-and-miss month to visit: warmer temperatures often means summer storms, not to mention head-spinningly bad traffic.

Booking Ahead

Like in most holiday hotspots, the peak months around Easter, Christmas, July and August mean maximum prices at hotels, cottages and campsites. If you want to bag a bargain, booking outside the peak times can bring big savings.

British Firework Championships (p72)

⊛ I LIVE HERE

SPRING SEAFOOD

Chef Rich Adams cooks stellar seafood at Argoe, his acclaimed restaurant in Newlyn (@argoenewlyn).

'Spring is really great for seafood in Cornwall, as several species come into season at this time of year – including two of my favourites, megrim sole and spider crab (or Cornish king crab, as it's been rebranded nowadays). Both are at their very best in spring, and you can pick them up fresh off the boats from Newlyn fishmongers or local fisher folk.'

THE GULF STREAM

A jet of warmth moving across the Atlantic from the Caribbean, the Gulf Stream is what gives the southwest its unusually mild climate. This is officially the UK's mildest corner: the Isles of Scilly has the warmest average temperatures, a balmy 11.6 °C.

Weather through the Year – Newquay

JANUARY	FEBRUARY	MARCH	APRIL	MAY	JUNE
Ave. daytime max: **9°C**	Ave. daytime max: **9°C**	Ave. daytime max: **11°C**	Ave. daytime max: **12°C**	Ave. daytime max: **15°C**	Ave. daytime max: **18°C**
Days of rainfall: 16	Days of rainfall: 13	Days of rainfall: 12	Days of rainfall: 12	Days of rainfall: 10	Days of rainfall: 11

SEA TEMPERATURES

While swimming in the southwest is hardly tropical, it's definitely warmer than up north: usually at least a couple of degrees in summer, but up to seven or eight degrees in winter. Best case: expect about 18°C in a warm summer, or around 7°C in a chilly winter.

The Big Events

The weirdest festival in the west, Padstow's **May Day** (p175) is rooted in a pagan rite to announce the arrival of spring. It involves two snapping 'osses, tooting street bands, scores of dancers and huge crowds of revellers. 🌊 **1 May**

The southwest's biggest music festival, **Boardmasters** (p165) attracts over 50,000 fans to the cliffs above Mawgan Porth, near Newquay. Meanwhile, top surfers and skateboarders compete for prizes. ☀ **August**

During the **British Fireworks Championships** (p72), the UK's top pyrotechnic experts battle it out in Plymouth Sound, staging incredible displays of light, sound and colour over the city. ☀ **August**

Summer is sailing season in the southwest, and many towns host their own maritime regattas. The largest of all is the **Dartmouth Royal Regatta** (p84), a week-long sailing celebration. ☀ **Late August**

Quirky Festivals

On **St Piran's Day** (p169), proud Cornish folk join parades across the county to honour their patron saint, St Piran, who is said to have brought Christianity to Cornwall. 🟢 **5 March**

Loosen up your vocal cords and join in with Jolly Roger during the **Falmouth International Sea Shanty Festival** (pictured right; p135), a celebration of salty nautical tunes. Big crowds and beer stalls throng Falmouth's quaysides. ☀ **June**

Observing a centuries-old custom, the locals of **Ottery St Mary** carry flaming tar barrels (p51) through packed-out streets, while paramedics and health-and-safety officials watch in horror. 🌊 **5 November**

Penzance holds its own spooky celebration on the winter solstice – **Montol Festival** (p191) is a pagan party that seems straight out of *The Wicker Man*. All hail the Lord of Misrule! ❄ **December**

COME RAIN OR SHINE

With 1500-odd hours of sunshine per year, Cornwall and Devon are one of the UK's top sun traps. The mild climate also means rain, between 1000mm and 1300mm per year – roughly the national average.

JULY	AUGUST	SEPTEMBER	OCTOBER	NOVEMBER	DECEMBER
Ave. daytime max: **19°C**	Ave. daytime max: **20°C**	Ave. daytime max: **18°C**	Ave. daytime max: **15°C**	Ave. daytime max: **12°C**	Ave. daytime max: **10°C**
Days of rainfall: 11	Days of rainfall: 12	Days of rainfall: 12	Days of rainfall: 15	Days of rainfall: 18	Days of rainfall: 17

LEFT: WILLIAM BARTON/SHUTTERSTOCK ©, RIGHT: PJ PHOTOGRAPHY/SHUTTERSTOCK ©

Wild camping, Dartmoor National Park (p112)

GET PREPARED FOR DEVON & CORNWALL

Useful things to load in your bag, your ears and your brain.

Clothes

Layers Even in summer, weather in southwest England can be unpredictable and change often. Dress in lightweight layers that can be easily adjusted as conditions change throughout the day.

Comfy shoes Hiking shoes are a must if you plan on hitting the coast paths or moorland trails. Even if not, the cobbled streets in historic areas and occasionally uneven rural roads call for comfortable walking shoes.

Raincoats Cornwall is sometimes called the 'wettest county in England'. Although that's untrue, the higher-elevation areas of Devon and Cornwall's moors do result in more rainy days than average.

Manners

A friendly rivalry exists between Devon and Cornwall. Praising one to someone from the other won't cause offence – but woe betide you if a Cornish person hears you prefer the Devonshire pasty!

Mild haggling is sometimes acceptable at markets but it's inappropriate – even impolite – elsewhere.

Brexit remains a contentious topic throughout England, probably best avoided if you don't want to spark a debate.

Wetsuits For surfing and other watersports, a wetsuit is usually a must. In summer, water temperatures reach around 15°C to 18°C, which is still too chilly to go without; in winter they drop to as low as 8°C.

📖 READ

Vanishing Cornwall (Daphne du Maurier; 1967) A lyrical history of Cornwall from the county's famed author.

Tarka the Otter (Henry Williamson; 1927) Classic children's novel recounting a wild otter's adventures in the Devon countryside.

And Then There Were None (Agatha Christie; 1939) Christie's finest and the best-selling crime novel of all time, set on Burgh Island.

The Salt Path (Raynor Winn; 2018) Memoir of a couple's journey walking the southwest coast while facing homelessness and terminal illness.

GET PREPARED

Words

Here are some of the unique colloquialisms and unusual phrases you might hear throughout Devon and Cornwall:

wasson? a greeting, short for 'what's going on?'

alright me/my luvver? informal greeting used by and for both men and women, similar to 'all right mate' or 'hello love'; all right my 'ansum (handsome) is used in a similar way

dreckly officially means 'directly' or 'very soon', but generally used to imply any unspecified time in the future

emmet Cornish name for a tourist

grockle also a tourist, in Devon this time (both are somewhat derogatory)

proper job good work, well done; sometimes used as a statement of affirmative or agreement

Kernewek, the Cornish language, is an ancient Celtic language that was almost entirely extinct by the end of the 18th century, but it underwent a revival in the 20th century and is now taught as a second language in some schools. Though little spoken these days, Cornish has heavily influenced the local dialect and is seen by many as an essential part of local identity and culture.

Practising these basic phrases may win you some local friends:

dydh da hello

meur ras thank you

▶ WATCH

War Horse (Steven Spielberg; 2011) WWI epic based on Michael Morpurgo's classic novel, filmed amid Dartmoor's tors.

Poldark (Debbie Horsfield; 2015–19) Brooding period drama series set in 18th-century Cornwall (Penberth Cove pictured above).

Doc Martin (Dominic Minghella; 2004–22) Martin Clunes plays a grumpy village doctor in this beloved series filmed in Port Isaac.

Sense and Sensibility (Ang Lee; 1995) This adaptation of Jane Austen's classic was filmed in Devon – notably Plymouth's Saltram House.

Devon and Cornwall (Will Coleman; 2019) Channel 4 documentary showcasing daily life in the southwest.

🎧 LISTEN

Port Isaac's Fisherman's Friends (Fisherman's Friends; 2010) Sea shanties and folk songs from a popular Cornish folk group.

Selected Ambient Works 85–92 (Aphex Twin; 1992) Debut album from the Irish-born, Cornwall-raised electronic musician.

People's Landscapes: A Tale of Tin (National Trust; 2019) Short podcast episode exploring the history of the Cornish Tin Coast.

Black Holes and Revelations (Muse; 2006) The biggest-selling album from Devonshire-born rock legends.

35

LEFT: DRONG/SHUTTERSTOCK ©; BELOW RIGHT: HUW FAIRCLOUGH/GETTY IMAGES ©;
FAR RIGHT: HUGH R HASTINGS/GETTY IMAGES ©

Cornish pasty

THE FOOD SCENE

The southwest is one of Britain's best foodie destinations, with a strong focus on slow, sustainable, seasonal and local.

There's no easier way to start a conversation in Devon or Cornwall than to engage a local on the subject of the two great regional debates: pasties and cream teas. With the exception of the weather, there's little that Brits love discussing more than food – and if there's a chance to adamantly and good-humouredly argue their side of a debate, all the better. In the southwest, the topics are pasties (who invented them, whose are better and where the crimped edge should be) and cream teas (who invented them and the correct order to apply jam and cream – see p223).

These two icons are just the tip of the iceberg when it comes to the southwest's culinary landscape. Thriving fishing industries and bustling harbours feed a rich seafood scene. Around 70% of Cornwall is farmland; some districts of Devon are over 80%. The region's produce is exceptional, and this is reflected at eateries across both counties, from Michelin-starred fine dining to humble beach shacks.

Local Produce

Before tourism took over, the southwest's fishing and farming industries were vital to the local economy. This is a land of quality dairy and sheep farms, just-caught seafood and independent producers. The region is awash with small-batch spirits distilleries, craft breweries and artisanal sauce makers – not to mention fantastic farm shops selling it all.

Best Devon & Cornwall dishes	CORNISH PASTY	DEVONSHIRE PASTY	CREAM TEA
	Beef, swede, potatoes and onions encased in D-shaped pastry with a crimped edge.	The difference is largely locational – though Devon doesn't have PGI status.	Scones, jam and clotted cream, served with tea.

Twice winner of the BBC Radio 4 Farmer of the Year, Guy Singh-Watson has been pioneering organic veg at Riverford Farm near Totnes for over 20 years, founding one of the UK's first vegetable subscription boxes. Riverford Field Kitchen's innovative farm-to-table dining experience is a frontrunner, but throughout the southwest, producers and eateries have long promoted the seasonal, minimal-mile, slow-food ethos.

Celebrity Chefs

In 1975, TV chef Rick Stein opened his Seafood Restaurant in Padstow. Today, he owns four eateries in the quaint Cornish village, and has become so synonymous with the culinary landscape that locals have nicknamed the place 'Padstein'. It's not meant particularly flatteringly, but Stein's restaurants and TV shows have done much to put Cornish cuisine in the national spotlight. One of his protégés, Nathan Outlaw, is responsible for two of the three Michelin-starred restaurants in Cornwall. Across the border, Hugh Fearnley-Whittingstall's River Cottage – star of the TV series of the same name – has long advocated seasonal, farm-to-table dining. Throughout both counties, renowned chefs like Paul Ainsworth, Mitch Tonks and Michael Caines are continuing the movement.

Paul Ainsworth at No 6, Padstow (p176)

Local Tipples

Cider is the iconic drink of the southwest, with producers big and small across both Devon and Cornwall. Scrumpy – cider's stronger, cloudier cousin – is also prevalent. More recently, the mild southwest climate has been put to use nurturing grape vines to produce some excellent sparkling wines, with some vineyards also producing whites and even reds. Devon's Sharpham Wines and Cornwall's Camel Valley are two of the best.

FOOD & WINE FESTIVALS

World Pasty Championships (*March*) Held annually in Cornwall, this one-day event sees entrants from around the world compete in a variety of categories.

Porthleven Food Festival (*porthlevenfood festival.com; April; pictured above*) A three-day harbourside feast of local food and drink in one of Cornwall's top foodie destinations.

Plymouth Seafood Festival (*September*) Celebrate Plymouth's sustainable seafood industry at this two-day harbourside festival.

Falmouth Oyster Festival (*falmouthoyster festival.co.uk; October*) An early autumn festival to celebrate the start of the oyster dredging season.

Dartmouth Food Festival (*dartmouthfood festival.com; October*) This free, family-friendly festival held along the River Dart is one of Devon's best.

FISH AND CHIPS	CRAB SANDWICH	LOBSTER	HOG'S PUDDING	MUSSELS
A British seaside staple: fried, battered fish served with chips.	Locally caught crab on granary bread.	Landed daily at harbours throughout the region.	Sausage made with pork, suet, oatmeal and, sometimes, offal.	Caught locally and cooked in a cider and cream sauce.

Specialities

Seafood

Shellfish Superb oysters, mussels, scallops, crab and lobster are all caught locally. Lundy and the Scilly Isles are particularly good for lobster.

Stargazey pie Baked pilchards, eggs and potatoes with fish heads protruding through the pastry lid.

Pilchards Once a vital industry, now being rebranded as 'Cornish sardines'.

Salcombe Smokies Salcombe's famous smoked mackerel.

Marsh samphire Coastal plant with a salty flavour, often partnered with seafood.

Laverbread Patties of seaweed and oats, usually served with bacon. A traditional Welsh dish popular on the north Devon and Exmoor coasts.

Local Cheeses

Cornish Yarg Nettle-wrapped, semi-hard and slightly tangy.

Sharpham Brie Sweet, soft brie made with Jersey cow's milk.

Quicke's Super-strong cheddar made near Exeter.

Clotted cream

Ticklemore Blues Devon (cow), Harbourne (goat) and Beenleigh (sheep), made near Totnes.

Cornish Blue Mild, creamy and gently sweet blue cheese from the edge of Bodmin Moor.

Sweet Treats

Splits Similar to scones, but lighter and made with yeast. Usually served sliced in half and filled with jam and cream.

Clotted cream Thick, decadent and a key component of cream tea. Made by heating cream until a crust forms on top.

Saffron cake Sweet, yeasted bun flavoured with saffron with dried fruit added.

MEALS OF A LIFETIME

Outlaw's Fish Kitchen (p179) Michelin-starred Port Isaac restaurant whose menu changes daily according to seasons, weather and the day's catch.

Coombeshead Farm (p183) The ultimate field-to-fork experience with hyper-seasonal menus in a working farm's rustic barn conversion.

Paul Ainsworth at No 6 (p176) Stylish Michelin-starred restaurant in Padstow with a focus on Cornish seafood.

Riverford Field Kitchen (p85) Completely farm-to-fork dining with seasonal, largely vegetarian menus.

Lympstone Manor (p61) Multi-course tasting menus at a Michelin-starred hotel restaurant near Exmouth.

Oyster Shack (p87) Iconic shabby-chic seafood shack on the Avon Estuary.

THE YEAR IN FOOD

SPRING

Salty **samphire** comes into season in May; look for it on fish dishes. Lamb is the meat of spring, often partnered with new potatoes and asparagus. For dessert, there's a British classic: rhubarb and custard.

SUMMER

Head to a 'pick your own' farm for raspberries, **strawberries** and cherries. Lobster and brown crabs are in season during summer, and salad leaves, radishes, peas and mint mean lots of fresh, light dishes.

AUTUMN

Oyster season starts in October: they're protected during summer when they spawn. Inland, this is the season for richly flavoured veg like mushrooms, squashes and leeks, and for cider-apple harvesting.

WINTER

On cold winter days, Britain's hearty, heavy dishes shine – especially the classic **roast dinner**. Some pubs and restaurants make good use of the autumn-winter game season; look for pheasant, rabbit and venison.

GAMMELMARK, SÖREN/IMAGE PROFESSIONALS GMBH/ALAMY ©

Seafood salad, Outlaws Fish Kitchen (p179)

LEFT: COLIN HAWKINS/GETTY IMAGES © RIGHT: PETER TITMUSS/SHUTTERSTOCK ©

Rock climbing, Dartmoor (p104)

THE OUTDOORS

The southwest is one big adventure playground. Hike the coast path, surf the breaks, clamber the tors or cycle the back lanes: it's a nonstop thrill.

With two national parks, pockets of wild, windswept moor, endless sandy beaches and a coastline that just seems to go on forever, Devon and Cornwall offer a plethora of outdoor pursuits. If you're an adrenaline junkie looking for some action, a dedicated rambler wanting to escape the summer crowds or a chilled-out kayaker searching for quiet waters, you'll find ample opportunity to indulge your passion here. Get sandy, get wet, get muddy – that's all part of the experience in the southwest.

Walking

Whether you're after an afternoon ramble or a week-long epic, there are unforgettable walks in store here. Without doubt, the region's most stunning routes can be found along the South West Coast Path – the twisting, up-and-down, clifftop roller-coaster of a trail that runs in an unbroken thread along the coasts of both counties. The official route covers 630 miles, but the Devon and Cornwall sections cover between 400 miles and 450 miles (depending on where you measure from). Even for hardcore hikers, it takes a good month to complete – but it's quite feasible to choose a section and tackle it in chunks. Inland, Dartmoor and Bodmin Moor are also hugely popular with hikers, while Exmoor offers the best of both worlds: coast and countryside.

Alternative Activities

HAND PLANING
Catch a wave with a miniaturised hand-held surfboard – wearing fins helps you gain speed. Try it at **Watergate Bay** (p169).

COASTEERING
Swim, scramble, climb, plunge and splash your way around the region's coastline, particularly in **north Devon** (p128).

ROCK CLIMBING
Strings of challenging crags stretch across Devon and Cornwall. **Dartmoor** (p110) and **Falmouth** (p145) have scores of pitches.

FAMILY ADVENTURES

Spot seals, dolphins and seabirds on a boat trip from St Ives (p192), Falmouth (p136) or Padstow (p172).

Visit Lundy Island (p125), a wildlife haven managed by the National Trust and its team of rangers.

Cycle the Camel Trail (p173), an easy day trip that follows the old train line from Wadebridge to Padstow.

Bodyboard on Cornwall's north coast; it's easy and fun. Watergate Bay (p169) has an excellent watersports centre.

Go rock-pooling (p171) on pretty much any beach: you'll uncover the most treasures just after a high tide.

Snorkel through sea grass on the beaches around Falmouth (p136), or book a snorkelling safari in Penzance (p201).

Take a dip in a lido, with two beauties to choose from: Penzance's Jubilee Pool (p201) and Plymouth's Tinside Lido (p72).

Surfing & Watersports

Few regions offer quite as much opportunity to get on, and in, the water. Cornwall and north Devon have the best surf in Britain, and the beaches around Sennen, Newquay, Bude and Croyde are all good places to learn the basics or hone your skills. Increasingly, other watersports are gaining popularity, too. Paddleboards and blow-up kayaks are ten-a-penny on the southwest's beaches in summer nowadays, but it's worth noting that the Royal National Lifeboat Institution (RNLI) has noticed a marked rise in incidents involving paddlers in recent years,

so it's essential to always be aware of the tides and wind direction. Better still, book a trip with a local guide or instructor who can help you paddle safely. Don't forget the region's rivers: they're perfect for exploring by kayak or canoe, and offer loads of wildlife-spotting opportunities. There's plenty to see under the water, too: all you need is a snorkel, mask and some fins.

Cycling

Cycling in Devon and Cornwall is superb, but let's be frank: you're not going to dodge a few hills. Quiet lanes and old bridleways make for pleasant, peaceful cycling, and there are a number of routes along former rail or tram lines, or around former mines or quarries, that allow you to escape most of the road traffic. Popular shorter routes include the 30-mile Tarka Trail through north Devon, the 11-mile Granite Way over Dartmoor, the 11-mile Coast to Coast Cycle Trail from Devoran to Portreath in Cornwall, and the 18-mile Camel Trail between Padstow and Bodmin Moor. For hardcore cyclists, National Cycle Route 3 connects the far west of Cornwall with the south coast, north Devon and the fringes of Exmoor. Mountain bikers are also pretty well served: Cardinham Woods near Bodmin, Exmoor and Dartmoor all have a decent range of trails.

BEST SPOTS

For the best outdoor spots and routes, see map on pages 42-3.

Sailing, River Fal (p139)

HORSE RIDING	SAILING	ZIP LINING	DIVING
Saddle up and trek multi-use trails and bridleways on **Dartmoor** (p109) and **Exmoor** (p118).	**Falmouth** (p136), **Salcombe** (p86), **Torquay** (p90) and **Plymouth** (p72) all offer the chance to learn the art of the sail.	The **Adrenalin Quarry** (p158) near Liskeard has Cornwall's longest run; it's not for vertigo-sufferers.	Wrecks litter the southwest coast. Hotspots include **Plymouth** (p72), the **Lizard** (p143) and the **Isles of Scilly** (p207).

ACTION AREAS

Where to find Devon & Cornwall's
best outdoor activities.

Lundy

*ATLANTIC
OCEAN*

Clovel

Bude
○

*Widemouth
Bay*

Port
Isaac ○
○ Camelford

Padstow ○
Wadebridge
○ Bolventor

Bodmin

○ Bolventor
4

Surfing

1. Newquay (p170)
2. Bude (p179)
3. Sennen (p200)
4. Croyde (p126)

Newquay ●

Perranporth ●

St Austell ●
Liskear

Looe ○

Fowey ○

3 Truro
Redruth

● St Ives

St Just-
in-Penwith
Hayle
Penzance ●

3
Sennen ○
Mousehole ○
Helston ●

Falmouth ●

*Land's
End*

*The
Lizard*

Cycling

1. Camel Trail (p173)
2. Granite Way (p109)
3. Coast to Coast Cycle Trail (p168)
4. Cardinham Woods (p184)
5. Tarka Trail (p127)

Bristol
Channel

Ilfracombe

Porlock

Minehead

Watchet

Croyde

Bridgwater

Exmoor
National
Park

Barnstaple

Taunton

Bideford

Chard

Tiverton

Cullompton

Honiton

Axminster

Okehampton

Exeter

Seaton

Lyme
Regis

Launceston

Range
Danger
Area

Dartmoor
National
Park

Bovey
Tracey

Sidmouth

Exmouth

Tavistock

Ashburton

Newton
Abbot

Buckfastleigh

Torquay

Saltash

Paignton

Tor
Bay

Plymouth

Brixham

Plympton

Devonport

Dartmouth

Start
Bay

English
Channel

Salcombe

Walking/Hiking

❶ South West Coast Path (p119)
❷ Dartmoor (p104)
❸ Exmoor (p114)
❹ Bodmin Moor (p181)

National Parks

❶ Dartmoor National Park (p104)
❷ Exmoor National Park (p114)

0   20 km
0   10 miles

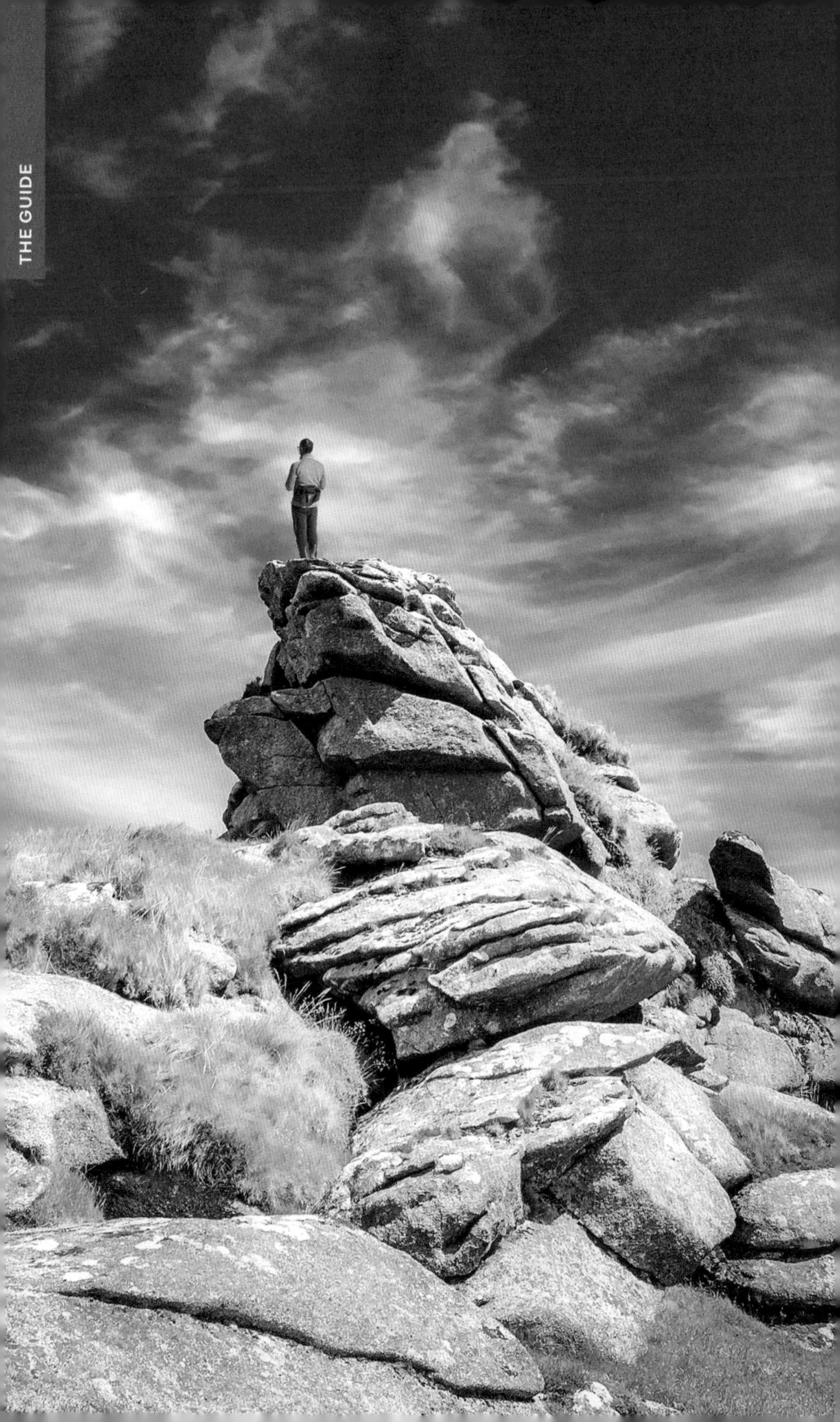

THE GUIDE

Chapters in this section are organised by hubs and their surrounding areas. We see the hub as your base in the destination, where you'll find unique experiences, local insights, insider tips and expert recommendations. It's also your gateway to the surrounding area, where you'll see what and how much you can do from there.

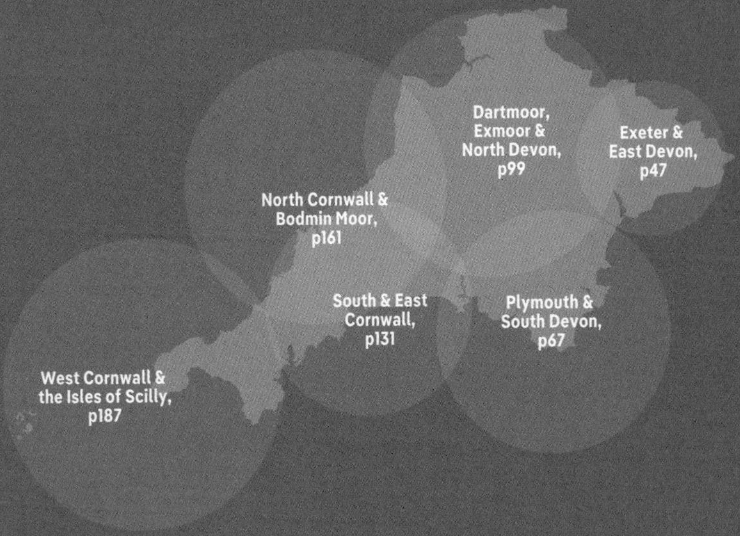

Dartmoor, Exmoor & North Devon, p99

Exeter & East Devon, p47

North Cornwall & Bodmin Moor, p161

South & East Cornwall, p131

Plymouth & South Devon, p67

West Cornwall & the Isles of Scilly, p187

Kilmar Tor, Bodmin Moor (p181)

Exmouth Beach

EXETER & EAST DEVON

CITY, COAST AND COUNTRYSIDE

Step through the gateway to the southwest to explore Devon's culture-filled capital, millennia-old coastline, quiet river valleys and thriving food scene.

From its source on Exmoor, the River Exe sets the pace for life in east Devon, feeding fertile farmland and cutting through the county's capital of Exeter on its journey south. This river once powered the industries that made the region rich long before tourism arrived; today it's a tranquil setting for outdoor pursuits, from the gentle – kayaking and biking – to the more thrilling, with prime kitesurfing conditions where it meets the sea.

All roads lead to Exeter, a Roman-founded city whose historic architecture forms a backdrop for a vibrant university town where independent businesses thrive. Here, the Exe provides a leafy urban oasis where once stood a bustling port. The Romans built their stronghold here because it was the lowest point where the Exe could be easily crossed: literally and symbolically the gateway to England's southwestern tip.

Along the Jurassic Coast, a different kind of history reigns. In 2001, the coastline between Exmouth and Dorset's Studland Bay was designated as the UK's first natural Unesco World Heritage Site. Just east of where the Exe spills into the sea, vivid rust-red cliffs rise, forming the oldest end of a 95-mile stretch of coast where the rock layers are a visible record of the entire Mesozoic era. What does that mean for those of us without a geology degree? Breathtaking cliff views, otherworldly rock formations and adventure.

SAVO ILIC/SHUTTERSTOCK ©

THE MAIN AREAS

EXETER	**EXMOUTH**	**JURASSIC COAST**
Ancient architecture meets vibrant culture.	Devon's oldest holiday resort.	Geology, fossils and coastal adventures.
p52	p58	p62

47

Find Your Way

East Devon encompasses a fairly small corner of the county. The coast stretches from Exmouth to the border with Dorset, while the interior between Exeter and Axminster is mainly rural countryside.

Witheridge

Tiverton

Exmouth, p58

This beloved seaside resort boasts 2 miles of sandy beach and excellent conditions for watersports, as well as nearby marshlands rich with birdlife.

Bickleigh

Exe

Exeter, p52

Devon's capital is home to Roman city walls, a Norman cathedral with a stunning Gothic facade, and a vibrant contemporary culture of independent businesses.

Newton St Cyres

Exeter

Dunsford

Topsham

Kenton

Moretonhampstead

Dartmoor National Park

Bovey Tracey

Exmouth

Budleigh Salterton

Dawlish

Poundsgate

Ashburton

Newton Abbot

CAR

Driving offers more freedom for coastal road trips and exploring rural areas, but it's better avoided in Exeter's busy city centre if possible. Be prepared for some narrow country lanes in places, and a fair bit of congestion around beach towns during summer.

BUS

Exeter is a transport hub, with a decent bus network extending along the coast and out into Mid Devon's towns and villages. For smaller towns in rural spots like the East Devon Area of Outstanding Natural Beauty (AONB), two or more buses may be required.

TRAIN

A direct train from London will have you in Exeter city centre in just over two hours. Trains also run between Exeter, Topsham and Exmouth, but for the rest of the coast you'll need to change for a bus.

Illminster

South Petherton

Chard

Crewkerne

Yarcombe

Drimpton

Beaminster

Honiton

Axminster

Marshwood

ittisham

Charmouth

Bridport

Lyme Regis

Burton Bradstock

ford

Seaton

Beer

Lyme Bay

Branscombe

dmouth

Jurassic Coast, p62
Boat trips, beaches, fishing and ancient quarries along a Unesco World Heritage Site where the cliffs tell a 180-million-year history.

English Channel

0   10 km
0   5 miles

Plan Your Days

Exeter has much to entice, but don't linger exclusively in the city. Drift along the coast in search of lazy beach days and adventure, or wander inland for countryside hikes and peaceful riverside towns.

PHIL FRIAR/SHUTTERSTOCK ©

Exmouth marina

A City Day Trip

Head straight for **Exeter** (p52), the gateway to Devon, to delve into its eclectic and historic city centre where Roman, Tudor and Georgian buildings jostle for space beneath the shadow of a towering Norman cathedral. Start with a **walking tour** (p55), taking in the 2000-year-old Roman city walls and more architectural gems on the high street, before ending at **Exeter Cathedral** (p53) to soak up the views with a rooftop tour.

On pleasant afternoons, slow down with a cruise along the **Exeter Canal** (p54) to a popular lock-side pub, then dine alfresco at the buzzing **Quayside** (p54).

Seasonal Highlights

Beach towns come alive in summer; seasonal businesses operate from Easter to October. Spring and autumn are ideal for hiking and nature, while thousands of birds winter in east Devon's marshlands.

JANUARY

New Year's Day Racing at Exeter Racecourse kickstarts the calendar with one of Devon's biggest sporting events.

APRIL

Easter sees the reopening of seasonal businesses, while the wetlands are alive with the songs of warblers and breeding lapwings.

JULY

Celebrating summertime and all things agriculture, the **Mid Devon Show** brings a fun, festival atmosphere to the countryside.

FROM LEFT: SIMON GALLOWAY - PA IMAGES VIA GETTY IMAGES ©, ERNI/SHUTTERSTOCK ©, DCURZON/SHUTTERSTOCK ©

A Long Weekend

Start with a day in **Exeter** (p52), then make your way down the river to **Exmouth** (p58). Devon's oldest holiday resort remains a popular seaside destination. You could easily spend the rest of the weekend on the beach here (which is long and glorious), but if you can tear yourself away, the rest of the **Jurassic Coast** (p62) is calling.

Discover millennia-old cliffs and stunning rock formations with a **Jurassic Coast cruise** (p63), then step back in time with a ride through the marshlands on **Seaton Tramway** (p65), before donning a hard hat to explore **Beer Quarry Caves** (p65).

If You Have More Time

Step back from the coast to explore east and Mid Devon's often-overlooked rural interior. Seek out Bronze and Iron Age earthworks and quiet hiking trails in the **East Devon Area of Outstanding Natural Beauty** (p60). Stop at vineyards and farm shops, or make a detour to **River Cottage** (p61) for a locally sourced feast.

Next, head along the River Exe through peaceful farmland. Visit **Powderham Castle** (p57) and the former port town of **Topsham** (p57), look for birdlife in the estuary marshes, then work your way north to sleepy, riverside **Tiverton** (p57) to visit one of Devon's most impressive stately homes.

AUGUST

Peak tourist season brings crowds, price spikes and a flurry of events – chief among them the **Sidmouth Folk Festival**.

OCTOBER

Migratory birds, including avocets and brent geese, begin to arrive on the marshes for the winter.

NOVEMBER

A centuries-old tradition sees **Ottery St Mary** residents carrying barrels of flaming tar through the streets on 5 November.

DECEMBER

A glittering, festive spread arrives on Exeter's Cathedral Green in the form of Devon's largest **Christmas market**.

EXETER

Around 2000 years ago, the Romans invaded present-day Britain and set about conquering the island. They established a stronghold at the lowest point at which the River Exe could be crossed, naming it Isca Dumnoniorum (thought to derive from a Celtic word meaning 'flowing water').

Centuries later, traces of the town's Roman walls still stand, alongside a Norman castle and twin-towered cathedral, a medieval guildhall and Tudor gabled architecture. This is a city that has lived many lives, leaving behind an attractive, eclectic centre where history comes alive on every street. Today, it's a lively university town with a buzzy nightlife, vibrant arts scene and a plethora of independent businesses.

Life here was once centred on the River Exe, which powered an early industrial area on the human-made Exe Island. Once a bustling trade port, Exeter Quayside is now a riverside leisure destination and a highlight for visitors.

TOP TIP

From local live music to large-scale festivals, there's always something going on in Exeter. Check *visitexeter.com* for a calendar of events to find out what's happening when you visit. Foodies shouldn't miss the weekly farmers market, held every Thursday on the junction of South St and Fore St.

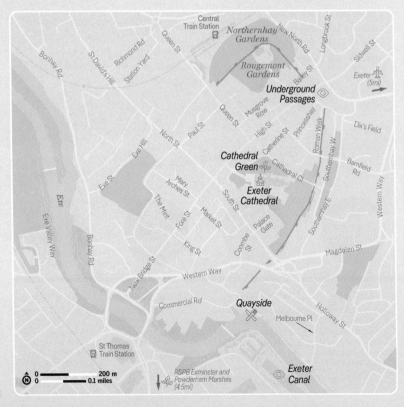

CRISTINA NIXAU/SHUTTERSTOCK ©

Exeter Cathedral

A Medieval Masterpiece

BE AWED BY EXETER CATHEDRAL

Exeter Cathedral – officially the **Cathedral Church of St Peter** – was built by the Normans on the site of a Saxon abbey in 1114 and rebuilt throughout the 13th and 14th centuries. Its blend of Early English and Decorated Gothic architectural styles showcases Exeter's long history, deserving lengthy exploration. The dazzling jewel in the cathedral's crown is its elaborate **West Front Image Screen**, covered with scores of carved figures depicting angels, kings, lords and saints. Carved in the 14th century, this masterpiece of medieval creativity would have once been entirely coloured: you can still see traces of red behind some of the figures. Inside, don't miss the exquisite fan-vaulted ceiling. A programme of special tours, including rooftop tower tours, runs throughout the year.

Step into History

WALKING TOURS WITH LOCAL EXPERTS

Dive into Exeter's many past lives with a local expert. Run by Exeter City Council, **Redcoat Tours** offers a diverse, year-round programme of free, funny and fascinating tours led by passionate locals clad in bright red blazers. Tour themes range from the city's Roman origins and historic architecture to ghosts and legends. For a solid overview of local history, start with the 'Heart of Exeter' or 'Introducing Exeter' tours. Occasionally, the Redcoat team run a special tour to tie in with a specific event, including Halloween ghost tours. Most walking tours depart from the **Cathedral Green**, with no booking required.

BEST MUSEUMS IN EXETER

Customs House
Built in 1680 at the height of Exeter's wool industry, now a visitors centre detailing the history of Exeter's quay.

Royal Albert Memorial Museum (RAMM)
The city's largest museum and art gallery with a diverse range of exhibits, from archaeological finds to fine arts.

Bill Douglas Cinema Museum
One of Britain's largest collections relating to the moving image, housed in Exeter University's old library.

Devon & Exeter Institution
Founded in 1813, this historic members-only library opens for public tours on Wednesday afternoons.

 WHERE TO STAY IN EXETER

Globe Backpackers
Dorms and private rooms in a converted 18th-century townhouse just outside the city centre. £

Townhouse
Cosy and seriously stylish B&B with friendly vibes, gorgeous decor and breakfast hampers in bed. ££

Southernhay House
Contemporary luxury, quirky decor and quality food in a beautiful Georgian townhouse. £££

Exeter Canal

BEST PLACES TO EAT IN EXETER

Red Panda
Southeast Asian street food from a colourful independent takeaway. £

Cork & Tile
Authentic Portuguese tapas and wine bar on Exeter's historic Gandy St. ££

Old Firehouse
Popular student hangout loved for its square pizzas, legendary Sunday roasts and live music. ££

Harry's
Family-run restaurant in a 19th-century Gothic building, with a diverse menu full of local produce. ££

On the Waterfront
Cool quayside restaurant and bar known for its tapas, pizzas and cocktails. ££

Going Underground
A GLIMPSE BENEATH THE CITY

Don a hard hat and get ready to duck on a tour of Exeter's **Underground Passages** – a system of 14th-century vaulted tunnels built to bring clean drinking water into the city through lead pipes. Squeeze through claustrophobia-inducing narrow passages, with the unnerving rumble of traffic overhead, to learn about this clever piece of medieval engineering. It's a unique experience; there's no similar publicly accessible system in Britain.

Rivers, Canals & Marshes
CRUISING THE RIVER EXE

Once the lifeblood of industry and trade in the city, today the River Exe lends Exeter a gentle, countryside atmosphere. The **Quayside** area is buzzing on sunny days, with plenty of options for alfresco dining and drinks. A short walk or cycle south, though, will have you in the tranquil surroundings of the parks and meadows that line the river and the **Exeter Canal**, which runs along the Exe to Topsham (p57). **Exeter Cruises** runs seasonal trips along the canal through this greenery as far as the Double Locks pub. To slow down and escape the city, rent a kayak, canoe or paddleboard and set off on a leisurely journey downriver. With a full day, you can paddle to the birdlife-rich **RSPB Exminster and Powderham Marshes**, the only place in Devon where lapwings still breed. Several companies around the quay offer equipment rentals; **Saddles and Paddles** also rents bikes to hit the Exe Estuary Trail.

GETTING AROUND

Exeter's centre is compact and fairly walkable, with plenty of footpaths, but expect a few hills and cobbles on some older streets. It's also a very bike-friendly city with numerous cycle routes. Day-trippers coming by car should use one of the three Park and Ride services to avoid driving in the city centre, which can get very congested.

This historic walking tour starts and ends at the exquisite **1 Exeter Cathedral** (p53). Wander past the Tudor architecture of **2 Cathedral Close** to pass beneath a green, wrought-iron **3 footbridge**. Turn left to walk one block along Southernhay Rd, then left again to connect onto the aptly named **4 Roman Walk**, featuring an impressive section of the Roman walls that encircled the town nearly 2000 years ago.

Cross over High St and head up Castle St for a look at the rosy-hued ruins of the Norman **5 Rougemont Castle**, built in 1068. Linger a while in the surrounding Rougemont Gardens and nearby **6 Northernhay Gardens**. Back on High St, follow it to the end, looking out for a pair of beautiful **7 Tudor merchant houses** at numbers 225 and 227, and the historic **8 Guildhall**, thought to date from at least 1330. Detour up The Mint to pass

9 St Nicholas Priory, one of Devon's oldest surviving buildings, which was founded as a Benedictine monastery in 1087.

Steep, cobbled and picturesque, **10 Stepcote Hill** leads down to the city walls' **11 West Gate**, as well as the medieval **12 St Mary Steps Church** and **13 The House That Moved** – a crooked Tudor building that was entirely moved in 1961 to avoid demolition. Cross busy Western Way to follow the scenic river path to **14 Exeter Quayside**, a historic trading port that is now a lively leisure destination where boutique shops are tucked into former warehouses. Reconnect with the city walls at **15 Water Gate** and follow them up Quay Lane, then cross the footbridge over Western Way and continue along the walls up Little Southernhay Lane.

Turn left to go back under the little green bridge, ending the walk at the cathedral.

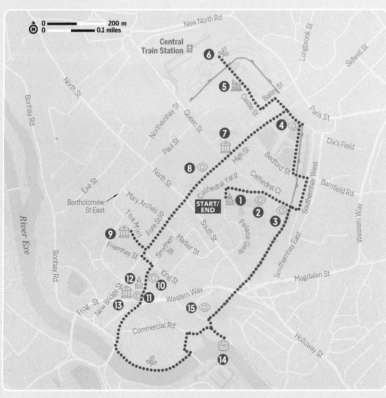

Beyond Exeter

Tiverton

Exeter Topsham

Flowing through Exeter on its way to the sea, the River Exe is the lifeblood of east and Mid-Devon.

Exeter owes much to the river it's named after. Up until the Industrial Revolution, the city grew rich from its booming wool industry – an industry that was quite literally fuelled by the Exe, powering fulling mills and carrying cloth for export from the quays at Exeter and Topsham. For centuries, the land around Exeter was filled with sheep farms, and Mid Devon is still a largely rural area. Following the Exe north leads through serene farmland and picturesque villages until it reaches the historic market town of Tiverton. South, towards Exmouth, protected marshlands provide crucial habitats for birds and other wildlife. Connecting it all, the Exe Valley Way is a 45-mile walking route following the river.

TOP TIP

Bring your bike: east Devon's flat canal paths are ideal cycling grounds, especially the Exe Estuary Trail.

Powderham Castle

MACIEJ OLSZEWSKI/SHUTTERSTOCK ©

DCUR2ON/SHUTTERSTOCK ©

Tiverton Canal Co

Castles & Canals

HIGHLIGHTS ALONG THE EXE VALLEY

Once the heart of Devon's fabric trade, **Tiverton** (a 30-minute drive from Exeter) boasts one of the Exe Valley's most charming days out. **Knightshayes Court**, designed in 1869 by the eccentric architect William Burges for local lace tycoon John Heathcoat-Amory, is a lavish, castle-like example of Victorian-Gothic architecture. It's also home to one of Devon's best gardens. Look up as you explore: Burges' elaborate ceilings were covered with plaster until the National Trust discovered and restored them. Back in town, head for the **Grand Western Canal** for a ride on one of Britain's last remaining horse-drawn barges, operated by **Tiverton Canal Co**.

Another canal lies downriver. At the top of the Exe Estuary, **Exeter Canal** is one of Britain's oldest waterways, dating from the 1560s. The canal connects Exeter with the estuary at Turf, where the imposing 14th-century **Powderham Castle** stands within an old deer park, surrounded by attractive gardens. To get there in the most romantic way possible, hop aboard the **Topsham–Turf Ferry** from the quaint port town of **Topsham**, then walk to the castle from the **Turf** pub. Topsham itself (20 minutes' drive from Exeter) blends historic maritime flavour with some fantastic independent shops and eateries. Look out for the 17th-century Dutch merchant houses on The Strand – one of them contains the **Topsham Museum**, filled with artefacts from the town's maritime past.

DEVON'S COUNTY SHOWS

England's summertime county shows combine agriculture with a fun, festival atmosphere.

These events were born as a way for farmers and breeders to showcase their livestock and crops through competitions. Today, they've evolved into tourist attractions with food stalls and entertainment, but the competitions – ranging from show jumping to sheep shearing – remain at the heart of things.

Devon has two of these farming festivals: **Devon County Show**, usually held in May, is the more traditional, while July's **Mid Devon Show** has more entertainment, including a music festival. Both offer a great chance to sample local food and drinks, shop and get a taste of English rural life.

 GETTING AROUND

Direct buses operated by Stagecoach run between Exeter and Tiverton, and to Topsham in the other direction. Connections to nearby villages are less convenient, if they exist at all. It is, however, possible to walk to both Powderham Castle and Knightshayes Court from Topsham and Tiverton, respectively, if driving is not an option.

EXMOUTH

Often said to be the oldest holiday resort in Devon, Exmouth has been a popular seaside destination since at least the 18th century. Like many other resorts along Devon's coastline, the town is dotted with Regency architecture and Victorian villas. Although some feel well-worn, the colourful, contemporary redevelopment around Exmouth Marina has breathed new life into the town.

Sitting at the mouth of the River Exe, Exmouth has the best of both worlds. There's a long sandy beach and rugged coastline to enjoy, as well as peaceful river-valley countryside begging to be explored on foot or two wheels.

Exmouth is also the gateway to the Jurassic Coast (p62), a playground for geologists and adventurers alike. The Unesco-listed coastline begins on the cliffs at the eastern end of town, marked by Orcombe Point, providing a dramatic backdrop for watersports, cliff walks and sea swims.

TOP TIP

Bring binoculars. The Exe Estuary is a haven for wildlife, including grey seals and otters, as well as wading birds like oystercatchers, lapwings and avocets. Along the coast, the cliffs shelter an array of gulls.

Hexadecagonal History

EXMOUTH'S QUIRKIEST COTTAGE

Lying just north of town, **A La Ronde** (pictured left) is one of Devon's most unique properties. This quirky 16-sided cottage was built in the 1790s by cousins Jane and Mary Parminter – two wealthy, unmarried women – following their Grand Tour of Europe. The eclectic design was inspired by their travels, and they filled the property with the curiosities and mementos they collected along the way.

HUGH WILLIAMSON/ALAMY ©

BEST CHILD-FRIENDLY DAYS

Donkey Sanctuary Sidmouth
Meet lots of rescued and retired donkeys on a working farm.

Crealy Theme Park
Rides, attractions, animals and live shows at Devon's largest family theme park, near Exeter.

Bear Town
Award-winning indoor role-playing venue in Cullompton where children up to age seven can play at 'grown-up' jobs.

World of Country Life
Meet and feed farm animals and get a taste of rural life through museums, vintage vehicles and more at this rural attraction near Exmouth.

For the Thrill-Seekers

ADRENALINE-PUMPING WATERSPORTS

Most visitors flock to Exmouth for its 2 miles of golden sand and the long, scenic promenade. But there's another, more thrilling side to this seaside town: Exmouth is one of south Devon's best watersports destinations. Kitesurfing and windsurfing are especially popular, thanks to the huge variety of conditions and wind directions. Known as the 'Duckpond', the **Exe Estuary** has flat waters and constant winds that make it a prime spot for beginners. **Edge Watersports** offers lessons from entry level to instructor training, as well as e-foiling and wingsurfing lessons for something a little different, plus equipment hire for those with experience.

Guided tours along the Jurassic Coast with **Sea Kayak Exmouth** afford an exciting, close-up view of the area's impressive red cliffs and striking geology, while gentler paddles up the Exe Estuary provide a chance to spot grey seals, sandpipers and avocets. Experienced kayakers and paddleboarders can rent gear from **Exmouth Watersports** to explore solo.

A BOAT RIDE AWAY...

Explorer Water Taxis runs a seasonal service between Exmouth and **Dalish Warren** (p97) in south Devon, where you can explore the nature reserve, unwind on the pristine white-sand beach or enjoy the rides at the retro amusement park.

GETTING AROUND

A train from Exeter can have you by the seaside at Exmouth in under half an hour. The town centre is compact and walkable, with a couple of hills and a long, flat promenade running all the way along the beach. The Stagecoach bus network connects Exmouth with other major towns along the Jurassic Coast.

Beyond Exmouth

Away from the coast, east Devon's interior is where you'll find some of the county's most beautiful countryside.

East Devon Area
of Outstanding
Natural Beauty • Colyton
• Sidbury
Exmouth

Visitors flock to Exmouth's seaside and surrounding coastline, too often overlooking east Devon's tranquil rural interior. That in itself is a selling point; this is an area where 'unspoilt' isn't just a marketing spiel but an accurate description. A designated Area of Outstanding Natural Beauty (AONB), this quiet corner of Devon is a true sleeper hit.

Stretching from Exmouth to the Dorset border, the East Devon AONB protects 103 sq miles of undulating hills and farmland, dotted with river valleys, heathland and pockets of woodland. Also protected are several declining species, including rare bats and butterflies. Slow down and explore a quiet region of breathtaking nature, criss-crossed by walking and biking trails.

TOP TIP

Seek out the region's farm shops to pick up excellent local produce – Darts Farm in Topsham is the biggest.

East Devon Area of Outstanding Natural Beauty

SAVO ILIC/SHUTTERSTOCK ©

JEANETTE TEARE/SHUTTERSTOCK ©

Thatched cottage, Sidbury

Outstanding Natural Beauty

COUNTRY WALKS AND BIKE RIDES

A quiet haven of nature, farming and simplicity on the very edge of Exmouth, the **East Devon AONB** is laced with footpaths and bridleways. The **East Devon Way** forms the backbone of these: a 40-mile walking trail charting a meandering inland course from Exmouth to the seaside town of **Lyme Regis**, just over the border in Dorset. Depending on your pace, it's possible to walk the whole thing in two days, but the official guide (eastdevonway.org.uk) splits the route into six stages – those who complete the entire walk get a certificate.

The route connects many of the AONB's gems, among them the village of **Sidbury** with its charming thatched cottages, and the ancient market town of **Colyton** on the River Coly.

The heathland of **Aylesbeare Common** is bursting with rare butterflies and birdlife, including Dartford warblers, stonechats and nightjars. There are Iron Age hillforts to explore for stunning views – **Woodbury Castle** overlooking the Exe Estuary and **Musbury Castle** in the Axe Valley – and Bronze Age barrows around **Farway**. Near the western end of the Way stands the **Cannington Viaduct**, part of the now-closed Lyme Regis branch line dating from around 1900.

For those who prefer two wheels, **The Buzzard** is an 80-mile regional cycling route taking in many of the same places, circling back via the **National Cycle Network Route 2** along the south coast.

BEST EAST DEVON FOOD & DRINK EXPERIENCES

River Exe Cafe
Unique, seasonal restaurant on a floating barge in the Exe Estuary. ££

Lympstone Manor
Tasting-menu experience at a Michelin-starred hotel restaurant from local chef Michael Caines MBE. £££

River Cottage
Set-menu dining events and cookery courses at Hugh Fearnley-Whittingstall's cosy Axminster restaurant. £££

Lyme Bay Winery
Makers of ciders, spirits and wines – samplings available at its Cellar Door shop.

Pebblebed Vineyard
This award-winning Exe Valley vineyard has tours, tastings and an annual community harvest.

GETTING AROUND

A car makes exploring the East Devon AONB easier, but expect some narrow country lanes and tight bends. For non-drivers, a public bus network exists but it's not extensive; you'll likely have to change in Exeter or Sidmouth, making journey times longer.

JURASSIC COAST

Across a 95-mile stretch of coastline in Devon and Dorset, the story of 180 million years is told. It's a story written in rock and stone, where cliff layers and prehistoric fossils reveal the secrets of a lost time. This is the Jurassic Coast: England's only natural Unesco World Heritage Site.

East Devon's stake of the Jurassic Coast is the oldest. The red sandstone cliffs here were formed in desert conditions during the Triassic period more than 200 million years ago – hence their vivid rusty hue – with the rocks getting younger as you move west through the Jurassic and Cretaceous periods.

Prepare to be awed by a coastline of not only huge geological importance but also of breathtaking landscapes, charming seaside towns, diverse wildlife and great seafood. Marvel at fossils discovered on local beaches, seek adventure on the coast paths and explore dramatic rock formations from the water.

TOP TIP

The erosion that shaped the Jurassic Coast also creates rockfalls and landslides. Pay attention to warning signs: if a path is closed, there's likely a good reason. Stay away from the bases of cliffs and the edges of clifftops, and avoid climbing or walking over landslide debris.

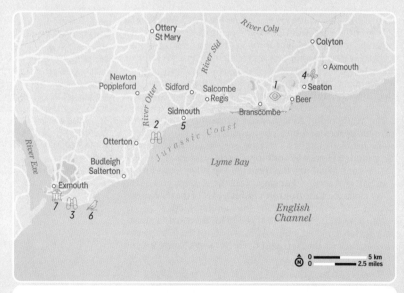

SIGHTS	2 High Peak	5 Sidmouth
1 Beer Quarry Caves	see 5 Jacob's Ladder Beach	see 5 Sidmouth Museum
see 5 Byes Toll House	3 Orcombe Point	6 Straight Point
see 5 Connaught Gardens	4 Seaton Wetlands	7 The Beacon

Orcombe Point

Triassic Views

GEOLOGICAL WONDERS FROM THE WATER

There's no better way to appreciate the Jurassic Coast than from the water. Set sail with **Stuart Line Cruises** for a trip along the Jurassic Coast on board the brightly painted *Pride of Exmouth*. Heading east from Exmouth, you'll enjoy exceptional views of east Devon's rust-red Triassic-era cliffs, with a chance of dolphin sightings in warmer months. How far you'll go depends on tides and conditions: usually Ladram Bay or Sidmouth. Highlights along the way include the Geoneedle at **Orcombe Point** – the official start of the Jurassic Coast – and **Straight Point**, a low headland that's home to a huge colony of kittiwakes, as well as shags and other gulls. Tide permitting, you may sail in between the rock stacks at Ladram Bay, overlooked by the towering cliff of **High Peak**. Stuart Line has a range of other offerings, including winter river and birdwatching cruises.

I LIVE HERE: FISHING IN BEER

Kim Aplin has been fishing in Beer since 1981 and leads fishing trips on board his boat, the *Sambe* E515 (fishinginbeer.co.uk).

'Beer is the best place for deep-sea fishing in east Devon. Here, you can catch mackerel, pollack, rock salmon, whiting in the winter and black bream in summer and autumn.

'When I take out angling groups for competitions, we can catch up to 11 species.

'The best place to try local fish is **Neil's Restaurant** in Sidmouth, or for lunch in summer, Beer pub **The Barrel of Beer**. If you want locally caught fish to cook yourself, visit **Beer Fisheries** on Beer beach – they can also deliver.'

 WHERE TO LEARN MORE ABOUT THE JURASSIC COAST

Fairlynch Museum
Learn about Budleigh Salterton's prehistoric red cliffs and view the Jurassic Coast's oldest fossil.

Sidmouth Museum
Triassic-era fossils alongside some interesting local history exhibits.

Fine Foundation Heritage Centre Beer
Discover local marine life and the story of Beer's famous stone at this beachside centre.

SMUGGLERS & WRECKERS

In 2007, the MSC *Napoli* was wrecked at Branscombe. Hundreds descended to scavenge the washed-up shipping containers, calling to mind the south coast's 'Wreckers' of the 18th and 19th centuries, some of whom deliberately lured ships to their doom.

Less menacing (and much more common) were smugglers, who landed illegal contraband like brandy, tea, tobacco and silk from the Channel Islands and France.

East Devon was a particular hotbed, especially Beer and Branscombe, with tunnels and caves along the coast used for storing contraband. One local gang was led by Jack Rattenbury (1778–1884) – supposedly nicknamed 'the Rob Roy of the West' – whose *Memoirs of a Smuggler* tells of his various adventures.

Ladram Bay

After the cruise, get closer to its highlights by walking the coast path – or taking to the water. Serene and picturesque, **Ladram Bay** is one of east Devon's top paddleboarding locations. The red-rock sea stacks that dot the bay are geological marvels, formed by millions of years of erosion.

From a paddleboard, at water level, their size is all the more impressive, and the calm waters of the bay are perfect for beginners. Board rental is available from **Ladram Bay Holiday Park**.

Timeless Charm

BEACHES AND BLUE PLAQUES

Nestled between two towering Jurassic Coast cliffs, **Sidmouth** was lauded for its timeless charm by Poet Laureate John Betjeman. The Regency-era resort has seen some distinguished visitors in its time, including Queen Victoria as a baby, and later her son Albert (the future King Edward VII). This rich history is captured by the **Blue Plaque Trail**, connecting 64 plaques that highlight heritage buildings and historic sights; the Sid Vale Association has a full list and

 WHERE TO STAY ON THE JURASSIC COAST

YHA Beer
Popular hostel and campsite in a large period property with beautiful gardens. **£**

Ladram Bay Holiday Park
Family-friendly park with holiday homes, camping and touring pitches, an indoor pool and other activities. **££**

Dukes Seaside Inn
Contemporary boutique rooms in a 19th-century inn at the centre of Sidmouth's esplanade. **£££**

map on its website. The **Sidmouth Museum** sells detailed guides and runs free guided town walks a few days a week.

Start on the Esplanade, where you can see a string of historic hotels, including the **Royal York Hotel**, Sidmouth's first purpose-built hotel. Peak Hill Rd, peeling away from the Esplanade at its western end, leads to several blue-plaque buildings, including **The Beacon**, a thatched-roof cottage built in 1842 and used as a hospital during WWI. Walk through **Connaught Gardens**, home to a pseudo-castle clock tower, for a view of **Jacob's Ladder Beach** – a great place to spend sunny days. At the eastern end of the Esplanade, walk along the River Sid as it carves below a wall of red cliffs to reach **Byes Toll House**, built in 1817 along with a new bridge to provide a more accessible crossing than the nearby ford.

Dig Deeper

EXPLORE A 2000-YEAR-OLD QUARRY

A pretty fishing village tucked beneath wooded cliffs, **Beer** sits on an impressive secret: a high-quality white-chalk limestone that lends itself perfectly to fine-detail carving. Beer stone was used to carve the Image Screen on Exeter Cathedral (p53), and was also used for other famous buildings across Britain including St Paul's Cathedral and Westminster Abbey in London. **Beer Quarry Caves** runs guided tours of the 2000-year-old quarry. Started by the Romans and used right up until the 1920s, the cavernous space was cut almost entirely by hand over the centuries, with pick-axe marks visible on almost every surface.

Trams & Marshlands

RIDE A VINTAGE TRAMWAY

Take a ride to a bygone age with **Seaton Tramway**. Running between seaside **Seaton** and the sleepy riverside town of **Colyton**, this fleet of restored historic trams follows the old Seaton branch line which once brought Victorian tourists to the seaside. Climbing the narrow, spiral staircase can feel a little like boarding a large toy, but these are genuine, life-sized electric trams: the oldest dates from 1904, and most others are from the 1960s.

The line heads through the scenic **Seaton Wetlands**, backed by densely wooded hills and rich with birdlife. Sit upstairs on the right (towards Colyton) for the best views, keeping your eyes peeled for buzzards, wading birds and otters.

WHY I LOVE THE JURASSIC COAST

Emily Luxton
(@em_luxton)

'There is nowhere in England I love quite as much as the Jurassic Coast. This is home; I was born and raised in Weymouth and spent my life walking these cliffs, fossil hunting on these beaches and paddleboarding on these waters.

There's so much to love: the geology, the seafood, the swashbuckling tales of smugglers… but most of all, that sense of adventure as you stand atop a windswept cliff looking out to sea.

One of my favourite walks here is a real toughie, but very rewarding: following the coast path from Seaton to Lyme Regis, through the unspoilt wilderness of the Undercliffs National Nature Reserve.'

GETTING AROUND

Driving is generally the easiest way to get around the Jurassic Coast, but there are some narrow country lanes and seaside towns that get fairly congested during summer. Stagecoach South West runs fairly regular bus services connecting most towns and villages along the coast. For walkers, the entire coastline is connected by the South West Coast Path.

Torcross and Slapton Sands (p84)

PLYMOUTH & SOUTH DEVON

PORTS, RIVERS AND RIVIERAS

Devon's southern coastline is long and diverse. Hop between classic seaside towns, historic harbours, tranquil estuaries and a sprawling coastal city.

South Devon feels like a land built for holidays. The county's bottom corner plunges southwards, as though to maximise the amount of coastline. At one end lies the English Riviera, with classic seaside resorts hugging the wide, east-facing expanse of Tor Bay. At the other end is the buzzing waterfront city of Plymouth (pictured right), known for its naval base, fishing industry and epic seafaring past, and currently undergoing a cultural makeover. Skirting the great lump of coast that lies in between are chic sailing havens, eco-conscious towns, beaches and rivers – lots of rivers.

The Dart, the Teign, the Kingsbridge Estuary and more meet the English Channel along Devon's south coast. Their wide estuaries create sheltered harbours like the ones at Dartmouth, home to an elite naval college, and Salcombe, an upscale yachtie hangout.

In 1620 the Pilgrims set sail for the New World from this very coast, just one of the innumerable momentous voyages that have set out from south Devon's ports. This is a land of seafarers, where life is tied to the coast and the rivers that lace it. But it's also holiday heaven, with a beach to suit every taste: family-friendly sands backed by arcades at busy resort towns, pristine swathes of white dunes, protected wildlife reserves and hidden coves that can only be reached on foot.

GORDON BELL/SHUTTERSTOCK ©

THE MAIN AREAS

PLYMOUTH	**DARTMOUTH**	**THE ENGLISH RIVIERA**
Waterfront city.	Rivers, sailing and	Classic British
p72	coastal adventures.	beach towns.
	p79	p90

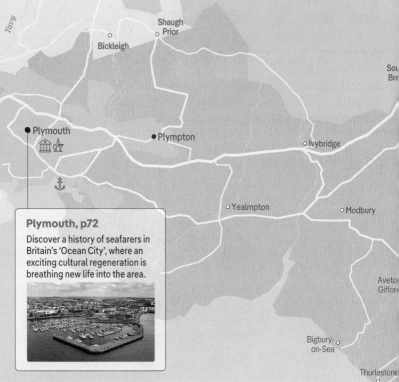

Find Your Way

Stretching from the waterfront city of Plymouth on the Cornish border to the edge of the River Exe in the east, Devon's southern region looks small on a map but it's richly varied.

Poundsg

Dartmoo
National
Park

Tavy

Shaugh
Prior

Bickleigh

Sou
Bre

Plymouth

Plympton

Ivybridge

Yealmpton

Modbury

Plymouth, p72

Discover a history of seafarers in Britain's 'Ocean City', where an exciting cultural regeneration is breathing new life into the area.

Aveto
Giffor

Bigbury-
on-Sea

Thurlestone

BUS

If you don't have a car, bus is the best option for reaching the towns along the south coast, though a change or two may be required for longer journeys or to reach less common destinations.

TRAIN

There are train stations at Plymouth, Totnes and the English Riviera, but you'll need a bus or taxi to connect with towns in between. The train from Plymouth into the Tamar Valley is one of the most scenic in the southwest.

CAR

Driving is the easiest way to explore the towns and beaches along the south coast, but be prepared for narrow, winding roads in rural areas. Some river crossings require a long drive inland to the nearest bridge – only the Dart has a car ferry.

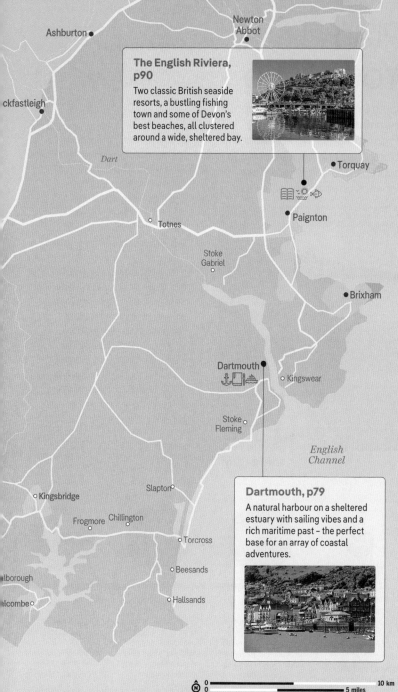

Ashburton

Newton Abbot

ckfastleigh

The English Riviera, p90

Two classic British seaside resorts, a bustling fishing town and some of Devon's best beaches, all clustered around a wide, sheltered bay.

Dart

Torquay

Totnes

Paignton

Stoke Gabriel

Brixham

Dartmouth

Kingswear

Stoke Fleming

English Channel

Kingsbridge

Slapton

Frogmore Chillington

Dartmouth, p79

A natural harbour on a sheltered estuary with sailing vibes and a rich maritime past – the perfect base for an array of coastal adventures.

Torcross

lborough

Beesands

alcombe

Hallsands

0   10 km
0   5 miles

Plan Your Time

South Devon is a diverse region, encompassing a bustling city, hidden beaches, wild coast paths, sailing hubs and popular seaside resorts. Choosing where to go depends on what appeals most.

Salcombe ferry

City Break

Arrive into **Plymouth** (p72) for a city break encompassing the main elements of the south coast: a thrilling maritime history, a thriving fishing industry and an ever-evolving cultural scene. Start with a **walking tour** (p75) to take in the historic sights and maritime monuments, particularly the Mayflower Steps – the point from which the Pilgrims set sail for North America.

On pleasant days, spend an afternoon relaxing at **Tinside Lido** (p74) or indulging in local watersports. Indoors, the **National Marine Aquarium** (p72) showcases local and exotic marine life. Round it all off with a tour of **Plymouth Gin** (p73), England's oldest working distillery.

Seasonal Highlights

Summer is when south Devon's beach towns shine, but spring and autumn are quieter and the ideal times for coastal hikes. Seasonal businesses generally open March to October.

MARCH
Businesses begin to reopen after winter and **spring blooms** bring colour to gardens like Overbeck's and Torre Abbey.

MAY
With spring in full swing, bluebells fill the woods and summer **migratory birds** like reed warblers arrive in the wetlands.

JULY
Regatta season kicks off with a three-day festival of yacht races in Plymouth, continuing in sailing towns throughout summer.

Seaside Weekender

If you have more time, add on a few days for the **English Riviera** (p90). Its much-loved resorts also make a good standalone destination for a beachy long weekend. Spend a day or two enjoying the retro seaside delights of **Torquay** (p90) and **Paignton** (p92) and Tor Bay's warm, sheltered waters.

Next, explore Torquay's connections with the world's most famous crime writer on an **Agatha Christie walking tour** (p94). Finally, hop on a ferry across the bay to explore the charming harbour in the fishing town of **Brixham** (p93), making sure to try local seafood at one of the restaurants.

A Week on the Coast

After a day in **Plymouth** (p72), head east. Time your arrival in Bigbury-on-Sea with low tide to walk across the beach to **Burgh Island** (p89), or take the Sea Tractor at high tide. Beach-hop (or hike) your way along the coast to the yachtie haven of **Salcombe** (p86), an ideal spot for sailing, watersports or cruising the **Kingsbridge Estuary** (p88).

Take a road trip along the unmissable **Start Bay** (p84), leading to **Dartmouth** (p79), another historic sailing town. Delve into this seafaring past on a **walking tour** (p82), then hire a boat or kayak to explore the **Dart Estuary** (p81).

AUGUST

Peak summer (usually) means great **watersports** conditions and beach weather – but also crowds and inflated prices.

SEPTEMBER

Fiction fans descend on Torquay for the **International Agatha Christie Festival**, and resorts quieten with kids back at school.

OCTOBER

Surfers flock to Bantham, where the waves are at their best, while **Dartmouth Food Festival** celebrates the southwest's finest.

DECEMBER

Historic homes host festive events, and **Dartmouth Steam Railway** runs the evening spectacle of a train clad in neon lights.

PLYMOUTH

Plymouth

Britain's 'Ocean City', Plymouth has long been a city of seafarers. A string of famous voyagers set out from here, among them the *Mayflower* Pilgrims and Captain James Cook. Most famously, Sir Francis Drake, the locally born explorer and hero of the battle against the Spanish Armada, began his circumnavigation of the globe from Plymouth. A privateer with links to the slave trade, Drake isn't exactly a cut-and-dry hero, but remains a crucial player in Plymouth's history.

Home to Europe's largest naval base and the second-biggest fresh-fish market in England, Plymouth is still intrinsically linked to the sea. That naval presence made the city one of the worst casualties of the WWII bombings, and hasty rebuilding created a city centre where functionality, rather than beauty, reigns. But pockets of historic architecture remain, while an ongoing waterfront regeneration and exciting new Cultural Quarter are creating a city that deserves a second glance.

TOP TIP

The city lies on Plymouth Sound, a deep, sheltered inlet in the English Channel where the rivers Plym and Tamar meet the sea. With the city centre spread along the waterfront, sometimes the most direct route from one side to the other is by ferry, rather than car or bus.

DATES FOR THE DIARY

Plymouth Regatta
A three-day yacht regatta in July, with competitive races and shoreside entertainment bringing a festival atmosphere to Plymouth Yacht Haven.

British Fireworks Championships
Held over two days in August in Plymouth Sound, this huge-scale fireworks display sees six professionals battle it out for the title.

Plymouth Armed Forces
An exciting summer event at The Hoe celebrating Plymouth's strong ties to the armed forces.

Plymouth Seafood Festival
Gather around Sutton Harbour for a late-summer celebration of all things seafood.

Open the Box

PLYMOUTH'S CULTURAL QUARTER

A dramatic grey and glass cubic structure containing a state-of-the-art museum and art gallery, **The Box** is at the forefront of Plymouth's ongoing cultural regeneration. Opened at the end of 2020, this architectural icon transformed the former museum, library and St Luke's church buildings, also creating a new public square – **Tavistock Place** – for performances and events. Alongside Plymouth University's Arts Institute, this exciting redevelopment forms the heart of Plymouth's new Cultural Quarter. Inside, the permanent exhibits tell the story of England's 'Ocean City', from vast ship figureheads in the lobby to the excellent '100 Journeys' exhibition showcasing the momentous voyages that have set out from Plymouth over the centuries.

Ocean City

LIFE ON THE WATER

At **Sutton Harbour** (pictured opposite page), two sides of Plymouth collide as the Barbican's historic, cobbled streets meet the sleek architecture of the redeveloped waterfront. The Barbican's former fish quay is now a hub of bars and restaurants, while across the harbour, Plymouth Fisheries remains one of the UK's most important fishing hubs, landing over 6000 tonnes of fish a year. Somewhat ironically, the **National Marine Aquarium** stands right next door. This is the UK's largest aquarium, with vast tanks

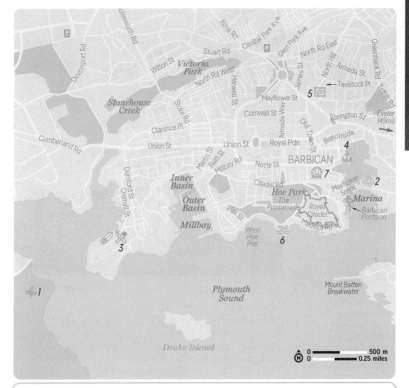

SIGHTS
1. Mount Edgcumbe
2. National Marine Aquarium
3. Royal William Yard

4. Sutton Harbour
5. The Box

ACTIVITIES
6. Tinside Lido

DRINKING & NIGHTLIFE
7. Plymouth Gin Distillery

showcasing marine life both local and exotic. Run by the Ocean Conservation Trust, it has a big focus on education, and ticket sales fund conservation and research projects.

Plymouth Boat Trips runs a ferry service connecting the Barbican with the manor house and country park at **Mount Edgcumbe** (p159) and with **Royal William Yard**, a Victorian naval yard whose waterfront warehouses have been repurposed into galleries, shops and restaurants. It also offers several cruises and a seasonal ferry to Cawsand in Cornwall.

 WHERE TO STAY IN PLYMOUTH

Imperial Hotel
Family-run hotel with lovely rooms and self-contained flats, five minutes from The Hoe. ££

Crowne Plaza
Comfortable rooms and an indoor pool at a popular chain hotel known for its excellent views. ££

Boringdon Hall Hotel & Spa
Grand country manor just outside Plymouth, with a spa, restaurant and stylish rooms. £££

I LIVE HERE

Jodie Pierre, local chef and owner of Maurish food stall (@areyoufeeling maurish), dishes up the details on Plymouth's foodie gem.

'Plymouth Market is undergoing a transformation at the moment, turning into more of a food court.

There are some great places to eat in the market now and it's bringing different clientele in. Maurish serves home-cooked Mauritian food, inspired by my dad who came from Port Louis. Other must-visit food stalls in the market are Taste of Thailand for authentic Thai food, Everest Flavours for Nepalese street-food snacks (don't miss their Everest Spicy Special), and At Kitchen or Tea and Bun for Asian cuisine. For dessert, try a bubble waffle from Kawaffle.'

SCOTT JENKIN/SHUTTERSTOCK ©

Plymouth Gin Distillery

On sunny days, head for **Tinside Lido**, a striking outdoor pool overlooking Plymouth Sound. An art-deco gem built in 1935, this seasonal saltwater pool is one of the city's most popular attractions. Experience the Sound's sheltered waters for yourself with a paddleboarding or kayaking session from **Mount Batten Watersports**, or try a lesson or guided adventure with **South West SUP** in Royal William Yard.

Naval Strength

ENGLAND'S OLDEST GIN DISTILLERY

At the heart of the historic Barbican district, Black Friar's building has been the home of **Plymouth Gin Distillery** since 1793, making it the oldest working gin distillery in England.

For nearly 200 years, its naval-strength gin was supplied to the Royal Navy whose officers mixed it into a 'medicinal' drink with lime juice, inventing the Gimlet cocktail. The building itself, a former monastery, dates from the early 1400s. It's worth a visit for the Refectory Bar's stunning beamed ceiling alone, but take one of the tours which run throughout the day for a glimpse of the Victorian still, an insight into the production process and a tasting.

GETTING AROUND

Plymouth's city centre is quite sprawling and can be hilly. The historic Barbican district has some cobbled and uneven streets. You can get between the waterfront areas by ferry or water taxi; the tourist office has a leaflet outlining all available water links. For longer distances, Plymouth Citybus is the main bus provider.

Discover Plymouth's sights and delve into its maritime history with this city centre walking tour, setting out from the striking Victorian **1 Guildhall** at the heart of the city. Follow Armada Way down to reach **2 The Hoe**, a clifftop park with unbeatable views of Plymouth Sound and several notable sights. Front and centre, the towering **3 Plymouth Naval Memorial** commemorates more than 23,000 sailors of WWI and WWII who have no known grave. Nearby stands a **4 statue of Sir Francis Drake**, explorer, privateer and mayor of Plymouth, who – according to popular legend – played bowls in The Hoe while awaiting the Spanish Armada in 1588. At the eastern end, heavy stone walls enclose the **5 Royal Citadel**, a 17th-century fortress still in use by the military today. Overlooking the sea is the iconic red-and-white **6 Smeaton's Tower**

lighthouse; originally built on Eddystone Reef in 1759, it was moved to The Hoe in the 1880s.

Pause for views from the top of the **7 Belvedere 'Wedding Cake'**, a grandiose Victorian structure with three tiers of colonnaded terraces, then take the steps down to follow the coast road around to **8 Sutton Harbour**. Here, the **9 Mayflower Steps** memorial marks the approximate site from which the Pilgrims set sail for North America in 1620. Follow Southside St into the **10 Barbican**, an area of cobbled streets, historic architecture and quirky shops. Return via the picturesque New St, passing the timber-clad **11 Elizabethan House** (dating from 1599) to end at the **12 Mayflower Museum**. Allow a little time for a visit to learn more about the story of the Pilgrim Fathers, as well as the history – and impact – of English colonisation.

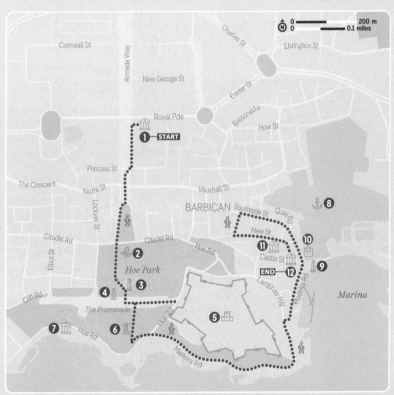

Beyond Plymouth

Tamar Valley Area
of Outstanding
Natural Beauty ● Plymouth

● Tavistock

● Wembury

Devon's biggest city lies within surprisingly easy reach of nature, from quiet beaches to tranquil river valleys.

Location is one of Plymouth's biggest selling points. Perched on the coast at Devon's western border, this waterside city is within day-tripping distance of some of the southwest's top attractions. The edge of Dartmoor is less than 20 minutes' drive, Cornwall is just a ferry ride across the Tamar, and south Devon's coastal highlights are all less than an hour away.

Moving eastwards from the city leads to some of the most underrated beaches in Devon, as well as some of the best views on the South West Coast Path. And tucked along the Devon–Cornwall border, the Tamar Valley Area of Outstanding Natural Beauty (AONB) is a rich landscape where heritage and nature collide.

TOP TIP

The Tamar Valley railway line from Plymouth to Gunnislake is known for its views: grab a window seat and enjoy.

West Hoe Pier and waterfront

Trails, Gardens & Heritage

ALONG THE TAMAR VALLEY

The rolling countryside of the **Tamar Valley AONB**, 20 minutes' drive from Plymouth, hides a wealth of heritage. Step into 700 years of history at **Buckland Abbey** – built by medieval Cistercian monks, it was converted into a grand estate by privateer and explorer Sir Richard Grenville in the 16th century and later sold to Sir Francis Drake. Learn more of his history and discover Elizabethan life, then enjoy a walk through the gardens and surrounding estate. Just down the road is another gorgeous garden – **Garden House**, built around a medieval vicarage. The 4 hectares of beautifully sculpted gardens here are a joy at any time of year, with wildflower meadows blooming in spring and summer and red hues in the Acer Glade in autumn.

Both these gems lie a short distance from **Drake's Trail**, a 21-mile cycling and walking route between Tavistock and Plymouth. Though named after the explorer, this trail is more about discovering the landscapes of the Tamar Valley. Highlights include the panoramic views of the wooded Walkham Valley from **Gem Bridge** and Isambard Kingdom Brunel's 341m-long **Grenofen Tunnel**. The route initially follows the **Plym Valley Trail** from Plymouth, passing by **Saltram House** – another historic property with delightful gardens to explore – and through the lovely **Plymbridge Woods**. This first stretch is ideal for a shorter, more leisurely day trip from Plymouth.

Scars of an Industry

TAMAR VALLEY'S MINING LANDSCAPE

Though tranquil today, the Tamar Valley once rang with the sound of over 100 mines. Tin, copper, silver-lead and arsenic were all mined here, shaping the landscape and leaving behind traces like **Wheal Betsy** (pictured), an abandoned tin mine near the village of Mary Tavy. **Tavistock**, a former stannary town on the edge of Dartmoor, was completely transformed by the 7th Duke of Bedford during the mid-19th century using profits from his mines, and quays sprang up along the Tamar to transport copper ore. **Morwellham Quay** was one of the busiest; today, it's a living museum where visitors can explore Victorian

THE GUIDE

PLYMOUTH & SOUTH DEVON: PLYMOUTH

HERO OR VILLAIN

Sir Francis Drake (1540–96) is intrinsically tied to Plymouth's history.

Born in Tavistock, he was brought up in Plymouth by relatives, the Hawkins family. Drake worked for the Hawkins fleet, whose ventures included the African Slave Trade, before making a name for himself as a privateer, plundering Spain's American colonies.

In 1580, the explorer returned from a three-year circumnavigation of the globe – the first Englishman and second person in the world to achieve the feat. Queen Elizabeth I backed the voyage and knighted Drake on his return.

Later, Drake played an important role in the victory over the Spanish Armada, destroying ships in a pre-emptive strike and serving as vice admiral in the battle.

 WHERE TO TAKE THE CHILDREN IN SOUTH DEVON

Dartmoor Zoo
Charity-run zoo and conservation centre known for its big-cat collection, about 20 minutes' drive from Plymouth.

Tree Surfers at Tamar Trails
Get the adrenaline pumping and test your limits with zip lines and treetop trails at this woodland centre near Tavistock.

Pennywell Farm
Popular family-friendly farm park near Totnes with animal encounters, shows and children's rides.

THE TAMAR BRIDGES

Forming the border between Devon and Cornwall, the River Tamar is one of the southwest's most significant waterways.

Northwest of Plymouth, two bridges span the river, literally and symbolically linking the two counties. Both are landmarks, particularly the Royal Albert Bridge. It was designed by the renowned Victorian architect Isambard Kingdom Brunel for the Great Western Railway, which he also engineered. It's still in use today, affording some unbeatable views of the Tamar as it carries trains west into Cornwall. The newer Tamar Bridge was added in 1961 to carry the A38 across the border. Visit the Bridging the Tamar visitors centre in Plymouth to learn more.

Rock pools, Wembury Beach

cottages and shops and take a ride on the underground Mine Train. Nearby, the **Tamar Trails Centre** is a starting point for 15 miles of walking and biking trails and bridleways that follow old mineral transport systems through the former mining landscapes.

Coastal Trails

WALKING THE SOUTH DEVON COAST

About 20 minutes' drive east of Plymouth, the section between the River Yealm and Bigbury-on-Sea is generally considered to have some of the best views on the South West Coast Path, but it's challenging. For something shorter, walk the coast path from **Wembury Beach** – one of the best rock-pooling spots in the area – to **Warren Point** on the Yealm, returning inland through the village. Pop into the **Wembury Marine Centre** to learn more about local beachside flora and fauna.

GETTING AROUND

Driving is generally the easiest way to explore the more remote countryside and coastal areas, but roads around the city can be congested, while further out you may need to navigate narrow country lanes. Plymouth Citybus operates services to Wembury on the coast (30 minutes) and up through the Tamar Valley to Tavistock (one hour).

DARTMOUTH

● Dartmouth

Rising high on Dartmoor, the River Dart widens into a sheltered tidal estuary for its final stretch, forming the natural harbour which is the backbone of life in Dartmouth. Spread along a hilltop on the west bank of the river, Dartmouth's crooked streets are rich with history. Many buildings date back to the 16th and 17th centuries; today, they house trendy eateries, swish art galleries and nautical clothing shops.

The Royal Navy arrived in Dartmouth in 1863 and still trains officers here at the UK's most prestigious naval college. But Dartmouth's maritime history goes much further back. In the 12th century, a flotilla of ships launched from here for the Second Crusades, and the Pilgrim Fathers initially set sail for North America from Dartmouth's Bayard's Cove in 1620 (relaunching from Plymouth when one of the ships sprang a leak). Today, Dartmouth is an attractive destination where river and sea meet.

TOP TIP

If visiting for a day, use the seasonal (March to October) Dartmouth Park & Ride car park on the outskirts of town to avoid driving into the town centre, which can get pretty congested, especially during summer. Two car ferries operate across the Dart.

Fortress Views

EXPLORE DARTMOUTH CASTLE

From its vantage point at the entrance to the estuary, the imposing limestone **Dartmouth Castle** (pictured) has been watching over Dartmouth and the River Dart for more than 600 years. The oldest parts of the fort date from 1388 – they were built during the Hundred Years' War to protect the town from potential French invasion. A booming sound-and-light show inside the Victorian-era point battery brings history to life. Don't miss the estuary views from the top of the gun tower; built in the 1490s, it's one of the oldest gun forts in England. You can walk to the castle, but the **Dartmouth Castle Ferry** is much more romantic.

 WHERE TO STAY IN DARTMOUTH

Bayard's Cove Inn
Boutique hotel and restaurant within a 14th-century Tudor inn with characterful, elegent rooms. **££**

Nethway Farm
Five beautifully decorated, family-run and sustainability focused holiday cottages in a peaceful setting. **£££**

Dart Marine
Stylish waterside retreat with calming, classic decor and views of the yacht harbour. **£££**

BEST RESTAURANTS IN DARTMOUTH

Alf Resco
Casual cafe with a tiny terrace and a museum-like interior full of eclectic maritime decor. £

Rockfish
Posh fish and chips and catch-of-the-day specials from the original branch of the popular southwest chain. Head to its harbourside takeaway for something quicker. ££

Angel
Relaxed fine dining and special tasting menus at a multi-award-winning riverside restaurant. £££

Andria
Chic contemporary restaurant with a Michelin Bib Gourmand, focused on modern European cuisine. £££

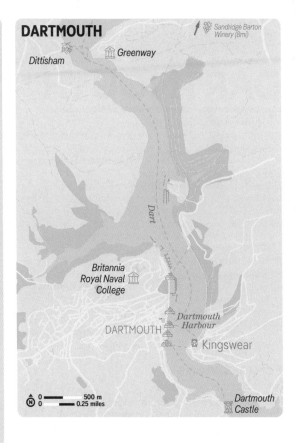

DARTMOUTH

Sandridge Barton Winery (8mi)

Dittisham

Greenway

Dart

Britannia Royal Naval College

Dartmouth Harbour

DARTMOUTH

Kingswear

0 — 500 m
0 — 0.25 miles

Dartmouth Castle

Dead Man's Folly

AGATHA CHRISTIE'S HOLIDAY HOME

MORE AGATHA CHRISTIE

Follow the **Agatha Christie Mile walking trail** (p94) in Torquay and visit the town's museum to learn more about the author's life and her connections with south Devon.

Just getting to **Greenway** feels like an adventure. The former holiday home of legendary local crime writer Agatha Christie lies in a remote spot above the River Dart, surrounded by beautiful gardens. It's possible to drive from Dartmouth, but the route is complicated and parking limited. Far more evocative is to take the small, twin-decked **Dittisham–Greenway Ferry** or to walk via the **Dart Valley Trail**. The attractive Georgian manor Christie called 'the loveliest place in the world' is still just as her family left it, filled with the author's collections and treasures. Don't miss the riverside boathouse, scene of the crime in the Poirot murder mystery *Dead Man's Folly* (1956).

River Dart, near Dittisham

Life on the River

WILDLIFE, CRUISES AND VINEYARDS

Flowing serenely through a deep wooded valley, the Dart Estuary is the final, tidal stretch of the River Dart. Rich in wildlife and dotted with waterside villages like idyllic **Dittisham**, the estuary is best explored from the water. **Dartmouth Steam Railway and Riverboat Company** runs a 90-minute cruise from Dartmouth to Totnes (and back) with an amusing, insightful commentary and unparalleled views from the top deck.

Alternatively, **Dartmouth Boat Hire** rents self-drive motorboats, enabling visitors to chart their own course to explore the estuary and its creeks. No licence is needed, but experience is required as navigating the tidal estuary can be tricky. As you cruise, keep your eyes on the treeline to spot birds of prey, including buzzards and peregrine falcons. At water level, you can see kingfishers, cormorants, grey herons and little egrets. Seals can be seen as far upriver as Totnes, and will often pop up to watch a boat pass. Otters live in the reeds along the banks, but are much more reticent; kayaking or paddleboarding offers a better chance of spotting them.

On dry land, walk the **Dart Valley Trail**, a 16-mile footpath from Dartmouth to Totnes through ancient woodlands. It passes within reach of **Sandridge Barton Winery**, home of Sharpham Wines – pop in for a tour and tasting!

GETTING AROUND

Dartmouth's small town centre is very walkable, although there are cobbled streets in the Bayard's Cove area and fairly steep hills as you move away from the water's edge. Driving in the town centre can be slow, with narrow roads and a one-way system to navigate. Two car and foot-passenger ferries – Higher Ferry and Lower Ferry – connect Dartmouth with the eastern bank of the River Dart; both accept card payments.

WALKING THROUGH HISTORY IN DARTMOUTH

Set out from Dartmouth's small **1 Inner Harbour**, pausing to admire the attractive row of historic buildings along its southern bank. Follow the riverside path to **2 Dart Marina Yacht Harbour**, enjoying views of colourful Kingswear on the opposite bank. Those with an interest in naval history may want to detour up to the **3 Britannia Royal Naval College**, or book a guided tour. Otherwise, skip the hill and wait for views of the imposing red-brick building from the other side of the river. Dating from 1905, it's the only remaining Naval Officer College in the country. From the marina, take the **4 Higher Ferry** across the river, then follow the Dart Valley Trail footpath south along the opposite bank, with the tracks of Dartmouth **5 Steam Railway** on your left. Climb into Kingswear along Brixham Rd, pausing at the top for a view of the Naval College across the thicket of masts in the estuary.

From Kingswear, take the **6 Lower Ferry** back across the river, and turn left onto the cobbled streets of **7 Bayard's Cove**, the quay from which the Pilgrims set sail for North America in 1620. Make your way down to explore the remnants of **8 Bayard's Cove Fort**, added during the reign of Henry VIII. Duck through the fort's archway, climb the staircase and turn right to follow Newcomen Rd (named for local Thomas Newcomen, who invented the first practical fuel-burning engine in 1712) back towards the harbour. Turn left up Duke St to pass the **9 Butterwalk**, a row of crooked 17th-century timber-framed merchant houses, then dive into the independent shops and galleries along crooked and colourful **10 Foss Street**. Finally, loop back to end at **11 Dartmouth Museum**, delving further into local history.

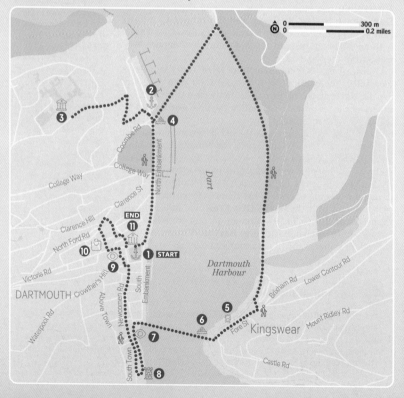

Beyond Dartmouth

Hit the south coast in search of clifftop walks, river valleys, watersports and some of south Devon's most beautiful beaches.

Totnes
Kingsbridge Estuary • Dartmouth
Burgh Island • • Start Bay
Salcombe

Beyond the Dart, several other estuaries punctuate Devon's southwestern coastline, feeding the fertile landscape of patchwork countryside that forms the South Devon Area of Outstanding Natural Beauty (AONB).

Most people head here for the coast, whether for relaxing beach days or more thrilling adventures. But the area is also dotted with pretty villages and characterful towns. Chic Salcombe appeals to a yachtie crowd, also boasting independent restaurants and a serene estuary that begs to be explored. Historic Totnes is a hippie haven, full of ecofriendly eateries and indie shops, while the market town of Kingsbridge offers an authentic glimpse of rural Devon life. Still, the rugged coastline is the star, featuring hidden coves, wild headlands and sandy beaches.

TOP TIP

Many car parks around south Devon use the RingGo app to accept online payments – download it for cash-free exploring.

Salcombe

UP.HILL.DOWN.DALE/SHUTTERSTOCK ©

83

REGAL REGATTAS

Summer on the south Devon coast means one thing: regatta season. These yacht and boat racing events have evolved into multiday festivals that pack out towns with spectators, sportspeople and revellers. Many incorporate fireworks displays and other entertainment, and celebrations go on into the night.

The oldest is Torbay Royal Regatta, which dates back to 1813. A blue plaque at the Royal Torbay Yacht Club commemorates the Regatta's 200th anniversary in 2012.

Dartmouth Royal Regatta, approaching its 180th year, is one of the biggest: a week-long celebration that always falls across the last Friday in August.

Finally, Salcombe has two major regattas, Salcombe Town Regatta and Salcombe Yacht Club Regatta.

Exercise Tiger Memorial, Slapton Sands

Beach Roads & Lost Villages

A START BAY ROAD TRIP

To truly appreciate **Start Bay**, you need to see it from above. Follow the meandering A379 coast road west from Dartmouth for 15 minutes for glimpses of the crescent-shaped bay. Descending from the village of Strete affords a fantastic view of **Slapton Sands** – a narrow strip of shingle beach with the sea on one side and the broad sweep of **Slapton Ley**, the southwest's largest freshwater lake, on the other. The road straightens out to cross the spit between the two; stop at the Memorial Carpark, halfway along, for a walk around the Ley and surrounding nature reserve. At the far end of the lake, stop in the village of Torcross to visit the **Excercise**

 WHERE TO HAVE A BEACH DAY NEAR DARTMOUTH

Blackpool Sands
Wide arc of shingle sand surrounded by evergreen woodlands with clear, calm waters.

South Milton Sands
A long stretch of golden sand watched over by the triangular arch of Thurlestone Rock.

Bantham Beach
Popular surfing beach, backed by towering sand dunes and the wildlife-rich Bantham Ham.

Tiger Memorial, a WWII Sherman Tank leftover from D-Day rehearsals. It was raised from the bottom of the ocean to stand as a tribute to the 639 American soldiers and sailors killed when a German torpedo boat sank the landing craft of their training mission. Beyond Torcross, the bay curves around to reach **Start Point**, a wild peninsula of rocky cliffs, tangled ferns and narrow country lanes, with the historic **Start Point Lighthouse** standing at its tip since 1836. The coast path here affords a view of **South Hallsands**, a 'lost village' swept away by a ferocious storm in 1917, leaving a handful of ruined stone cottages clinging precariously to the cliff.

Historic Buildings & Hippie Vibes

ETHICAL, ALTERNATIVE TOTNES

At the top of the Dart Estuary, about 25 minutes' drive from Dartmouth, **Totnes** is a charming market town packed with historic buildings and incredible Tudor architecture. It's also one of the most ethical places in Britain: in 2006, Totnes was one of the first towns in the UK to declare itself a Transition Town, and became a Fairtrade Town in 2011. **Riverford Farm**, birthplace of the organic-veggie-box subscription service, lies nearby. Totnes' High St is crammed with zero-waste shops, local crafts boutiques and vegan cafes. Historic highlights include **Totnes Castle**, a Norman 'motte and bailey' castle with a 13th-century stone keep; the colonnaded Tudor buildings near the top of High St; **Totnes Museum** with its Elizabethan Garden; and the ancient **Guildhall**, tucked away down a leafy side street behind the church.

Pick Up a Paddle

KAYAKING THE RIVER DART

One of the best ways to explore Devon's estuaries is on a kayak (pictured right) or paddleboard. Moving quietly at water level offers a chance to get much closer to the river's wildlife than you would in a boat. Rent a kayak or board from **Totnes Kayaks** in Stoke Gabriel, and follow the tide up or downriver, keeping your eyes peeled for otters, seals, kingfishers and more. Rentals are available seasonally and guided trips can be arranged year-round. Totnes' **Canoe Adventures** runs year-round voyages and overnight wild-camp adventures in 12-seater wooden canoes.

WATERSPORTS ON THE SOUTH COAST

Bantham Surfing Academy
Beginner and improver lessons plus beachside board rental at one of the south coast's best surf beaches.

Sea Kayak Devon
Dartmouth-based company offering skills courses and guided kayaking trips along the coast. Explore hidden sea caves and secret coves that can't be reached any other way.

Sea Kayak Salcombe
Rent kayaks, paddleboards and surf skis on South Sands beach to make a splash in the sheltered bay.

 WHERE TO EAT IN TOTNES

Wild Fig
Deli and cafe with seasonal, locally sourced food and great veggie and vegan options. £

Big Kebabski
Award-winning independent pop-up specialising in vegetarian and vegan kebabs with a twist. £

Riverford Field Kitchen
An ecofriendly, farm-to-table dining experience with veg-centric seasonal menus. ££

I LIVE HERE

Guy Erlacher-Downing, coordinator of *@TransitionTown Totnes* (TTT) and resident of a local, off-grid permaculture cooperative, explains what it means to be Transition.

'A Transition Town is any community that recognises the potential that local-level action has for positive change. Totnes has long been a place of pioneers and creative, community-oriented people. So, as people became aware of the emerging global climate and energy crises, instinctively they set about organising themselves locally to do something about it.

In 2005, the Transition Network was born to support Transition initiatives worldwide. TTT enables locals to take positive community action in response to global crises, through participatory and educational projects promoting a low-carbon, sustainable, economically resilient and healthy society.'

By Rail, River & Road
STEAM TRAIN AND RIVER CRUISE

Explore the Dart Valley by bus, riverboat and steam train on a day trip that harks back to the romantic early days of seaside tourism. **Dartmouth Steam Railway and Riverboat Company**'s Round Robin ticket sees you travel from Paignton to Kingswear by steam train – with stunning coastal views as you chug away from the seaside town – and then by riverboat up the Dart to Totnes, spotting seals and birdlife along the way. Finally, connect back to Paignton by bus. The three stages of the ticket can be done in any order.

School for Grown-Ups
DISTILLERY-HOPPING AND SPIRIT SCHOOLS

Perhaps it's the presence of England's oldest working gin distillery in Plymouth (p73), or maybe it's the soft Dartmoor water they use. Whatever it is, Devon's distillery scene is strong – and growing stronger. Fans of small-batch gin will find dozens of local distilleries (many offering tours), but there are also Devonshire rums and whiskies to try. **Salcombe Gin** is a relative newcomer but firmly established as one of Devon's best. Visit its riverside distillery (40 minutes' drive from Dartmouth) for a tour and tasting or, better still, its Gin School where you'll use a mini copper still to distil your very own bottle. A similar experience is offered by **Devon Gin School** at The Shops at Dartington (30 minutes' drive). Next door, the **Devon Rum School** is run inside an old yellow school bus.

Beach-Hopping & Boutique Shopping
A CHIC YACHT HAVEN

Dartmouth is not the only sailing town in south Devon. About 45 minutes' drive southwest, at the mouth of the Kingsbridge Estuary, lies **Salcombe**. Pretty and chic, Salcombe appeals to a middle-class market, but the idyllic beaches and surrounding nature are for all. For shopping, head to **Fore Street** – a long stretch of historic stone cottages running parallel to the river, packed with nautical clothing brands, upscale boutiques and more galleries than any town could possibly need. Island St is home to several of Salcombe's independent producers, including the iconic **Salcombe Dairy** ice-cream and chocolate factories, and Salcombe Gin. If you have time, short visits to the **Maritime Museum** and

 WHERE TO ENJOY A SECLUDED SWIM NEAR DARTMOUTH

Macely Cove
Lesser known golden-sand beach tucked between Gammon Head and some steep cliffs.

Ayrmer Cove
Remote sand and shingle beach with rock pools overlooked by low white cliffs.

Mattiscombe Sands
Follow the coast path past Start Point Lighthouse to reach this crescent-shaped sandy cove.

NEVILLE CLAYTON/SHUTTERSTOCK ©

Dartmouth Steam Railway

BEAUTIFUL ESTATES & GARDENS

Overbeck's Garden
Clinging to the cliffs above Salcombe, a hidden paradise of layered subtropical gardens surrounds an early-20th-century manor house.

Coleton Fishacre
An evocative country house near Kingswear, with 1920s art-deco interiors and a tropical garden overlooking the sea.

Dartington Estate
Visit this 485-heactare charity-owned country estate for walks in the Grade II–listed gardens or the Deer Park. Don't miss The Shops at Dartington, a mini village packed with boutiques and independent businesses.

Lifeboat Museum provide insight into the town's long nautical history.

But it's what lies beyond the town centre that brings most people to Salcombe: boating on the tranquil estuary, cliff walks on the dramatic coastline and – above all – the sheltered sandy beaches. Closest to town, **South Sands** and **North Sands** sit on a small bay, overlooked by the ruined tower of Salcombe Castle. From March to October, you can take the **South Sands Ferry** to the beach from Salcombe, while the blink-and-you'll-miss-it **East Portlemouth Ferry** runs all year to the string of small, sandy coves awaiting along the Kingsbridge Estuary's east bank.

STEAM TRAIN TO DARTMOOR

South Devon Railway is another beautiful steam-train ride in the Dart Valley, running from Totnes to Buckfastleigh on the edge of **Dartmoor National Park** (p104).

 WHERE TO EAT SEAFOOD NEAR SALCOMBE

Oyster Shack
Casual eatery on the Avon Estuary with a daily changing menu specialising in shellfish. **££**

Crab Shed Salcombe
Quayside seafood restaurant where fresh crab is sustainably harvested by local day-fishing boats. **££**

Winking Prawn
Colourful, casual beachside restaurant with locally sourced food and summer evening BBQs. **££**

BEST SOUTH COAST WALKS

Prawle Point
Devon's southern-most point has rugged cliffs and a dramatic history of shipwrecks. Expect epic views: the name comes from an Old English word for 'lookout'.

Bolt Head
A small, adventurous headland with jagged rocks and an idyllic beach at Starehole Bay.

Kingswear to Brownstone Battery
Follow the Dart Estuary to a WWII battery with views of the Dragon's Tail rocks.

Bolberr Down
A relatively flat section of coast west of Salcombe, where the heathland is full of wildflowers in springtime.

LEFT: MARK NAYLOR/SHUTTERSTOCK ©; RIGHT: MAXIAN/GETTY IMAGES ©

Burgh Island Hotel

Boat Trips & Snorkel Spots

SET SAIL ON THE KINGSBRIDGE ESTUARY

Like the Dart Estuary (p79), the scenic **Kingsbridge Estuary** is a haven for wildlife, but unlike the Dart, it has very little freshwater input – which means sea life thrives here. The seagrass meadows found along the lower shores are home to seahorses, fan mussels and the permanently attached stalked jellyfish. When the tide is in, these underwater jungles are prime snorkelling spots. Larger marine animalls, including dolphins, seals and basking sharks, also visit these rich foraging grounds. Spot them from the shore or from a boat, kayak or paddleboard, always passing slowly and giving animals as much room as possible. **Whitestrand Boat Hire** in Salcombe has a fleet of small motor boats which can be

WHERE TO SIP LOCAL DRINKS NEAR DARTMOUTH

The Cove
Hope Cove beach views, local spirits and ever-changing taps featuring the UK's best craft beers.

Bull Inn, Totnes
This ethical pub in Totnes serves organic wines, local beers and seasonal special cocktails.

Kings Arms
Devon-brewed ales and cider and epic sea views at a community-owned clifftop pub in Strete.

rented by the hour or day. No experience or qualifications are needed, so anyone can get out and explore the estuary and its many creeks. At high tide, you can head up Southpool Creek to visit **Millbrook Inn** for lunch, or all the way along the estuary to **Crabshell Inn** in Kingsbridge.

If driving your own boat sounds like too much responsibility, the **Salcombe–Kingsbridge Ferry** is a perfect alternative. This leisurely, 40-minute cruise aboard the bright-red *Lady Mary* will take you upriver to the sleepy market town, where you can visit the **Cookworthy Museum of Rural Life** for a glimpse of Devon's past.

Windswept Island Walks

WALK TO A WILD ISLAND

Just off the coast from family-favourite Bigbury-on-Sea (45 minutes' drive from Dartmouth) lies a south Devon landmark, the wild and windswept **Burgh Island**. With its rocky coastline and tiny hidden coves, this tidal island makes an adventurous day out. At low tide, you can walk there across a spit of sand stretching out from Bigbury; at high tide, hitch a ride on the Sea Tractor. Designed in 1969 and the only one in the world, this bizarre-looking vehicle is operated by **Burgh Island Hotel**, a striking art-deco hotel that's almost as famous as the island itself. When you're on the island, follow the cliff path uphill to the remains of a huer's hut. Fisherfolk once kept watch for pilchard shoals here, crying out to raise the alarm – the apparent origin of the phrase 'hue and cry'. End with a drink at one of England's oldest taverns, the 14th-century **Pilchard Inn** (supposedly haunted by a smuggler's ghost).

Find Your Sea Legs

LEARN TO SAIL

If you've always fancied finding your sea legs, book yourself onto a course at one of the local sailing schools. With its sheltered estuaries and long history as a port town, Salcombe (pictured right; p86) is the ideal spot to learn. **Salcombe Dinghy Sailing** offers two-day courses for both absolute beginners and more experienced sailors looking to improve.

DEVON'S VANISHING ROAD

Life in south Devon is tied to the rivers, and nowhere is that more apparent than on the aptly named Tidal Rd along the River Avon.

When the river swells at high tide, the surrounding marsh is completely submerged along with the road itself. Despite warning signs, more than one motorist has found themselves stuck after blindly following a satnav onto the drowned road.

Residents have to plan around the tides; while most can use an alternative lane at high tide, some houses can only be accessed by a footpath. At low tide, though, this is one of the most scenic drives in south Devon, meandering with the river alongside marshes full of wading birds.

GETTING AROUND

South Devon's many rivers can slow down coastal drives. A car ferry runs across the Dart Estuary, but most other rivers require a long inland trip to the nearest bridge. Drivers should also be ready for some country lanes and steep hills. A fairly decent bus network exists, with Stagecoach South West and Tally Ho! Coaches covering most of south Devon's highlights between them.

THE ENGLISH RIVIERA

Looking out at the glittering spread of Tor Bay, it's easy to see how the English Riviera became one of Britain's most popular seaside resort areas. Spread along the wide bay, Torquay, Paignton and Brixham owe their thriving tourist industry and collective name to the Napoleonic Wars (1803–15). With France blockaded by the Royal Navy, the wealthy turned to the warm, sheltered waters of Tor Bay as a replacement for the French Riviera.

As its popularity boomed, the Victorians transformed Tor Bay, building grand villas and parks. Today, the glamour and glitz have faded a little, but the area remains a beloved seaside destination. Torquay, an interesting mix of shabby and chic, retains a hint of its former grandeur, while cheap-and-cheerful Paignton's retro seafront plays more to families and coach-holiday crowds. To the west, Brixham's working fishing harbour feeds Tor Bay's growing foodie reputation.

Er
Ri

TOP TIP

Torquay can be reached by direct train from London in around three hours, and a decent public transport network around the English Riviera and beyond makes exploring without a car fairly easy.

Beside the Seaside

RETRO BRITISH BEACH VIBES

With 22 miles of coastline and over 20 beaches to explore, there's no better way to spend a sunny day on the English Riviera than beside the sea. Start with a walk along **Torquay**'s Victorian seafront, with its wide, palm-lined promenade and numerous gardens. The historic **Princess Pier** (built in 1890; pictured left) and neighbouring **Princess Gardens** are perhaps the most iconic sights, named for Queen Victoria's fourth daughter Princess Louise. Torquay's most popular beach is **Torre Abbey Sands** – a sandy, tidal beach overlooked by one of Torbay borough's most historic buildings, Torre Abbey (built in 1196). Rent a kayak or paddleboard from **Wesup Abbey Sands** to make the most of the bay's calm waters, or lose yourself amid the abbey's attractive gardens above.

 WHERE TO TAKE THE CHILDREN ON THE ENGLISH RIVIERA

Paignton Zoo
A conservation charity runs this innovative zoo with animals and plants from around the world.

Babbacombe Model Village
1.5 heactares of gardens dotted with hand-crafted model scenes, including some famous British landmarks.

Splashdown Quaywest
Outdoor waterpark with slides and tyre rides right next to Goodrington Beach.

THE ENGLISH RIVIERA

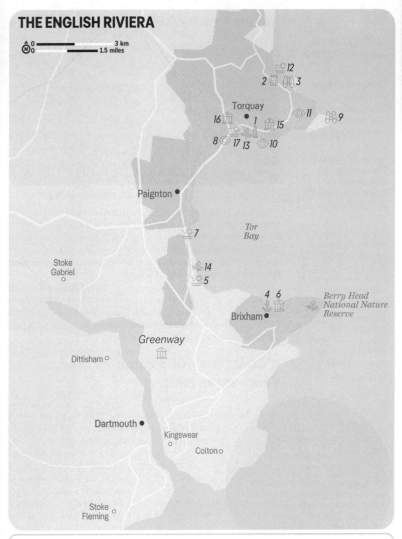

SIGHTS

1	Agatha Christie Memorial Bust	**7**	Goodrington Beach	**13**	Princess Gardens
2	Babbacome Cliff Railway	**8**	Grand Hotel	**14**	Saltern Cove
3	Babbacombe Downs	**9**	Hope's Nose	**15**	Torquay Museum
4	Brixham Harbour	**10**	Imperial Torquay	**16**	Torre Abbey
5	Broadsands Beach	**11**	Kents Cavern	**17**	Torre Abbey Sands
6	Golden Hind	**12**	Oddicombe Beach		

BEST HISTORY & QUIRKY MUSEUMS

Torquay Museum
The Agatha Christie collection and Explorer's Gallery steal the show at this eclectic museum.

Brixham Heritage Museum
Discover Brixham's maritime history: fishing, shipbuilding, smugglers and sea rescues.

Bygones
Step back in time in Torquay among life-sized reproductions of a Victorian street, period rooms and a wartime trench.

The Real Crime Museum
Small, quirky museum in Torquay with intriguing exhibits from the world of crime.

Berry Head National Nature Reserve

LORETTA DAMSKA/SHUTTERSTOCK ©

The long, pink-hued beach at **Paignton** also boasts a grand Victorian pier, but this one is steeped in seaside nostalgia – it's home to an amusement arcade and funfair rides. Despite a slightly tired feel, the retro vibes and sandy beaches continue to appeal to families, especially the golden sands of **Goodrington Beach** and **Broadsands Beach**.

For a vintage seaside day out, head for the **Babbacombe Cliff Railway**, a 1920s funicular that will transport you down to the rust-red shingle sand at **Oddicombe Beach**. Pause in the clifftop gardens at **Babbacombe Downs** before descending for views along the coast as far as Dorset.

A Coastline 400 Million Years in the Making

GEOLOGY, NATURE AND CLIFF WALKS

GO JURASSIC

East of the English Riviera is the the Unesco-listed **Jurassic Coast** (p62), which stretches 95 miles from Exmouth to Dorset's Studland Bay and is known for rock formations and fossils from the Triassic, Jurassic and Cretaceous periods.

Torbay borough was designated as a Unesco Global Geopark (englishrivierageopark.org.uk) in 2007, one of just two 'urban' geoparks in the UK. What makes the English Riviera special is its rich geological heritage, but also the nature thriving in the sheltered bay's microclimate. Endangered bats roost in caves and seahorses nest amid underwater seagrasses. Spanning some 400 million years, the area's geology covers four time periods: Devonian, Carboniferous, Permian and Quaternary. What that means to non-geologists is a dramatic coastline to explore, either on foot or

WHERE TO STAY ON THE ENGLISH RIVIERA

The 25
Adults-only boutique B&B in Torquay with quirky, glitzy decor that's over the top in the best way possible. £££

Meadfoot Bay
Tranquil adults-only hotel with elegantly decorated rooms and one of Torquay's top restaurants. ££

Hoburne Devon Bay
Popular, family-friendly holiday park overlooking Goodrington Beach, with heated outdoor pool and kids' entertainment. £

from the water by kayak or cruise. Key sites include the clifftop **Berry Head National Nature Reserve**, ideal for walking; **Hope's Nose**, known for its Devonian limestone and spectacular views; and **Saltern Cove**, home to the only underwater Site of Special Scientific Interest in the country.

Back to the Stone Age

TORQUAY'S PREHISTORIC CAVES

Step back in time within the rust-hued tunnels of **Kents Cavern**, a remarkable cave system directly beneath Torquay and one of the key sites of the English Riviera Unesco Global Geopark. The hour-long guided tours feel tailored towards younger audiences, but the maze of rock galleries and chambers hides a fascinating history. Bones of prehistoric mammals, including giant cave bears and sabre-toothed tigers, have been discovered here, as well as tools and bones from ancient humans going back over 500,000 years, making this the oldest known human dwelling in Britain.

Ferries & Fisherfolk

DISCOVER BRIXHAM'S FISHING INDUSTRY

At the western end of Tor Bay, **Brixham** is the smallest town on the English Riviera, and has a very different feel to Torquay and Paignton. Strings of multicoloured fisher cottages are packed haphazardly onto hillsides overlooking **Brixham Harbour**, around which life here revolves. This busy, working harbour is home to one of the UK's largest fishing fleets – as well as a slew of restaurants making full use of those daily catches. There's also a life-sized replica of the **Golden Hind**, the ship on which Devon-born explorer Sir Francis Drake circumnavigated the globe in the late 1500s.

From spring to autumn, you can take the **Western Lady** ferry from Torquay to arrive into Brixham Harbour onto the New Pier, a stone's throw from the famous **Fish Market**. Usually, only buyers and fisherfolk can visit the auction, but you can book a market tour – with fish breakfast – through the neighbouring **Rockfish** restaurant, with all proceeds supporting the Fishermen's Mission charity. Get a more hands-on experience of Brixham's fishing industry on a two-hour mackerel fishing trip with **Funfish Trips**. The company also runs dolphin-spotting 'seafaris' and sunset cruises. On land, several harbourside shops can sell you a crab line, bucket and bait: while away an hour or two fishing for crabs off the harbour's edge.

 WHERE TO KAYAK AND PADDLEBOARD IN TOR BAY

Broadsands Beach
Perfect for beginners; also a good launch for paddles to Crystal Cove or Elberry Cove.

Anstey's Cove
Small inlet overlooked by jagged rocks at Long Quarry Point; rentals available on the beach.

Fishcombe Cove
Sheltered inlet surrounded by limestone cliffs and semi-ancient woodland; better for experienced paddlers.

AGATHA CHRISTIE

Dame Agatha Christie (1890–1976) was born Agatha Miller in Torquay's Barton Rd. During WWI, she worked as a nurse at the Red Cross Hospital in Torquay Town Hall. Working in the Dispensary equipped Christie with a knowledge of poisons that helped her kill off numerous characters, including the victim of her first novel, *The Mysterious Affair at Styles* (1920).

After divorcing Archibald Christie in 1926, Christie married archaeologist Sir Max Mallowan in 1930 and accompanied him on several expeditions. These provided new settings for novels like *Murder on the Orient Express* (1934) and *Death on the Nile* (1937), although she continued to set many works in Devon, specialising in 'murders of quiet, domestic interest'.

Agatha Christie Memorial Bust

Seaside Sleuthing

WALK THE AGATHA CHRISTIE MILE

Torquay was the birthplace of Agatha Christie, probably the world's most famous – and most prolific – crime-fiction writer. Christie wrote over 80 novels and plays and created two of literature's best-loved detectives: the moustachioed Hercule Poirot and the sharp-eyed Miss Marple, setting many of their adventures in Devon.

Fans of the 'Queen of Crime' should start with the **Agatha Christie Mile**, a walking route connecting various locations linked to the author's life and novels. A free route guide is available at the English Riviera Visitor Information Centre. The walk leads along the bay between two iconic Victorian hotels, the **Grand Hotel** and the **Imperial Torquay**. The latter appeared as the setting for the last chapter of Miss Marple's final case, *Sleeping Murder* (1976). Along the way, you'll pass seven Agatha Christie plaques and a **Memorial Bust**, as well as many of Torquay's key historic sights. At **Torre Abbey** gardens, don't miss the fascinating Potent Plants Garden. This collection of poisonous and pharmaceutical plants is a celebration of Christie's specialism: over half of her fictional murders involved poisonings.

AGATHA CHRISTIE FANS

The highlight for Agatha Christie fans is her stunning River Dart holiday home, **Greenway** (p80). To get there in romantic style, take the **Dartmouth Steam Railway** (p81) to Dartmouth, where a ferry service departs for Greenway.

The Agatha Christie Gallery at **Torquay Museum** has notes, photographs and memorabilia, as well as props from the TV adaptations of Poirot and Miss Marple. Finally, the week-long annual **International Agatha Christie Festival** celebrates the author's life and legacy with a flurry of events and performances.

GETTING AROUND

Torquay is fairly sprawling and hilly, so exploring the wider town on foot can get tiring. Thankfully, Stagecoach operates a good network of regular buses. There are also good services between Torquay, Paignton and Brixham (journey times are about 30 minutes), so visitors can avoid driving in the congested town centres. It's also possible to walk from Torquay to Paignton along the seafront in around an hour (and from there on to Brixham).

Beyond the English Riviera

Escape the resorts in search of seafaring history, secluded beaches, historic castles and an emerging food scene.

Dawlish Warren
National Nature
Reserve
Teignmouth •
• Shaldon
Marldon •
The English
Riviera

Before the seaside resorts and tourist traps, the south Devon coast was an area of huge maritime importance. Life here depended on trading, shipbuilding and fishing – these industries have left a clear mark, especially around the River Teign, which meets the sea a few miles northeast of Torquay after a 31-mile journey from Dartmoor. Strike out from the English Riviera to discover a dramatic coastline of vivid red cliffs and intriguing history featuring smugglers, shipwrecks and the last successful invasion of England, or uncover ghost stories at castles further inland. Nature lovers will find plenty to entice, from hidden beaches and unusual geological formations to abundant birdlife in the Exe Estuary's marshlands.

TOP TIP

Be aware that many of the beaches along this coast don't have lifeguards, especially the more remote spots.

Black-tailed godwits, River Exe

CHRISTOPHER NICHOLSON/ALAMY ©

THE GLORIOUS REVOLUTION

The last successful invasion of England happened at Torbay.

In November 1688, William of Orange (later William III of England) landed in Brixham to launch his Glorious Revolution, then marched to Newton Abbot where he declared his intention to become King of England.

The Dutch prince was husband of Mary, daughter of English King James II, and his invasion was requested by several Protestant lords, who feared the Catholic James II and his new son (now heir to the throne ahead of Mary) would elevate Catholicism in England.

William and Mary ruled as joint sovereigns until his death in 1702; today, a plaque at St Leonard's Tower marks the spot of his first declaration.

Berry Pomeroy Castle

Castles, Gardens & Ghost Stories

A CASTLE-FILLED DAY TRIP

Two castles lie less than 20 minutes' drive from the English Riviera. Just north of the pretty village of Marldon, **Compton Castle** is a medieval manor dating back to the early 12th century and fortified in the 1520s following French raids on Plymouth. On open days (which vary), you can explore the castle and wander the gardens – don't miss the medieval-style knot garden. To the southwest, **Berry Pomeroy Castle** is perhaps the more intriguing. Often called the 'most haunted place in Britain', this ruined Elizabethan mansion stands within the 15th-century defences of the Pomeroy family castle. Never completed, and abandoned by 1700, the evocative ruin has long been the subject of chilling ghost stories and unnerving legends. One tale tells of the White Lady, the ghost of Lady Margaret Pomeroy, said to have been imprisoned and starved to death in the tower dungeons by her jealous sister.

 WHERE TO GO FOR A SECLUDED SWIM ON THE ENGLISH RIVIERA

Maidencombe Beach
A small, secluded sandy beach framed by red cliffs, with steep steps and safe swimming.

Ness Cove Beach
Access to this mainly shingle beach is through a historic smugglers' tunnel in Shaldon.

Dawlish Warren Beach
Overlooking the Exe Estuary, this Blue Flag beach sits on a sandbank backed by dunes.

Sand Dunes & Mudflats

SEEK NATURE AT DAWLISH WARREN

Every autumn, up to 23,000 birds arrive in the **Exe Estuary** to overwinter. Many of them flock to the grasslands, salt marshes and mudflats of **Dawlish Warren National Nature Reserve**, one of the southwest's best birdwatching locations centred on a 1.5-mile-long spit of white sand dunes. In spring and summer, visit for the tranquil beach and abundant wildflowers. For a day trip, walk the 6-mile coast path there from Teignmouth, returning by train (20 minutes).

Explore a Reinvented Resort

A BEACH TOWN REINVENTING ITSELF

Self-styled as 'the gem of south Devon', **Teignmouth** (a 25-minute drive from Torquay) has all the trappings of a British seaside resort: a wide prom lined with a string of Georgian terraces and a classic Victorian **Grand Pier**, complete with amusement arcades. Although the town feels a little less grand these days, the pink sands of **Teignmouth Beach** still draw in summer crowds and the rowing-boat-cluttered, riverside **Back Beach** has a quaint, ramshackle charm. As far back as the 14th century, Teignmouth was a major port and shipbuilding centre; it still has a busy, working port, lending the riverside a gritty, industrial air. Head to the **Teign Heritage Centre** to delve into this maritime history – highlights include an Edwardian bathing machine and the remains of a wrecked 16th-century Venetian vessel. Modern-day Teignmouth is busy restyling itself as an art and food destination, particularly around the **Teignmouth Arts Quarter**, an emerging area of art galleries, boutique shops and independent eateries.

TASTE OF THE TEIGN

Fed by the thriving fishing industry and fertile valleys surrounding the River Teign, Teignmouth's food scene is growing.

There are mussel and oyster beds on the river, thanks to the Teign's high water quality, and local fisherfolk catch crabs, scallops, lobster and more along the coast.

The verdant countryside on either side of the estuary is home to orchards and farms, as well as the Red Rock Brewery and Old Walls Vineyard near Bishopsteignton.

Discover local produce at Teignmouth Farmers Market on the last Saturday of every month, or download a *Taste of the Teign Trail* map from *visitsouthdevon.co.uk* to set out on a foodie adventure around the Teign Valley.

England's Oldest Ferry

HISTORIC FERRY RIDE TO SHALDON

Across the mouth of the River Teign from Teignmouth, the pretty village of **Shaldon** lies in the shadow of a towering hulk of red rock known as **The Ness**. Although the vessel itself dates from the 20th century, the **Teignmouth–Shaldon Ferry** (pictured right) has been shuttling across the river since at least 1296 and possibly as far back as Saxon times, making it one of the oldest passenger ferries in England.

 GETTING AROUND

Great Western Rail operates regular, direct trains covering the short distance from Torquay to both Teignmouth (20 minutes) and Dawlish Warren (35 minutes), and on from there towards Exeter and Exmouth. It's also possible to walk via the South West Coast Path: Torquay to Teignmouth is around 8 miles and features some steep climbs.

Wild flowers, Hound Tor (p104)

DARTMOOR, EXMOOR & NORTH DEVON

SHORES AND MOORS

Welcome to Devon's wild side: rolling moorlands, dramatic coastal trails, unique beach towns and adventures to suit every taste.

In the 1970s, the South West Coast Path opened – an epic long-distance trail starting in Minehead and marching along the coasts of Exmoor and north Devon to skirt the entire southwestern corner of England. But the paths themselves are much older than that. Until 1913, the route was used by coast guards and excise officers patrolling for smugglers.

These first sections are some of the toughest of the whole trail. This is a coastline of lurching ups and downs, choice surf and dramatic rocky coves. Dotted along it are seaside towns bursting with Regency and Victorian architecture, postcard-perfect villages spilling history from every cobble and beaches to suit every taste. And wildlife – lots of wildlife. Dolphins, porpoises and seals are all common sightings on both north Devon's and Exmoor's coasts, while Exmoor's interior is so rich with fauna that you can actually go on safari. One of England's more underrated national parks, this is a place to truly get away from it all.

Further south, Dartmoor feels like another world entirely – a wilderness of sweeping, heather-strewn moorlands dotted with twisted rock formations. Sitting on a vast granite plateau, these upland moors provide a suitably epic setting for adventures big and small.

At a glance, north Devon, Exmoor and Dartmoor don't seem all that similar. But all three call to adventurous spirits, nature lovers and those simply seeking a little peace and quiet.

THE MAIN AREAS

DARTMOOR	EXMOOR	ILFRACOMBE
Wilderness and adventure.	Rolling moors and epic shores.	Beaches, boat tours and seafood.
p104	p114	p121

Exmoor, p114

One of the UK's smallest national parks, known for its iconic wild ponies, roller-coaster coast paths, Dark Sky Reserve and autumn stag rut.

Ilfracombe, p121

The gateway to the north coast, this lively seaside resort has an emerging art scene, a working harbour and beaches, accessed via tunnels.

Watchet
Williton
Minehead
Portlock
Wheddon Cross
Exford
Simonsbath
Lynmouth
Blackmoor Gate
Brayford
Withypool
Exmoor National Park
Dulverton
Brushford
Bampton
Tiverton
Bickleigh
Cullompton
Kentisbeare
Honiton
Exe
Witheridge
Chulmleigh
East Leigh
Crediton
South Molton
Barnstaple
Taw
Braunton
Woolacombe
Croyde
Ilfracombe
Appledore
Bideford
Great Torrington
Torridge
Meeth
Hatherleigh
Shebbear
Holsworthy
Kilkhampton
Hartland

10 km
5 miles
0
0
N

Find Your Way

The destinations in this chapter cover a vast area of north, mid and south Devon. Exmoor pairs well with the north coast, extending across the border into Somerset, while Dartmoor is just an hour to the south.

FROM LEFT: A G BAXTER/SHUTTERSTOCK ©; CHARLES BOWMAN/SHUTTERSTOCK ©; PETER TURNER PHOTOGRAPHY/SHUTTERSTOCK ©

Dartmoor, p104

A vast wilderness of high moors, lush wooded valleys and roadside views that feel like driving in a car ad. Hiking, biking and adventure await.

BUS

A decent public transport system exists across all three regions, with additional seasonal bus services like the Exmoor Coaster and Dartmoor Explorer in key tourist destinations. For longer journeys, a change or two may be required.

TRAIN

Barnstaple's train station acts as a transport hub for the region, but you'll need to change to a bus to reach the rest of the north coast and Exmoor. Dartmoor's closest stations are Okehampton and Newton Abbot.

CAR

Driving in the national parks, as well as rural parts of the coast, can prove a challenge. Roads are often narrow and hills are steep, especially on Exmoor. Go slow, take care and be prepared for sheep in the road!

Sidmouth
Budleigh Salterton
Topsham
Kenton
Exmouth
English Channel
Dawlish
Torquay
Paignton
Newton Abbot
Dunsford
Bovey Tracey
Moretonhampstead
Easton
Ashburton
Dart
Buckfastleigh
Widecombe-in-the-Moor
Poundsgate
Totnes
South Brent
Chagford
Dartmoor National Park
Two Bridges
Yelverton
Shaugh Prior
Bridestowe
Lydford
Tavistock
Tavy
Plymouth
Henford

Plan Your Time

North Devon is a place for beach-hopping, road trips and adventure; Exmoor and the north coast blend together nicely for this. The wildernesses of Dartmoor, in the south, feels a world apart – literally and figuratively.

Standing stones, Merrivale (p108)

Seaside Weekender

Find a seaside town to base yourself in. Colourful **Ilfracombe** (p121) is liveliest, but the chilled-out surfing scene and sandy beach at **Croyde** (p126) make it a strong contender. Start with a day spent beachside: take a boat tour, learn to surf or try **coasteering** (p128).

Make your way to the **Taw-Torridge Estuary** (p127) to cycle the riverside **Tarka Trail** (p127) and explore the vast sand-dune systems at **Braunton Burrows and Northam Burrows** (p127). From here, the cliff paths and remote beaches of the **Hartland Peninsula** (p128) and the absurdly scenic village of **Clovelly** (p128) are a short hop away.

Seasonal Highlights

Summer usually means better beach weather, though autumn brings prime surf conditions and the national parks have something to entice in every season. Many tourist businesses close from October to March.

JANUARY
A chance of snow on Dartmoor's peaks. Long winter nights afford fabulous **stargazing** in both national parks – when it's clear!

MAY
Carpets of bluebells lend a splash of colour to **woodland walks** on Dartmoor and the Hartland Peninsula.

JULY
Generally good weather for **beach days** and coastal activities – but also peak tourist season, bringing crowds and price hikes.

FROM LEFT: ARTHUR CAUTY/SHUTTERSTOCK ©, ASC PHOTOGRAPHY/SHUTTERSTOCK ©, TRAVELLIGHT/SHUTTERSTOCK ©

A Week in the North

Start with a few days exploring the north coast, then set sail for an adventurous day trip to tiny **Lundy Island** (p125). Hop along the coast to **Lynton and Lymouth** (p119) for another day trip soaking up their seaside charm.

Next, spend a day or two (or more) road-tripping around **Exmoor** (p116). Stay the night in the national park to make the most of its **Dark Sky Reserve** (p118). Take a **wildlife safari** (p115) to see the iconic red deer and wild ponies, go **horse trekking** (p118) or embrace Exmoor's hills with some **mountain biking** (p118).

Dartmoor Diversion

Dartmoor (p104) can be tied in with the previous itineraries, but also works well as a standalone destination. Kick off with a **road trip** (p106) around the national park for epic views, stopping at top attractions. From the Bronze Age settlements and stone circles of **Grimspound and Merrivale** (p108) to the 20th-century **Castle Drogo** (p111), there's a lot of history here.

Spend at least a day **hiking the moors** (p104), then book an adventure activity: climbing, caving, or white-water **kayaking on the River Dart** (p110) can all be tried here. Round off busy days by the fire at one of **Dartmoor's cosy pubs** (p111).

AUGUST
Nothing says summer in England like a **carnival**. Ilfracombe, Hartland and Moretonhampstead all have one.

SEPTEMBER
Food festivals lessen the pain as summer slips away. Barnstaple has the north coast's biggest.

OCTOBER
Eerie bellows and clashing antlers sound the arrival of Exmoor's stag **rutting season**. On the coast, it's seal pup season.

NOVEMBER
Autumn is the best season for **surfing** in north Devon, with things getting choppier in November.

DARTMOOR

Dartmoor is a land of contrasts – it's bleak yet beautiful, remote but rich in heritage. On the heather-clad, granite-strewn moors, it's possible to feel like the only person on Earth one moment, then find yourself sipping local beer by the fire in a crowded pub the next.

It's also a land of magic, where pixies, witches and beasts roam the moors and the imagination runs rampant. Seemingly every mossy woodland and oddly shaped rock has a legend attached to it, every historic edifice a ghost story or two.

The 368-sq-mile national park contains south England's largest area of moorland, but also plunging gorges, dense woodland and winding rivers. These diverse landscapes shelter a wealth of wildlife and have inspired artists for generations, from Sir Arthur Conan Doyle to Steven Spielberg, who filmed *War Horse* here. For the visitor, they provide epic backdrops for hiking, biking and adventure.

TOP TIP

Weather changes fast on Dartmoor, even in summer. The high plateau is generally wetter, windier and colder than the rest of Devon, and mist is a common hazard. Plan well, carry the right equipment and don't hesitate to turn back if the weather deteriorates.

Get Your Hiking Boots On

ADVENTURES ON TWO FEET

BEST WALKS

Lydford Gorge
The deepest gorge in the southwest, home to a 30m waterfall and a magical whirlpool.

Wistman's Wood
Easy stroll from a pub to a mossy oak woodland straight from a fairy tale.

Bellever Forest
Waymarked trails in a dense pine forest: climb Bellever Tor and explore Kraps Ring Bronze Age village.

Princetown Railway Track
Follow the old railway to King's Tor, passing two abandoned quarries, Swell Tor and Foggintor.

Yes Tor and High Willhays
The two highest points on Dartmoor – 619m and 621m above sea level, respectively.

Dartmoor is hiking heaven. Its vast, wild landscapes are criss-crossed by trails, from epic multiday treks to gentle riverside strolls. Explore abandoned granite quarries, plummeting gorges and ancient settlements (p198), or climb tors for sweeping views across the moors. Start at one of the three **National Park Visitor Centres** (Postbridge, Princetown and Haytor) for maps and recommendations. For those with limited mobility, **Miles Without Stiles** routes are stile-free and usually suitable for all-terrain mobility scooters; find a full list at *dartmoor.gov.uk*.

Encircling the national park, the **Dartmoor Way** is a waymarked 108-mile circular route, with the optional High Moorland link forming a figure-eight loop. If a 10-day hike sounds a bit much, many shorter circular walks use sections of the Way, like the trail from Chagford to Fingle Bridge along the wooded slopes of **Teign Gorge**. For a walk that's pure Dartmoor, the moorland trail from **Haytor** to **Hound Tor** takes in disused quarries, a clapper bridge and a medieval settlement.

Walking the high moors affords views that could have been lifted straight from a fantasy movie, but stick to waymarked trails or book a guide (**Dartmoor's Daughter** or **Walk Climb Dartmoor**) unless you know how to use a map and compass. Be aware that the military has several training ranges on Dartmoor – check firing times at *gov.uk*.

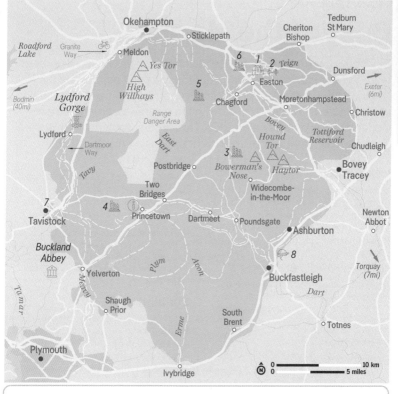

SIGHTS

1 Castle Drogo
2 Fingle Bridge
3 Grimspound
see 7 Guildhall Heritage Centre

4 Merrivale Prehistoric Settlement
5 Scorhill Stone Circle
6 Spinster's Rock
7 Tavistock

SHOPPING

see 7 Pannier Market

TOURIST INFORMATION

8 Pridhamsleigh Cavern

Starry, Starry Night

ADVENTURES AFTER DARK

Dartmoor's vast, sparsely populated landscapes provide prime **stargazing** conditions. On clear nights, head for remote hilltop car parks like the ones at Haytor, Hounds Tor and Holming Beam; *gostargazing.co.uk* has a full list and a light-pollution map. Castle Drogo's Piddledown Common is good spot for both stargazing and nocturnal wildlife, as it comes alive with badgers, bats and tawny owls.

JACKO WATSON/SHUTTERSTOCK ©

ROAD TRIP

Best of the Moors

Driving on Dartmoor may induce flashbacks of your hazard perception test – prepare for cattle grids, river crossings and animals on the road. But the national park is a joy to discover on four wheels – especially snaking across the high moors, with the cinematic, granite-strewn wilderness falling away alongside. This circular route takes in several Dartmoor highlights, from an ancient bridge to a towering tor.

1 Princetown

At first glance, Dartmoor's highest village seems a little bleak, partly due to the towering granite walls of its infamous 19th-century prison. Visit the **Dartmoor Prison Museum** for its fascinating history; the artefacts here include prisoner-made goods and handmade weapons.

The Drive: Cutting across the high moors (10 minutes), the B3212 is one of Dartmoor's best roads: two lanes, gently winding and dazzlingly scenic.

2 Postbridge

Slow down as you approach the road bridge for a view of the ancient **clapper bridge** – a simple, 13th-century granite structure – on the right. There's a lay-by opposite the pub, or park at **Bellever Forest** for a lovely river walk.

The Drive: Ignore your satnav if it directs you up Adley Lane, which is a farm track; instead go via Moretonhampstead (30 minutes). The last section towards the castle is hilly and often single-lane.

3 Castle Drogo

After exploring the faux-medieval **Castle Drogo** (p111), which was actually constructed in the 20th century, be sure to wander across the estate grounds for a view of wooded Teign Gorge from Sharp Tor.

OARFLAND/ALAMY ©

Castle Drogo

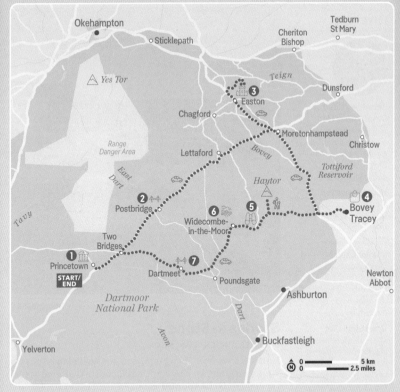

The Drive: The A382 may be an A-road, but it frequently narrows to one lane, snaking as much as the river it follows (30 minutes).

4 Bovey Tracey

This riverside market town sits at the gateway to Dartmoor. Shop for local crafts at **MAKE Southwest** or for local produce on the high street. You can also visit Devon's only whisky distillery (p113) for a tour and tasting.

The Drive: The B3387 is narrow in spots as it meanders uphill through a tunnel of trees (10 minutes).

5 Haytor Rocks

Dartmoor is home to over 160 tors (p109), but **Haytor** is the most famous. Walk up to the rocks for far-reaching views across Dartmoor to the south coast. Time permitting, there are several great walking trails here, including the circular walk to nearby **Hound Tor**.

The Drive: Watch out for sheep on the road as it undulates up over the moor, then descends into a wooded valley (five minutes).

6 Widecombe-in-the-Moor

A cluster of granite cottages and cosy pubs nestled in a scenic valley, **Widecombe** is one of Dartmoor's prettiest villages (p110) – and certainly the most popular. St Pancras Church's impressive 40m tower has given it the nickname 'Cathedral of the Moors'.

The Drive: This section (20 minutes) is almost entirely single-track. There's a shallow river to ford at Ponsworthy (if flooded, go the long way round), then a steep uphill to the B3357.

7 Dartmeet

En route back to Princetown (about 10 minutes) you'll pass Dartmeet, where the East Dart and West Dart rivers meet to flow southwards. There's another clapper bridge here, alongside the 18th-century road bridge.

I LIVE HERE

Sebastien Coell, a Devon-based landscape photographer (scoellphotography.co.uk), shares Dartmoor's most photogenic locations.

Holwell Lawn Tor
A classic photo spot with a large hawthorn tree which looks like part of the tor.

Brentor Church
This hilltop church appears to rise out of the earth and teeter on the edge high above everything else.

Great Staple Tor
These photogenic stacks appear almost artificial with the rocks perfectly bal-anced on top of one another.

Emsworthy Red Barn
In spring, Emsworthy Mire enables some great bluebell photography with the red-roofed barn in the background.

Bowerman's Nose
At the right angle, this tor looks like a man, said to be a hunter turned to stone by witches.

Grimspound

Stories in Stone

UNCOVER ANCIENT DARTMOOR

Humans have been living on Dartmoor's wild lands for over 6000 years, and traces of ancient Brits are scattered across the moors. **Grimspound** is one of the best examples: the remnants of a Bronze Age settlement dating from around 1500 BCE, with more than 20 stone huts enclosed within a stone wall. It's difficult not to feel awed as you walk among the shapes of ancient human dwellings – many with the doorways still visible. In the north of the park, **Spinster's Rock** is one of Dartmoor's most ancient monuments. An early Neolithic portal dolmen (megalithic tomb) with a large granite slab balanced on three smaller rocks, it dates from between 4000 BCE and 3000 BCE. Just off the B3357, **Merrivale Prehistoric Settlement** is a ceremonial complex built between 2500 BCE and 1000 BCE. Three stone rows, a stone circle and several standing stones pepper the landscape, all overlooked by the impressive King's Tor.

 WHERE TO WATCH THE SUNSET ON DARTMOOR

Sheeps Tor
West-facing views across Burrator Reservoir towards the Tamar Valley.

Windy Post Cross
A medieval granite cross beside a small stream between Princetown and Tavistock.

Merrivale Stone Rows
On the western slopes of thc moors with views across Tavistock towards Cornwall.

On Your Bike

HIT THE CYCLING TRAILS

Dartmoor's cinematic landscapes are a joy to explore on two wheels. There's an extensive network of routes, bridleways and byways, covering everything from challenging mountain trails to gentler paved paths. Note that cycling is only permitted on designated routes and bridleways.

One of the best is the 11-mile **Granite Way**, running along an old railway line from Okehampton to Lydford. Paved, traffic-free and mostly flat, this popular route crosses the 165m-long **Meldon Viaduct**, affording spectacular views of Meldon Reservoir's dam. For moorland views and majestic tors, try the ride from Princetown to **Burrator Reservoir**. There are two route options: one follows the old Princetown Railway past granite quarries, the other crosses open moorland on permitted bridleways via **Ditsworthy Warren**. Find downloadable maps for all three routes and many others at *visitdartmoor.co.uk*.

For more intrepid cyclists, the 90-mile **Dartmoor Way** circuits the national park, taking in winding country lanes, meandering moorland crossings, old railway tunnels and a host of attractions.

Dartmoor Bike Park provides a different kind of biking experience. Located within the woodlands at **River Dart Country Park**, near Ashburton, the bike park has a range of mountain bike trails and terrains to suit riders of all abilities. For more Dartmoor bike trails, visitors centres sell the invaluable *Dartmoor for Cyclists* map.

DARTMOOR LEGENDS

Dartmoor's legends are so prolific that they've become part of the map itself.

The Grey Wethers stone circles are supposedly a petrified shepherd and his flock, 'wethers' being an old name for sheep. 'Grim', as in Grimspound (p108), is an Anglo-Saxon word for Devil; a local name for him, 'Old Dewer', is found in Dewerstone (p110), from which the devil drove travellers to their deaths with a pack of Wisht Hounds from Wistman's Wood. Similar stories of demon dogs are scattered throughout the moor: it's said that Hound Tor (p104) inspired Arthur Conan Doyle's famous *The Hound of the Baskervilles*. The website *legendarydartmoor.co.uk* has an extensive collection of local stories for some bedtime reading.

Adventures on Horseback

BRIDLEWAYS AND HORSE TREKKING

With miles of bridleways to explore, Dartmoor is an excellent horse-riding destination. For new visitors, the southeast has several easy rides and gentle slopes, while for experienced riders, southwest Dartmoor's remote high moors are an unbeatable adventure. Several stables offer guided horse trekking: family-run **Cholwell Riding Stables**, between Tavistock and Lydford, caters for riders of all levels.

 WHERE TO RENT BIKES ON DARTMOOR

Granite Way Cycle Hire
Friendly, knowledgable staff and quality bikes, right by the train station in Okehampton.

Devon Cycle Hire
Direct trail access to the Granite Way with a funky cafe to fuel up, near Okehampton.

Dartmoor Bike Hire
Bike hire and cafe at the start of the Wray Valley Trail, near Moretonhampstead.

PRETTIEST TOWNS & VILLAGES

Widecombe-in-the-Moor
Picturesque cluster of grey stone buildings and an impressive church tower nestled in a moorland valley.

Lustleigh
Thatched cottages and a 13th-century church tucked into the wooded Wray Valley – often called the 'prettiest village in Dartmoor'.

Chagford
Wonky thatched cottages, an eclectic mix of independent shops and the distinctive 'Pepperpot' market house.

Ashburton
Ancient stannary town rammed with antique stores, galleries and local crafts.

Lydford
Quiet countryside village with a medieval castle and Saxon town defences.

Of Rocks & Legends

CLIMB A TOR OR TWO

Dartmoor's tors are legendary. Though they look like they were dropped upon the landscape by a giant hand, these free-standing, hilltop outcrops of granite were formed from molten rock some 280 million years ago and left exposed by millennia of erosion.

The bizarre shapes of these stacks and monoliths have inspired humankind for centuries. Some were used as places of worship by Dartmoor's ancient inhabitants, others have inspired folklore and legends that persist to this day. Amid the wilds of Dartmoor, it's easy to believe that the figure-shaped **Bowerman's Nose** is a hunter turned to stone by witches, or that the scattered stacks at **Vixen Tor** were once home to the evil witch Vixana.

There are more than 160 tors on Dartmoor. Some, like the face-shaped **Combestone Tor**, can be seen from the road, while others require a walk. For the best views, try **High Willhays** (the highest point in the park), **Leather Tor** or **Black Tor**.

Adventures Rock

CLIMBING, KAYAKING AND CAVING

Dartmoor's bleak-yet-beautiful moors, towering granite tors and shivering purple heaths are the perfect settings for adventure.

Experienced climbers will find some sensational crags to tackle. Some of the best spots include the tors at **Haytor** and **Bonehill Rocks**, the stark rock walls of **Foggintor Quarry** and the enormous, legendary crag of **Dewerstone**, aka the Devil's Stone. Beginners can book a course or guided climb with qualified instructors.

Adventures also lie below the rocks. Southeast Dartmoor is home to several limestone caves, many of them important roosting sites for greater and lesser horseshoe bats. **Pridhamsleigh Cavern** (known as 'Prid') is one of the best. Experienced cavers can pay at the honesty box to access (with a cave survey), but this is also a popular spot for novice cavers on guided tours.

For adventures of a more watery nature, kayaking and canoeing are permitted on the **River Dart** below Dartmeet from 1 October to 31 March each year. In winter, the raging river has some of England's best mid-grade white water, offering a thrilling challenge for experienced canoeists and kayakers.

 WHERE TO STAY IN DARTMOOR

Dartmoor Shepherds Huts
Tranquil, family-run campsite alongside a stream with simple but good facilities and shepherds huts. **£**

River Dart Country Park
Popular holiday park with caravan and camping pitches and plenty of family-friendly attractions. **£**

Dartmoor YHA
Dorms, private rooms and camping at a comfortable hostel in a central location, a mile south of Postbridge. **£**

Foggintor Quarry

Castle & Gorge

ENGLAND'S LAST CASTLE

It may look the part of a medieval fortress, with its portcullis and arrow slits, but there's an oddly unweathered quality to **Castle Drogo**. This was, in fact, the last castle built in England, constructed between 1911 and 1931 for self-made millionaire Julius Drewe and designed by the renowned architect Edwin Lutyens. Drogo was surprisingly state-of-the-art for its time, with electric lights, a switchboard, even a lift – all powered by renewable energy from a hydro turbine on the River Teign.

From the castle, you can set out on one of Dartmoor's most atmospheric walks around and into the plummeting Teign Gorge (p104), crossing the river at **Fingle Bridge**. A map and directions are available from the visitors centre.

BEST PUBS AROUND DARTMOOR

Dartmoor Inn, Lydford
Slate-floored 16th-century inn with local ales and a daily menu of seasonal classics. ££

Warren House Inn, Postbridge
Legendary pub halfway along the B3212 where the fire has remained lit since 1845. ££

Three Crowns, Chagford
Part-thatched inn with 13th-century features and a modern atrium dining room. ££

Rugglestone Inn, Widecombe-in-the-Moor
Log fires and home-cooked food in a wisteria-clad stone property beside the moors. ££

Cornish Arms, Tavistock
Classic British dishes with a modern twist have earned this pub a Michelin Bib Gourmand. £££

Cottages at Blackadon Farm
Stylish, sustainable self-catering cottages with luxurious touches and unbeatable views on the edge of Dartmoor. ££

One Drake Road
Expect a warm welcome, characterful rooms and fabulously eclectic decor at this intimate Tavistock B&B. ££

Bovey Castle
Luxurious rooms, gorgeous period features and a spa in a grand country manor. £££

WHY I LOVE DARTMOOR

Emily Luxton
@em_luxton

'I still remember the first night of my first school trip to Dartmoor as a shy 11-year-old. Hyped up by ghost stories, we ventured out into the inky blackness of the moors for a moonlit walk beneath an impossibly dense swathe of stars.

That trip, perhaps that very moment, sparked a lifelong addiction to travel that I've never been able to kick. On Dartmoor, I discovered that adventure could exist in real life. We went rock climbing, horse riding and squeezing through the mud-slicked gaps of bat-haunted caves. I came home filthy (my poor mum), exhausted, giddy from the thrill – and very much in love!'

MATT GIBSON/SHUTTERSTOCK ©

Wild camping

Off-Grid Adventures

WILD CAMPING

Dartmoor is the only place in England where wild camping is widely permitted. This is the ultimate off-grid experience: hike out to your own private patch of wilderness, set up a tent and spend the night beneath Dartmoor's glittering starry skies.

The permission is currently in flux, after a court ruling in January 2023 overturned a historically accepted right to wild camp in all parts of the National Park. However, wild camping remains permitted in certain areas under a new agreement with local landowners - as long as you stay no more than two nights and follow the National Park Authority's Code of Conduct. Visit *dartmoor.gov.uk* for a map, regulations and the latest news on the situation.

WILD CAMPING UPDATES

Scan the QR code for information on wild camping on Dartmoor.

WHERE TO BOOK YOUR ADVENTURE ON DARTMOOR

Adventure Okehampton
A huge range of activities and courses including climbing, kayaking, orienteering, bushcraft and more.

Crag 2 Mountain
Princetown-based operator offering caving, rock climbing and mountaineering sessions along with navigation training.

Walk Climb Dartmoor
Guided hikes, navigation training and climbing lessons from beginner to intermediate; based in Liverton.

Ugborough Moor is delightfully remote, while the moors northwest of Princetown are a little closer to civilisation, with tors and quarries offering some shelter. Navigational skills are a necessity, as is having the right equipment. Do thorough research and remember to 'leave no trace': no open fires or BBQs, take all your litter home, and don't pollute rivers or streams.

Local Tipples

DISCOVER DARTMOOR'S DRINKS

Dartmoor Whisky Distillery in Bovey Tracey is Devon's only whisky distillery. A tour and tasting here pairs well with a day adventuring on the moors. Other local drinks to look out for in pubs are Dartmoor Brewery ales and Black Dog Gin.

Take a Dip

COOL OFF WITH A WILD SWIM

On sunny days, a cooling dip in one of Dartmoor's rivers and natural pools is hard to beat – especially after a long hike. **Sharrah Pool** on the River Dart is one of the best spots, reached by ambling through Holne Woods. Alternatively, some of the abandoned quarries like **Foggintor Quarry** and **Haytor Quarry** have been filled with serene pools. Always put safety first: read the safety guide at *wildswimming.co.uk* before your first dip.

Mining & Markets

EXPLORE TAVISTOCK'S HERITAGE

Tavistock, Devon's only World Heritage town, forms the eastern gateway to the **Cornwall and West Devon Mining Landscape**. A former stannary town, where mined tin was weighed and stamped, Tavistock was completely transformed by mining profits. An informative exhibition at the **Guildhall Heritage Centre** covers this mining history and Tavistock's past, including a glimpse of the Victorian prison cells and courtroom. Next door, the historic **Pannier Market** was built in 1860 – but Tavistock's market has been held continuously for over 900 years. Today, it's a good place to pick up locally made goods, especially at Tuesday's craft market.

WILDLIFE ON DARTMOOR

The largest upland area in southern England, Dartmoor's diverse landscapes are rich with wildlife.

Animals range from the small – like the rare blue ground beetle and globally threatened marsh fritillary butterfly – to the iconic Dartmoor pony. These hardy little ponies have lived on the moors for centuries; the Miniature Pony Centre is a good place to meet them. Sheep are prolific (and often in the roads), as are highland cows.

The rivers have always been strongholds for otters, although you have to be very lucky to spot one. In summer, the moors are home to rare birds, including cuckoos and skylarks, while meadow pipits and stonechats can be seen (and heard) year-round.

MINING LANDMARKS

Tavistock was the centre of the **Tamar Valley** (p77) mining landscape. Tavistock Canal was built in the early 1800s to transport copper; today, you can walk the towpath as far as the Grade II-listed Lumburn Aqueduct.

GETTING AROUND

Dartmoor's public transport network is sadly less than comprehensive. Bus services exist between most towns and villages, although often only a few times a day, so a little planning is required to explore without a car. Two additional bus services – Dartmoor Explorer and Haytor Hoppa – run seasonally. If driving, be prepared for single-lane roads, tight bends, narrow bridges and animals in the road. The speed limit on the moors is 40mph.

Exmoor

EXMOOR

One of England's smallest national parks, Exmoor packs surprising diversity into its 267 sq miles. Here, you'll find windswept moors, wooded river valleys and rolling farmland – not to mention the highest coastline in England and Wales. Named for the River Exe, which rises here, and famed for its eponymous native ponies, Exmoor is an often-overlooked corner of the southwest which, once discovered, is impossible to forget. Although the majority of the national park lies across the border in Somerset, this magical place deserves to be explored as a whole.

Wildlife is one of Exmoor's biggest draws. The park's famous red deer population – one of England's biggest – was historically protected exclusively for royal hunting. A royal forest until 1818, today Exmoor remains a largely unspoilt landscape, where adventure is in the air, night skies are dazzling affairs and rare-wildlife sightings are an everyday occurrence.

TOP TIP

Phone signal can be a rarity on the moors. Download offline maps to your phone or satnav before setting out, in case you lose service while driving to your destination. For hiking and biking, a paper map or offline version is essential.

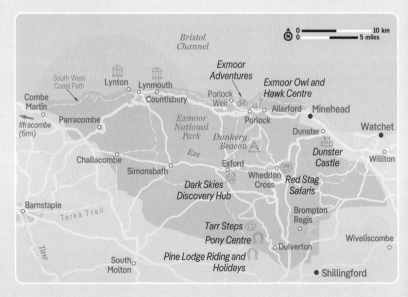

Red deer, Exmoor National Park

Wild Encounters

WILDLIFE & NATURE

Exmoor's diverse landscapes and habitats mean an abundance of flora and fauna, from the famous inhabitants like red deer and Exmoor ponies to rare butterflies and unusual lichens. Hop in a 4WD and get off-road with a local expert on a wildlife safari. Taking dirt tracks into forests and over the moors allows for some brilliant close-ups of wildlife, including those gorgeous red deer. Guides know the best places to spot wildlife to make sure you see everything – just remember to bring binoculars. Both **Red Stag Safari** and **Exmoor Wildlife Safaris** offer half-day wildlife safaris on the moors.

A short visit to the charity-run **Exmoor Pony Centre** near Dulverton affords the chance to meet the park's iconic animals up close. Entry is free, but spending a little in the shop – or booking a grooming session or pony ride – supports efforts to protect this rare and endangered pony species.

Across the moors, near the picturesque village of Allerford, the **Exmoor Owl and Hawk Centre** offers another hands-on wildlife encounter. A taster session or flying experience sees you landing one of the centre's beautiful birds of prey on your gloved hand for the ultimate up-close encounter. This is not a zoo; visitors can only come for the flying experiences or to watch the twice-weekly flying display (Wednesdays and Saturdays).

WILDLIFE ON EXMOOR

The Exmoor pony is the park's most famous species: a hardy breed of semi-feral ponies who roam freely across the moors.

Britain's largest land mammal, the majestic red deer, has lived on Exmoor for hundreds – possibly thousands – of years.

Smaller, but equally notable, are the many species of butterflies and moths, including the high brown fritillary, one of the UK's fastest-declining species.

Woodlands shelter owls and rare lichens, while Exmoor's rivers are home to otters, kingfishers and – in autumn – leaping Atlantic salmon returning to their spawning grounds.

Birdwatchers can look out for a variety of raptors – including buzzards, red kites and kestrels – as well as starlings, stonechats and wading birds like sandpipers and oystercatchers.

 WHERE TO BASE YOURSELF IN NORTH DEVON

Exford
Rural village clustered along the River Exe in an ideal location at the heart of Exmoor.

Dulverton
Historic market town on the River Barle with lots of good food options.

Lynton & Lynmouth
For sea views, harbourside restaurants and direct access to the South West Coast Path.

Coast to County Loop

This road trip connects some of Exmoor's prettiest villages, while looping through a myriad of different landscapes for such a short route. Wind your way through ancient woodland dense with ferns and moss, over heather-strewn moors and along windswept cliffs with views across the Severn Estuary to Wales. It's possible to squeeze this trip into one day, but far more enjoyable to spread it over two or three.

1 Dunster

With its rosy-hued stonework and thatched cottages tucked between forested hills, this is one of Exmoor's prettiest villages. Wander through the medieval centre to explore the quirky high street and 17th-century octagonal **Yarn Market**. The 13th-century **Dunster Castle** is perched on a hilltop above the river that powers the estate's working watermill. Most of the lavish country home you see today was added in the 1800s.

The Drive: The coast-hugging A39 is more direct, but detour inland (25 minutes) via Wheddon Cross and over Dunkery Beacon for one of the best views in Exmoor.

2 Porlock

Porlock's high street is worth a pit stop for its independent shops, but the coastal village of **Porlock Weir** is the real gem. Drive or walk the 1.5 miles to the coast to explore Porlock Weir's tiny, tidal harbour, surrounded by pretty stone cottages and a handful of intriguing shops and galleries.

The Drive: Take the cliff-hugging toll road from Porlock (£3) for sea views glimpsed between pines, then rejoin the A39 for one of its most impressive sections (30 minutes).

PETER TITMUSS/SHUTTERSTOCK ©

Lynton & Lynmouth cliff railway

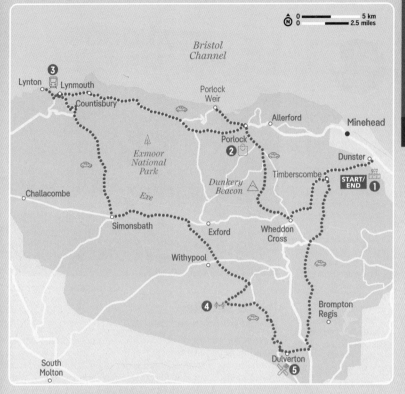

3 Lynton & Lynmouth

These twinned villages, at the foot and top of a cliff, are separated only by height. You could easily while away an afternoon at this romantic seaside stop but, if pressed for time, the main attraction is the **cliff railway** (p119) between the two.

The Drive: Follow the B3223 across open moorland towards Simonsbath for one of the best drives in Exmoor (40 minutes). From Liscombe on, it's a narrow one-lane road between high hedgerows.

4 Tarr Steps

Thought to be medieval, this is Britain's longest **clapper bridge** – a simple, stone bridge spanning 55m across the River Barle. Local legend holds that it was built by the devil, who still sunbathes there occasionally. If the five-minute stroll from the car park isn't long enough, there are several signposted trails through the surrounding nature reserve.

The Drive: Northmore Rd snakes beneath the dense canopy of Barle Valley's ancient woodland (15 minutes); it's generally two lanes, but narrow in spots with some sharp bends.

5 Dulverton

Known as the gateway to Exmoor, Dulverton is one of the park's larger towns, home to the **Exmoor National Park Centre**. The topsy-turvy town centre contains a scattering of antique stores and bookshops, as well as several popular pubs and restaurants.

I LIVE HERE

Dan French, founder and director of Exmoor Adventures (*@exmoor adventures),* shares his mountain-biking tips.

Mountain biking on Exmoor is simply fantastic: a huge variety of trails, great views...and it's quiet! For the best routes, try Dunkery Beacon, Exmoor's highest point. There are amazing descents off the top, leading down into the ancient oak woodlands of Horner. Open rocky bridleways quickly descend into tight, steep trails heading into the valleys. Top tips:

Download a route from *exmoor adventures.com.*

Prepare for all weathers.

Give bikes a check-over before heading out.

Carry a spare tube, pump, multitool, food and a drink.

Start with a climb, so you get to finish with a descent!

STEPHEN DOREY/ALAMY ©

Cycling to Dunkery Beacon

In the Saddle

EXPLORE EXMOOR ON HORSEBACK

Slow down and reconnect with nature on a guided horse-trekking tour. With over 300 miles of bridleways across a diverse mix of terrain, Exmoor is one of England's best riding destinations. Several local stables cater for beginners as well as experienced riders. Seek red deer on a quiet hack through fairy-tale woodlands, or feel the wind in your hair as you canter across open moorland. Keep your eyes peeled; the quiet approach of a horse allows for close-up glimpses of local wildlife. **Pine Lodge Riding and Holidays**, in the south of Exmoor, is particularly good for beginners thanks to the patient staff and almost direct access to off-road trails.

Dark Starry Nights

STARGAZE IN EPIC DARK SKIES

On clear nights, Exmoor's inky skies provide a spellbinding display for stargazers. Thanks to the local authority's efforts to limit light pollution and protect these dazzling nightly displays, the park was designated as Europe's first

 WHERE TO RIDE HORSES IN NORTH DEVON

Exmoor Riding
Barefoot riding for experienced riders, with a focus on holistic horsemanship and reconnecting with nature. Based in Allerford.

Pine Lodge
Various guided rides including options for beginners, riding holidays and safari day rides; near Dulverton.

Brendon Manor
A range of guided treks for all abilities, across open moorland and into river valleys; near Lynton.

International Dark Sky Reserve in 2011. Download a free *Astronomer's Guide* from the National Park Authority (exmoor-nationalpark.gov.uk), or pick up guides and rent telescopes (£25 for a night) from the National Park Centres at Dulverton, Dunster and Lynmouth. The **Dark Skies Festival**, held in October, sees a flurry of fun and educational events, while the **Dark Skies Discovery Hub** at Exford hosts guided stargazing events and presentations throughout the year.

Victorian Seaside Engineering

LYNMOUTH–LYNTON CLIFF RAILWAY

One clustered around a harbour and grey stone beach, the other perched on the cliffs above, the twin villages of **Lynton** and **Lynmouth** create a romantic seaside setting. Move between the two towns on the **Lynton and Lynmouth Cliff Railway**, the world's highest and steepest fully water-powered railway. This feat of Victorian engineering opened in 1890 and is one of just three examples of its kind left in the world. Hop into one of the two emerald-green carriages to speed up the 152m elevation in a matter of minutes – enjoying views of Lynmouth and the surrounding coastline as you go.

At the top, explore Lynton's Old Town, particularly the shops and galleries around Queen St and the surprising, Tudor Revival facade of **Lynton Town Hall**. A short visit to **Lynton Toy Museum and Shop** offers a nostalgic trip back to childhood, or discover local history at the quirky **Lyn and Exmoor Museum** inside the town's oldest house.

Follow the zigzagging cliff path back down to Lynmouth (or ride the railway again) to explore the harbour and browse the independent shops along the pedestrian Lynmouth St. For more local history, the free **Lynmouth Flood Memorial Hall** is worth a look – the small museum and model village is dedicated to the devastating flood that swept through Lynmouth on 16 August 1952.

Coastal Trails

EMBARK ON ENGLAND'S LONGEST JOURNEY

Just east of Exmoor, the seaside town of **Minehead** marks the start of the **South West Coast Path**, a 630-mile walking route that skirts the entire southwestern corner of the country. On the promenade in Minehead, the start of England's longest footpath is marked by a bronze sculpture of two giant hands holding a map. Most guides

BEST PUBS AROUND EXMOOR

Ancient Mariner, Lynmouth
Fun gastropub with local drinks and food plus eclectic maritime memorabilia. ££

Royal Oak, Withypool
This 18th-century pub has beamed ceilings, log fires and a great selection of local gins. ££

Ship Inn, Porlock Weir
Twinned with Porlock's Ship Inn, the white-washed 'Bottom Ship' has a seaside beer garden. ££

Tarr Farm Inn, Tarr Steps
Cosy 17th-century inn known for award-winning locally sourced food. £££

Masons Arms, Knowstone
Just outside the national park, this 13th-century inn holds one of Devon's only Michelin stars. £££

 WHERE TO STAY IN NORTH DEVON

Westermill Farm Holidays
Sustainable campsite on a peaceful working sheep farm on the banks of the River Exe. £

Dunkery Beacon Country House Hotel
Sweeping countryside vistas and an award-winning restaurant set this cosy country hotel apart. ££

Exmoor Forest Inn
Food-led hotel and restaurant run (and fed) by local farmers with chic country-manor vibes. £££

MORE GREAT WALKING SPOTS

Valley of Rocks
A dramatic rocky landscape with sheer cliffs, spectacular rock formations and friendly wild goats.

Dunkery Beacon
The highest point in Exmoor at 519m, this heather-clad sandstone hill provides exceptional views.

Watersmeet
A gentle stroll alongside the East Lyn River through a steep, forested gorge.

Doone Valley
The peaceful, rural setting of RD Blackmore's novel *Lorna Doone*.

Tarr Steps Woods
This nature reserve is an important conservation area. Look out for otters in the River Barle.

PETER TURNER PHOTOGRAPHY/SHUTTERSTOCK ©

South West Coast Path (p119)

break the route into 52 one-day sections, the first three of which follow the coastline of Exmoor National Park, one of the path's more challenging sections. The first day, from Minehead to Porlock Weir, sees you summiting **Selworthy Beacon** (308m) for views of Wales across the Bristol Channel and across the national park towards Dunkery Beacon. If three full days of walking sounds a bit much, there are plenty of shorter circular walks; check *southwestcoastpath.org* for route guides and maps.

For Thrill-Seekers

PUSH YOURSELF WITH NEW CHALLENGES

On the sea road outside Porlock Weir, **Exmoor Adventures** offers mountain bike and e-bike rental, as well as biking tours and lessons among Exmoor's imposing hills. That's all alongside an exciting array of other adventure sports. Try your hand at kayaking or paddleboarding with an introductory session; experienced paddlers can spot wildlife on a guided trip through Porlock Bay's flooded marshlands. Those looking for a land-based adventure can also have a go at archery, tree climbing and rock climbing.

GETTING AROUND

Car is the most convenient way to explore Exmoor, but it's not the only option. With planning and patience, it's possible to explore a fair amount of the national park by public transport. The coastal towns and attractions are connected by the Exmoor Coaster (First Bus), an open-top hop-on/ hop-off bus running between Watchet and Lynmouth. Several other bus services connect the rest of the park, but these tend to be infrequent, with some only running on certain days. Walking, biking and horse riding are zero-footprint ways to reach some of the more remote areas.

ILFRACOMBE

Like so many towns on the British coast, Ilfracombe turned into the town it is today thanks to the Georgian fashion for sea bathing. Expansion began in the early 1800s, with a bathhouse, bathing pools and terraces for taking the sea air all built to encourage tourism. But it was the arrival of the railway to nearby Barnstaple in 1854 that sealed the deal, ushering in Ilfracombe's heyday as a popular Victorian resort.

Before any of that, though, Ilfracombe was a port town. Its natural harbour was a significant safe port on the Bristol Channel, in use since at least the 12th century. Today, top-notch restaurants and boutique galleries are clustered around that picturesque harbour, evidencing Ilfracombe's emerging food and art scenes. This is still one of Devon's most popular seaside towns, with plenty to entice, from its beaches and bathing pools to watersports and boat trips.

TOP TIP

The Bristol Channel's tides are the second most variable in the world, after Canada's Bay of Fundy. Whole beaches can disappear at high tide, leaving walkers and rock-poolers cut off – always check tide times before setting out. Stick to beaches with lifeguards and learn your beach flags (p221).

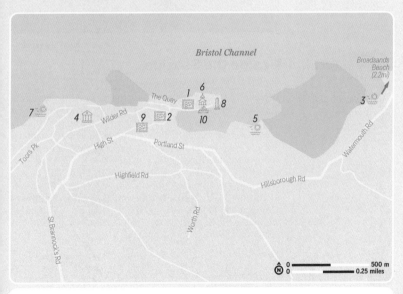

SIGHTS
1 Aluna Collective
2 Fleek Gallery
3 Hele Bay
4 Ilfracombe Museum
5 Rapparee Cove
6 St Nicholas Chapel
7 Tunnels Beaches
8 *Verity*

DRINKING & NIGHTLIFE
9 Fore Street

BEST ILFRACOMBE RESTAURANTS

Lynbay Fish and Chips
Queue for the locally caught fish and chips at this popular harbourside spot. £

Take Thyme
Local seafood and great wines dominate this cosy restaurant's menu. Order Lundy lobster if it's on the specials menu. ££

Stacc
Colourful seafront cafe known for great cakes, coffee and cocktails. £

Slice of Devon
Takeaway pizza by the slice, plus seafood specials like crab-loaded fries. £

Antidote
Intimate restaurant just off the quayside with a locally focused menu and a Michelin Bib Gourmand. ££

LEFT: ANDY SAGE/SHUTTERSTOCK ©; RIGHT: CARL_FORBES/ALAMY ©

Tunnels Beaches

Beside the Seaside

BEACHES AND BATHING POOLS

Ilfracombe's grey shingle beaches aren't exactly beauty spots, but they provide sheltered swimming on a blustery coastline, and the rocky coves of this once-grand Victorian resort hold a certain rugged charm. Visit the **Tunnels Beaches** for a unique seaside experience. In 1823, a team of miners hand-carved 160m of tunnels through the cliffs to reach the beaches – you can still see pickaxe marks on the walls. These cliff-backed coves now boast modern toilets, changing rooms and a cafe alongside the Victorian bathing pools. Nearby **Rapparee Cove**, at the foot of a steep cliff, was the site of a famous shipwreck in 1796, while the sheltered waters of **Hele Bay** are popular with families and paddleboarders.

 WHERE TO STAY IN ILFRACOMBE

Ocean Backpackers
Relaxed and friendly hostel in an ideal harbourside location. £

Beach Cove Coastal Retreat
A cluster of luxurious beach-hut-style holiday lodges perched above the sand at Hele Bay. £££

Wildercombe House
Family-run guesthouse in a Victorian residence with characterful rooms and fantastic bay views. £££

Smugglers & Sea Life

EXPLORE BY BOAT

There's been a port at Ilfracombe since at least the 12th century. The town's restaurants still depend on this working harbour, but more common than fishing vessels these days are boat tours for tourists. Hop aboard the bright-yellow *Ilfracombe Princess* for a cruise, or experience the thrill of a RIB ride with **Ilfracombe Sea Safari**, leaping over waves at up to 20 knots. Pass smugglers' caves and silver mines in the cliffs, or take a longer cruise in search of seals and dolphins. As you sail away from Ilfracombe, look out for the tiny, hilltop **St Nicholas Chapel**, built for local sailors in 1361.

Art by the Ocean

DIVE INTO ILFRACOMBE'S ART SCENE

In 2012, Damien Hirst gave Ilfracombe a gift that many of the town's inhabitants would rather return. Hirst's 20m-tall bronze statue **Verity** stands on the harbourside: naked, pregnant, holding aloft a huge sword and flayed on her sea-facing side to reveal sinew, fat and unborn foetus. Whether you think it's an eyesore or an allegory for truth as the artist affirms, Hirst's divisive statue feels like the herald of Ilfracombe's vibrant art scene. A slew of galleries and studios have popped up in the last few years, and the annual **Ilfracombe Art Trail** sees artists and craftspeople opening their homes, studios and galleries for visitors to explore. **Fore Street** is emerging as a hub for indie shops and art galleries, while elsewhere in town the **Aluna Collective** and **Fleek Gallery** sell works by local artists. Those less interested in modern art may prefer the historic paintings, photographs and engravings in **Ilfracombe Museum**. This eclectic collection of artefacts pertaining to local history is a great place to while away an hour, especially on rainy afternoons.

Snorkel in a Hidden Bay

ESCAPE TO BROADSANDS BEACH

Known locally as 'Little Thailand' for its forest-topped cliffs and turquoise waters, formerly 'secret' **Broadsands Beach** (pictured right) is increasingly popular, though the 240-odd steps are still enough to put off less determined beachgoers. Pack a snorkel to enjoy the reef and clear waters.

BEST CHILD-FRIENDLY DAYS

Ilfracombe Aquarium
There's a focus on local aquatic environments at this small pier-side aquarium housed within the old lifeboat house.

Watermouth Castle
The grounds of this imposing 19th-century country house hide a miniature theme park.

Exmoor Zoo
Meet the only pair of black leopards in the UK at this popular charity-run zoo, where ticket sales help fund breeding programmes and conservation work.

GETTING AROUND

Ilfracombe's centre is small and can easily be explored on foot. That said, the town is built on hills and has some steep streets. You'll find plenty of parking in the town centre, especially around the harbour area, but during summer these fill up fast. The larger carparks at Larkstone Lane and Hillsborough Rd are a short walk from town and make a good alternative. Stagecoach and Filer's run regular bus services to Barnstaple and along the coast.

Beyond Ilfracombe

Lundy Island
Ilfracombe
Hartland Peninsula
Croyde
Taw-Torridge Estuary
Clovelly

Heading west from Ilfracombe leads to an enticing and varied coastline dotted with beaches, clifftop trails and choice surf.

North Devon's coastline is often overlooked in favour of the south coast beaches and the Cornish surf towns further west. But this area is home to one of the southwest's best surfing beaches, an Area of Outstanding Natural Beauty (AONB) and an abundance of unspoilt nature.

A Unesco Biosphere Reserve encompasses the entire north coast, taking in several vital Marine Conservation Zones. Wildlife thrives here, from the huge seal colonies on Lundy Island to the tiny, rare sand lizards that hide among grass-tufted sand dunes.

Beaches range from sheltered pockets of white sand to rocky tumbles that call for adventures big and small. Inland, there are historic stately homes, riverside bike rides and pretty villages to explore.

TOP TIP

Many North Devon car parks use the RingGo app to accept online payments – download it to make exploring easier.

North Devon coastline

ALEXEY LOBANOV/SHUTTERSTOCK ©

MARK CAUNT/SHUTTERSTOCK ©

Grey seal

Island Escape

SET SAIL FOR BRITAIN'S GALAPAGOS

Chances are, you'll spot a few **Lundy Island** locals before you even step off the boat. This tiny Bristol Channel island, roughly two hours by ferry from Ilfracombe, is home to a population of around 180 Atlantic grey seals, and the inquisitive creatures seem to love people-watching as day-trippers disembark. Lundy is car-free, wind-buffeted and deliciously remote – the main draws are its castaway feel and abundant wildlife. In addition to seals, there are puffins, Lundy ponies and feral goats. From March to November, visitors can hop aboard MS *Oldenburg,* a 1950s ferry whose timetable and departure point (Ilfracombe or Bideford) varies with the tides. In winter months, this is replaced by an infrequent helicopter service.

Day-trippers should stick to the south. From the village, you can walk to the west coast's dramatic granite cliffs and back around the southern tip in under an hour. The island wardens run seasonal guided walks, Rockpool Rambles and Snorkel Safaris, timed with ferry arrivals. Climb the narrow spiral staircase of **Old Light** – a historic lighthouse built in 1820 – for views of the entire island. Lundy's facilities are sparse: there's just one pub (the **Marisco Tavern**) and a village shop, but this adds to the escaping-it-all flavour, and you may find a day trip isn't quite enough. If so, there are several accommodation options for an off-grid escape, all managed by the Landmark Trust.

PERFECT NORTH COAST BEACHES

Westward Ho!
Cheerfully retro family favourite with sandy beach, arcades, mini golf and a rock swimming pool.

Combe Martin
A breakwater makes for flat water in the bay. At low tide, a rocky path leads to the caves of former silver mines.

Woolacombe and Putsborough Sands
Two beaches merge into a 3-mile sweep of golden sand.

Saunton Sands
Long sandy beach with mellow surf, backed by vast dunes.

Barricane Beach
Tiny cove strewn with exotic shells carried by the Gulf Stream from the Caribbean.

WHERE TO LEARN LOCAL HISTORY IN NORTH DEVON

Lundy Museum
Tiny, single-room museum with archaeological finds and exhibits about the island's history.

Museum of Branstaple and North Devon
Social and natural history, geology and art collections tell the stories of north Devon.

North Devon Maritime Museum
Small museum in a Georgian house in Appledore, covering the area's seafaring past.

I LIVE HERE

Jasmine Bennett, North Devon Project Coordinator for surf therapy charity The Wave Project *(@wave projectuk)*, shares what makes Croyde special.

'North Devon is an amazing surf destination: we have world-class waves with a backdrop of stunning scenery.

The sandbanks at Croyde cause the waves (on a good day) to have this perfect hollow form. There's also Saunton for a chilled longboard wave or Putsborough for shelter from a southerly wind.

Water has a psycho-logically restorative effect, and the fact that surfing is so challenging enables children at The Wave Project to build resilience and leave our sessions with a real sense of achievement, key contributors to good self-esteem. More importantly, it's fun!'

Surfing, Woolacombe Beach

Surf's Up

DEVON'S SURF TOWN

In the quaint coastal village of **Croyde** (a 25-minute drive from Ilfracombe), whitewashed thatched cottages meet laid-back surfer vibes. The choice waves on Croyde's crescent of sandy beach have been drawing surfers here since the 1920s. Today, the town – set within an AONB, a Marine Protected Area and the UK's only World Surfing Reserve – is north Devon's surfing hub.

Experienced surfers can hit the waves at **Croyde Beach** or one of the nearby spots like **Saunton Sands**, **Woolacombe** or **Barricane Beach**, depending where the surf is. For beginners, there are several surf schools in town; **Surfing Croyde Bay** and **Surf South West** are two of the best.

 WHERE TO RENT A SURFBOARD IN CROYDE

Ralph's Surf Shop
Small, locally run surf and hire shop beloved for its friendly, knowledgeable staff.

Little Pink Shop
Everything you need for surfing and watersports in a fun, hot-pink boutique.

Surfing Croyde Bay
Surf school with board rental, warm indoor changing, and a beach-chic bar on-site.

If surfing is more of a spectator sport for you, watch the pros from Surfing Croyde Bay's funky sea-view cafe. Or, walk the cliff path around to **Baggy Point** for views of the bay, returning via Putsborough for one of the area's best coastal walks. Back in the village, refuel with a pub lunch at the **Thatch** – a local institution – or one of the many food trucks and pop-ups that scatter Croyde in summer.

The **Museum of British Surfing** lies a stone's throw from Croyde, in Braunton. Step in on your way to or from the beach for an impressive collection of memorabilia and surfboards (the oldest from 1919), which tell the story of British surfing.

Dunes, Rivers & Beaches

ESTUARY EXPLORATIONS

Two rivers – one rising on Dartmoor and the other away in the west near Meddon – meet near Braunton to create the wide **Taw-Torridge Estuary** before spilling into Bideford Bay, about 40 minutes' drive from Ilfracombe.

Facing each other across the estuary are two vast expanses of sand dunes. Backing the popular Saunton Sands beach, **Braunton Burrows** (pictured below) is one of the largest dune systems in the British Isles (approximately 1000 hectares). These are home to a diversity of plants and wildlife, including rare orchids, butterflies and reptiles. Look out for mock concrete landing craft among the tufted dunes – remnants of military training for the WWII D-Day invasion. **Northam Burrows** is smaller but equally scenic, grazed by free-roaming sheep and home to England's oldest golf course. Both are beloved by birdwatchers; look out for curlews, oystercatchers and lapwings in winter.

Two of north Devon's prettiest villages are found nearby. On the Torridge's western bank lies **Instow**, with its small beach, grassy sand dunes and fantastic food scene. Across the river, **Appledore** is a colourful fishing village that embodies the word 'quaint', where every other building is painted a different pastel hue – Irsha St, Bude St and One End St are a few of the best examples. A small, seasonal ferry runs between the two at high tide, or there's a gentle 6-mile river walk, crossing at Bideford.

TARKA TRAIL

Exmoor, north Devon and Dartmoor are linked by the Tarka Trail – a mammoth, 180-mile figure-of-eight walking and cycling loop inspired by the route taken by the title character in Henry Williamson's 1927 novel *Tarka the Otter*.

Starting in Barnstaple, the trail heads up through Exmouth, along the north coast, then all the way down to Okehampton on the northern edge of Dartmoor, ending with a ride on the scenic Tarka Line railway.

The cycling section starts in Braunton and follows a disused Victorian railway path 30 miles south to Meeth. Traffic-free and tarmacked, the gentle 6-mile cycle along the Taw-Torridge Estuary from Barnstaple to Instow makes for a lovely day out.

 WHERE TO EAT IN INSTOW AND APPLEDORE

Glorious Oyster
Colourful beachside shack for just-caught seafood, with picnic tables tucked behind Instow's sand dunes. ££

Hocking's Dairy Ice Cream
Historic ice-cream factory and an iconic Appledore brand with a fleet of cream-coloured vans. £

Johns of Instow
Deli and cafe with a range of local produce and locally roasted coffee. £

BEST GARDENS

RHS Rosemoor
There's something beautiful to see all year round – plus a summertime Flower Show to rival Chelsea's – at this historic, 26-hectare garden in the Torridge Valley.

Broomhill Sculpture Gardens
More than 150 sculptures are dotted throughout the gardens and ancient woodlands of the historic Broomhill Estate, north of Barnstaple.

Arlington Court
North of Barnstaple, this 19th-century manor house sits on extensive grounds with a human-made lake, woodlands and formal Victorian garden. Don't miss the impressive National Trust Carriage Museum, housed in the stables.

Postcard Perfection

IS THIS DEVON'S PRETTIEST VILLAGE?

With whitewashed cottages zigzagging down the forested slopes of a plummeting cliffside towards a curved harbour, **Clovelly** feels like it was designed purely with postcards in mind. The steep cobbled streets can't accommodate cars, so the centre of **Clovelly Historic Village** is strictly pedestrianised, lending an enticing 'lost in time' feel. Deliveries are dragged downhill on wooden sledges; the Clovelly donkeys, who once carried supplies in and fisherfolk's hauls out, now spend their days posing for photos at the historic stables. Make your way downhill past craft workshops and quaint shops to reach **Clovelly Quay**, where the sea wall affords the best views of the hill-hugging town. Clovelly's two museums are worth a short visit: the **Kingsley Museum** (former home of *The Water Babies* author Charles Kingsley) and the cramped and atmospheric **Fisherman's Cottage**.

Park at the visitors centre, about an hour's drive from Ilfracombe, to visit the privately owned village. There's a fee to enter – tickets also include the nearby **Clovelly Court Gardens**, a Victorian kitchen garden with restored greenhouses.

Make a Splash

GIVE COASTEERING A GO

North Devon's rugged coastline provides some perfect spots for the thrilling sport of coasteering. Don a wetsuit and helmet to get up close and personal with the cliffs, climbing rock faces and leaping into the sea. **Active Escape** runs coasteering sessions at Hele Bay (a 10-minute bus ride from Ilfracombe), while **Surfing Croyde Bay** will have you clambering over the cliffs and gullies at Baggy Point.

History, Hiking & Hartlands

DISCOVER THE HARTLAND PENINSULA

A rugged jot of land at the very edge of Devon, about an hour's drive from Ilfracombe, the **Hartland Peninsula** is an often-forgotten area of unspoilt coastline, sleepy farmland and pockets of ancient woodland. Hit the coast paths for hiking; try the circular trail through **Brownsham Wood** to **Mouthmill Beach**, where you can hop over rock pools to reach the triangular arch of **Blackchurch Rock**. For a challenge, the section of the **South West Coast Path** from Hartland Quay to Bude is considered one of the toughest parts of the trail.

 WHERE TO EAT IN CLOVELLY

Post Office
Award-winning Devon pasties from a takeaway counter inside the post office. **£**

Cottage Tea Rooms
Enjoy harbour views from the cobbled, plant-filled terrace at this quaint cottage tearoom. **££**

Red Lion
This 18th-century quayside pub has a scattering of outdoor seats overlooking the harbour. **££**

Clovelly

BEST CREAM TEAS IN NORTH DEVON

Docton Mill Gardens and Tea Rooms
Voted best cream tea in Devon, surrounded by charming gardens and a historic mill on the Hartland Peninsula. £

May Cottage Tea Rooms
Lovely little tearoom in a traditional thatched cottage in the heart of Croyde. £

Nectary Restaurant
Switch jam for honey at this award-winning restaurant on a working honey farm. £

Coffee Cabin
Amazing homemade cakes and seaside chic vibes on Appledore's quay. £

Fremington Quay Cafe
Popular riverside stop on the Tarka Trail, with great views. £

Head to **Hartland Point** for unbeatable views across the Bristol Channel to Lundy Island, directly opposite. It's not possible to walk right to the point, but follow the coast path up to the **Coastguard Station** to look down at the 19th-century lighthouse perched on rust-coloured cliffs. Bring binoculars – seals often hang out on the beaches below.

It's not all about hiking and nature, though they tend to steal the show. Don't miss the striking 12th-century **Hartland Abbey**, a monastery until the Dissolution when Henry VIII gave it to the keeper of his wine cellar. West-facing **Hartland Quay** is a cracking sunset spot, with its jagged rocky ledges adding a touch of foreground drama. These rocks have been responsible for many a shipwreck over the centuries; stories of these are recounted in the **Hartland Quay Museum**.

GETTING AROUND

Driving is generally the easiest way to explore, but in peak season congested roads and packed car parks can be an issue. In some areas, especially around the Hartland Peninsula, expect narrow country lanes which may prove a challenge for those not used to them. Stagecoach operates regular bus services connecting most towns and beaches on the coastline, including a seasonal open-top bus.

Lantic Bay, Fowey (p153)

SOUTH & EAST CORNWALL

CORNWALL'S GENTLER SIDE

It might lack the granite cliffs and sea-blown grandeur of the north coast, but Cornwall's southern side has ample charms of its own: sleepy creeks, green fields, quaint harbours and gardens galore.

Greener and gentler than the stark granite cliffs of the north and west, the south coast presents a more pastoral side to the county. It's riven by a trio of great river estuaries – the Helford, the Fal and the Fowey – along with numerous sheltered valleys with unique microclimates that enable unusual and exotic plants to flourish, nurtured by the balmy breezes of the Gulf Stream.

It's perhaps no surprise, then, that many of Cornwall's most famous gardens are found here, including Trebah, Heligan, Trelissick and Glendurgan, as well as the futuristic biomes of the Eden Project (pictured), built at the bottom of an abandoned clay pit near St Austell. A century or so ago, Cornwall's south coast was alive with maritime traffic, and its atmospheric harbour towns would have been thronged with tall ships, clippers, fishing sloops and schooners. Sadly, they're all long gone these days, to be replaced with a summertime tidal wave of yachts and pleasure boats. Still, these old towns – places like St Mawes, Fowey, Mevagissey and Falmouth, once the home port of the Packet Service – are full of salty atmosphere, and pretty, too. For the south coast's wilder aspect, head for the Lizard, Roseland and Rame peninsulas, where you'll find big cliffs, remote beaches and fine coast walks to while away as many days as you can spare.

THE MAIN AREAS

ATLANTIC
OCEAN

0 ___ 10 km
0 ___ 5 miles

Watergate Bay   ○ Porth

Newquay ●

Cubert ○

Mount ○

Truro, p147

Cornwall's capital city is
best known for its mighty
cathedral, and it makes a
good base for exploring the
county's central heartland.

Perranporth ●

Trevellas ○

St Agnes ○

Porthtowan ○   Blackwater ○

Mawla ○

Tresillian

Truro ●

Redruth ●

Camborne ●

A39

Trelissi
Garder

Troon ○   ○ Four Lanes

○ Devoran

● Hayle

Praze-an-
Beeble ○

Penmarth ○   Longdowns ○

Penryn ○

Portscat

Leedstown ○

Porkelis ○   Hernis ○

Flushing ○   Falmouth
Bay

Townshend ○

Nancegollan ○

Falmouth ●   St Mawes ●

Godolphin
Cross ○

Rose
Penin

Helston ●

Constantine ○

Mawnan ○

Breage ○

Porthleven ○

Mawgan ○   ○ Helford

○ Garras

Falmouth, p136

A rich maritime history and a
buzzy arts scene combine to make
this waterfront town an essential
stop. Beaches, boat trips, scenery,
walks – Falmouth has it all.

Gunwalloe ○

English
Channel

Mullion ○

Cadgwith ○

Lizard ○

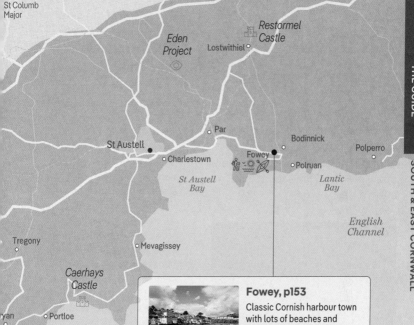

St Columb Major

Eden Project

Restormel Castle

Lostwithiel

Par

St Austell

Charlestown

Fowey

Bodinnick

Polperro

Polruan

St Austell Bay

Lantic Bay

English Channel

Tregony

Mevagissey

Caerhays Castle

...ryan

Portloe

Fowey, p153

Classic Cornish harbour town with lots of beaches and coast walks on its doorstep. It's also handy for jaunts to the Eden Project, Heligan and southeast Cornwall.

BUS

If you're not on a strict time schedule, it's perfectly possible to get around by bus – and if you don't have your own car, it's pretty much the only way to get to rural areas like the Lizard and the Roseland.

TRAIN

The main train line between London and Penzance stops at Truro, St Austell and Par, from where onward buses shuttle to the Fowey area. There are also useful branch lines: Truro–Falmouth and Liskeard–Looe.

CAR

There's no doubt that a car brings maximum freedom in this part of Cornwall, but parking can be tricky (and often pricey) in larger towns like Falmouth, Truro and Fowey.

Find Your Way

From Porthleven to the Tamar, the area covered in this chapter spans around 80 to 90 crow-flying miles – but count on quite a bit more thanks to the circuitous roads, especially around the Lizard, Roseland and Rame peninsulas.

Plan Your Time

The south coast is a place, you don't want to hurry. Hike to quiet beaches, putter along in boats, explore the creeks and, above all, allow plenty of time for at least a swim a day.

Gyllyngvase Beach (p136)

If You Only Do One Thing

Spend a day in **Falmouth** (p136). It's a lively, creative town with loads of ways to while away your day – including a **Tudor castle** (p137), a brilliant **maritime museum** (p137), some excellent **pubs** (p139) and a trio of pleasant **beaches** (p136) that are great for snorkelling and paddleboarding. Falmouth is also an ideal launchpad for taking a **boat trip** (p139) across the water to Flushingor St Mawes, a longer trip upriver via **Trelissick Gardens** (p148) or a **wildlife adventure** (p139) in search of dolphins and basking sharks.

PETER TITMUSS/SHUTTERSTOCK ©

Seasonal Highlights

Summer is obviously the focus of travel in this region, but there are interesting events happening throughout the year – from oyster celebrations to pasty-making contests.

MARCH

Bakers battle it out to master the perfect crimp during the **World Pasty Championships** in early March, staged at the Eden Project.

APRIL

One of Cornwall's biggest feasts occurs during the **Porthleven Food Festival**, which attracts big-name chefs and pop-up food stalls.

MAY

The biggest day of the year in Helston, **Flora Day** is part street dance, musical parade and floral pageant.

FROM LEFT: PAUL_BRIGHTON/SHUTTERSTOCK ©, HUGH R HASTINGS/GETTY IMAGES ©, CHRISTOPHER ISON/ALAMY ©

A Long Weekend

With a few more days to spare, a visit to the **Lizard Peninsula** (p143) should figure high on your list – a dramatic landscape that's home to some of Cornwall's wildest cliffs, prettiest villages and most secluded beaches. Bring a pair of binoculars for spotting wildlife around the Lizard's cliffs. You should also have the time to visit a few of the area's subtropical gardens, like **Trebah** (p140), **Glendurgan** (p140) or Cornwall's real-life secret garden, the **Lost Gardens of Heligan** (p157), along with the county's most iconic modern landmark, the incredible **Eden Project** (p157).

A Week of Exploring

Extra time will enable you to explore a few more rural corners of the Cornish south coast, including the bucolic **Roseland** (p141), which offers the enticing prospect of pleasant coastal towns, golden beaches and seemingly endless green fields. Ideally, you should also squeeze in some time for exploring further along the coast, perhaps via the historic harbour of **Charlestown** (p155) to yacht-filled **Fowey** (p153), or the quiet, little-explored and little-known southeast corner around the **Rame Peninsula** (p159).

JUNE
The quaysides echo with hearty sailors' songs during the **Falmouth International Sea Shanty Festival**.

AUGUST
Parades take over the streets during **Falmouth Week**, while sea vessels flock to **Fowey Royal Regatta**.

OCTOBER
Feast on fresh oysters, mussels and other crustaceans during the **Falmouth Oyster Festival**, which also hosts cookery classes.

DECEMBER
Giant withy (wicker) lanterns are carried through Truro's city centre during the **City of Lights** parade to mark the festive season.

FALMOUTH

Falmouth

Few seaside towns in Cornwall boast such an arresting location as Falmouth, overlooking the broad River Fal as it empties into the English Channel. Surrounded by sea, Falmouth is an appealing jumble of lanes, old pubs, slate roofs and trendy cafes – and with its clifftop castle, sandy beaches and excellent maritime museum, it's an ideal base for exploring Cornwall's south coast.

Historically, the town made its fortune during the 18th and 19th centuries. Between 1689 and 1851, this was the home port for the Packet Service – the vital communications link that underpinned the smooth running of the British Empire. Sadly, the days of the tea clippers, trading vessels and privateers have long passed, and these days the town is supported by a lively tourist trade and student crowd from nearby Falmouth University. Nevertheless, the docks remain an important centre for ship repairs – spot the cranes as you walk to Pendennis Point.

TOP TIP

Falmouth gets busy in summer and parking can be tricky, but the Ponsharden Park & Float/Ride service allows you to park your car on the outskirts and catch a boat into town. Handy buses shuttle from the main square, the Moor, to locations around town, including the beaches.

WHY I LOVE FALMOUTH

Oliver Berry
@olivertomberry

Falmouth has everything I love most about Cornwall: sea, beaches, cliffs, gardens and amazing views, along with a fascinating history and a strong sense of community.

I've lived here for a long time but I never get tired of exploring the town's old lanes, alleyways and opes – not to mention its brilliant pubs. And when I want to escape, there are so many secret spots along the River Fal to take refuge from the summer crowds. Where are they? Now that would be telling.

Beach Time

SEA SWIMMING, SUP AND SNORKELLING

Falmouth's trio of beaches are the town's main summer draw. All three can be reached on foot via the coast path or by bike (although you won't be able to get away without tackling some hills en route).

Nearest to town (and busiest) is **Gyllyngvase Beach**, known to locals as Gylly – a flat, sandy stretch about half a mile from the centre of Falmouth, with the popular Gylly Beach Cafe on-site. The area further towards Pendennis is known as Castle Beach, and generally stays quieter. **Swanpool Beach** lies about 20 minutes' walk away via the coast path; it's a popular swimming spot, and also has a lagoon just inland from the beach. **Maenporth Beach** is the furthest of the three, 3 miles or so from Falmouth along the coast path. Needless to say, there are numerous other little coves to discover on the way (including a super-secret nudist beach), but you'll need local knowledge to find many of them.

Hiring a kayak or SUP is a great way of exploring the coast. There are places to hire SUPs and kayaks at all three beaches, and each has its own cafe nearby. **WeSup**, based at Gylly, offers a memorable sunrise tour, plus yoga sessions and SUP retreats. The beaches also offer good snorkelling at high tide.

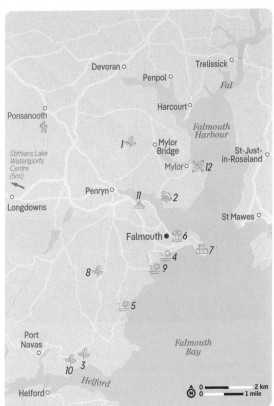

SIGHTS
1 Enys Gardens
2 Flushing
3 Glendurgan Garden
4 Gyllyngvase Beach
5 Maenporth Beach
6 National Maritime Museum
7 Pendennis Castle
8 Penjerrick Garden
9 Swanpool Beach
10 Trebah Garden

ACTIVITIES
11 AK Wildlife Cruises
12 Falmouth River Watersports

Ships & Castles

DEEP DIVE INTO FALMOUTH'S PAST

Falmouth's Tudor fortress, **Pendennis Castle**, stands formidably atop Pendennis Point commanding a widescreen view over the harbour mouth and the whole of Falmouth Bay. It was built as part of Henry VIII's massive 16th-century castle-building program, and designed to work in tandem with its sister fortress across the river at St Mawes: any vessel entering the Carrick Roads without permission would have been shredded by cannon fire, although

FOR CASTLE & COUNTRY HOUSE FANS

Castle connoisseur? Then you'll definitely want to visit **St Mawes** (p151) and **Restormel** (p157). Country-house crazy? Don't miss **Trelissick** (p148), **Caerhays** (p152), **Port Eliot** (p159) and **Mount Edgcumbe** (p159).

WHERE TO FIND WATERFRONT PUBS NEAR FALMOUTH

Pandora Inn
On the banks of Restronguet Creek, this thatched inn is one of Cornwall's landmark pubs, in situ since the mid-1600s.

Ferryboat
Lovely pub on the Helford River. The picnic tables have dreamy river views; inside, it's all wood, slate and open plan.

Shipwright's Arms
A posh gastropub across the river in Helford village. The food is great, but it gets very busy in summer.

I LIVE HERE

Will Hazell, of Falmouth Uncovered (falmouth uncovered.co.uk), offers fascinating history tours. A few of his favourite nooks and crannies:

Killigrew Monument
A granite pyramid built in 1737 to honour the Killigrews, the family of blood-soaked pirates who founded Falmouth. Universally ignored by locals and tourists alike.

Custom House
This grand building was the base for customs officers waging war against Cornish smuggling. It's now a pizza restaurant, but you can still see the 'King's Pipe' (a chimney used to burn contraband tobacco) outside.

Beerwolf Books
This brilliant pub-bookshop occupies a building that once belonged to the Falmouth Packet Service, which carried mail across the Atlantic for nearly 200 years.

National Maritime Museum

ironically the fortress only saw real action during the Civil War. The circular walk up to the castle from town is lovely, and takes you past Gyllyngvase Beach, Castle Beach and Falmouth Docks: take a picnic for when you reach the point. Along the way, you'll find the remains of various fortifications and gun emplacements on the wooded slopes around the castle, along with a number of secluded little coves that are perfect for a cooling dip.

The town's other historical must-see is the **National Maritime Museum**, a sister outpost of the original in London's Greenwich. Imaginative displays focus on Falmouth's history as a port, and on the broader impact of the sea on history and culture. The centrepiece is the five-storey Flotilla Gallery, where an array of small vessels ranging from rowboats to rescue craft are suspended from the ceiling. Don't miss the view from the top floor of the Lookout tower, offering a 360-degree panorama across the entirety of Falmouth Bay.

 WHERE TO EAT IN FALMOUTH

Star & Garter
Gourmet gastropub focusing on nose-to-tail dining. The menu is meat-heavy, so vegetarians might struggle. ££

Hooked on the Rocks
Seafood restaurant in a grand spot beside Swanpool Beach. ££

Meat Counter
Burger joint that turns out the best patties in town – including veggie and vegan options. £

Messing About on the Fal

THE QUEEN OF CORNISH RIVERS

Along with the Helford and the Fowey, the **River Fal** is one of Cornwall's great tidal river systems. It's astonishingly deep in places, and strong tidal currents mean that in a matter of hours, upriver sections transform from stinky mudflats to deep blue water. Lined with overhanging oaks, inlets and creeks, it's a fascinating place to explore by boat – either self-piloted or tour-guided. It's also awash with history – tales of pirates, sea captains and smugglers cling to the riverbanks (during WWII, the Fal served as a secret staging post for troop ships heading for the beaches of Normandy).

Falmouth's Princess of Wales Pier is the embarcation point for boat trips. The best are the **Enterprise Boats**, provided by the Fal River Company, which offer various river routes to Trelissick Gardens, Truro and St Mawes, and provide informative commentary on the local wildlife and history. Alternatively, you can rent your own motorboat from **Falmouth Boat Hire** on Custom House Quay, but make sure to check the tides: getting stuck in the Fal's glutinous mudbanks does not a fun holiday make.

The river and coastline are also fantastic for spotting wildlife. Depending on the season, there's birdlife galore, from cormorants and curlews to snowy egrets. Further out to sea, you may have a chance of spotting dolphins, porpoises, basking sharks, seals and even minke whales. **AK Wildlife Cruises**, run by the unflinchingly enthusiastic Captain Keith, is the best operator.

Nature's Bounty

TAKE A WILD-FOOD TOUR

Local foraging expert Matt Vernon runs fascinating guided walks in search of wild (and free) grub through his company **Cornish Wild Food**. You can join a group tour or organise your own private foraging session. Depending on the season, you might discover fungi, wild salads, berries or edible flowers. Matt also makes his own wild gin. He runs trips in various areas of Cornwall, so check the website to see what's on.

BEST SPOTS FOR A PINT IN FALMOUTH

Beerwolf Books
A boozer and bookshop rolled into one. You can even bring your own grub.

Moth & Moon
Lovingly renovated old pub off the Moor, with a secret hillside garden.

Chain Locker
The classic Falmouth drinking hole: loads of harbourside tables.

Working Boat
A good sundowner spot under the Greenbank Hotel.

Cornish Bank
Former bank on the town's main street, now a brilliant gig venue.

Verdant Brewery
A corking craft brewery with a flashy taproom on Tregoniggie Industrial Estate, which also does good pizzas.

MORE PUBS

Check out our three tips for top **waterfront pubs** (p137) within easy driving distance of Falmouth.

Harbour Lights
The only place for fish and chips in Falmouth. Accept no alternative. £

Pizza Please
Hipster pizza in a quaint Penryn courtyard, just along the river from Falmouth. ££

Orgia
Tapas-style dining in a wine bar on Falmouth's main street. ££

BLOOMING BIVALVES

The tradition of oyster farming on the Helford and Fal rivers has existed for over five centuries.

By the mid-19th century, helped by the arrival of the railway, Cornish oyster fisheries were supplying markets across Britain, a trade which flourished for the next 100 years. The industry suffered a catastrophic decline in the late 1980s, after the introduction of a parasite from the US devastated stocks of native British oysters.

Thankfully, oyster production is up and running again on the Helford, although recent problems with pollution and Brexit export rules haven't helped.

You can guzzle some local oysters at the Falmouth Oyster Festival in October.

Into the Vale

WANDER AN OLD GUNPOWDER WORKS

The sleepy village of **Ponsanooth** lies in a wooded valley about 5 miles from Falmouth. It's worth a stop for the lovely woodland walks at **Kennall Vale**, a former gunpowder works. You'll see the remains of crumbling buildings half-hidden among the trees, and there's an oak-lined pool which is great for bird-spotting.

While in Ponsanooth, take the time to visit the brilliant brewery nearby, **Dynamite Valley**. It offers a range of delicious brews, from golden ales to rich stouts, and has its own taproom.

How Green Is My Valley

FALMOUTH'S GLORIOUS GARDENS

The sheltered coastline around Falmouth harbours several classic Cornish gardens, brimful with exotic species and horticultural wonders. They can probably be just about covered in a day, but a couple of days is preferable: Glendurgan and Trebah together make for a fun day's bike ride.

Grandest of them all is **Glendurgan**, 7 miles southwest of Falmouth, established by Alfred Fox in the 1820s to show off his plant collection from the far corners of the empire – from Himalayan rhododendrons to Canadian maples and New Zealand tree ferns. Now owned by the National Trust, the gardens tumble down a stunning valley and offer breathtaking views of the Helford; they have their own ornamental maze. The walk along the river from the Ferryboat Inn via Durgan village is delightful, and passes several secluded beaches that offer great swimming.

Next door and accessible via the coast path is **Trebah**, planted in 1840 by Charles Fox, Alfred's younger brother. It's less formal, with riotous rhododendrons, gunnera and jungle ferns lining the sides of a steep ravine leading down to the quay and shingle beach.

There are several other gardens worth seeking out around Falmouth. **Enys** is famous for its spring bluebells, while **Penjerrick** is two gardens in one: exotic jungle plants in the Valley Garden, and rhododendrons, magnolias and camellias in the Upper Garden.

GARDENER'S WORLD

Learn more about the background of the southwest's wonderful gardens in our essay **The Great Gardens of Devon & Cornwall** (p241).

WHERE TO SLEEP IN FALMOUTH

Merchants Manor
A venerable town hotel turned boutique beauty: expect bold fabrics, indulgent colour schemes and fun prints. **£££**

Highcliffe B&B
Vintage furniture and upcycled design pieces give each room here its own feel. **££**

Greenbank Hotel
The queen of Falmouth's hotels, with a knockout position beside the boat-filled estuary. **£££**

HELEN HOTSON/SHUTTERSTOCK ©

Abandoned gunpowder works, Kennall Vale

Over the Water

CATCH THE FERRY TO FLUSHING

Directly across the water from Falmouth (a ferry shuttles over regularly from Princess of Wales Pier), the handsome village of **Flushing** was once the home of many sea captains, who built fine seafront houses here. It also has a good beach for paddling and swimming and a couple of great local pubs.

It makes for a fun afternoon trip, especially if you factor in a walk around Trefusis Point to **Mylor**, a centre for yachting and watersports. You can hire boats, canoes and paddleboards from **Mylor Boat Hire** and **Falmouth River Watersports**; the **Mylor Sailing School** offers tuition if you dream of seaborne adventures.

BEST CAFES IN FALMOUTH

Espressini
Falmouth's best espresso spot, run by coffee maestro Rupert Ellis. £

Stones Bakery
Incredible bread, pastries and cakes and sweet treats on the old High St. £

Nude Canteen
Super-tasty veggie poke bowls, wraps and cakes. £

Sabzi
Chic canteen-style dining; mix up your lunch box to eat in or to go. £

Solskinn
A bookish spot on the 1st floor of the Poly, Falmouth's arts centre. £

Dark Pony
Quality coffee just off the Moor; handy while waiting for a bus. £

GETTING AROUND

Falmouth sits at the end of the railway branch line from Truro. Local buses shuttle around town and the surrounding area, including the beaches; see *gocornwallbus.co.uk* for details and timetables. For buses to other towns such as Helston, Redruth and Truro, consult *firstbus.co.uk/cornwall*. Falmouth also has its own electric bike scheme, provided by Beryl Bikes.

Car parks in Falmouth fill up quickly in summer, so consider using the Ponsharden Park & Float/Ride service (p136). Most boat and ferry services leave from Princess of Wales Pier, including the Flushing Ferry and St Mawes Ferry, which are both operated by Fal River Cornwall. Depending on the tide, boats to St Mawes occasionally leave from Custom House Quay, next to the Chain Locker pub. For faster journeys, you can also book the Falmouth Water Taxi to most destinations along the river.

Beyond Falmouth

Cornwall's southern coastline takes a sudden wild turn around the Lizard, where fields and heaths plunge into a melee of black cliffs, churning surf and sawtooth rocks.

Stithians Lake • Mabe
Helston • • Falmouth
Porthleven • • Helford
Lizard Point

Cut off by the Helford River and encircled by treacherous seas, the Lizard Peninsula is an ill-famed graveyard for ships, and it retains a raw, untamed edge. Wind-lashed in winter, in summer its clifftops blaze with wildflowers, and its beaches and coves are perfect for a wild swim. Lizard village and the foodie haven of Porthleven make good bases. While here, keep an eye out for the Cornish chough, the red-billed, crow-like bird featured on the county's coat of arms; once all but extinct, it's re-established itself on the cliffs since being reintroduced.

Look out for the Lizard's weirdest sight as you cross Goonhilly Downs: a cluster of gigantic satellite dishes, until recently a hub for UK telecommunications.

TOP TIP

National Trust membership is handy on the Lizard, especially if you're planning on visiting Kynance Cove, as you get free parking.

Kynance Cove

LEFT: LUKASZ SUCHOCKI/SHUTTERSTOCK ©; RIGHT: PHILIP BIRD LRPS CPAGB/SHUTTERSTOCK ©

Cliffs, Coves & Choughs

MAINLAND BRITAIN'S SOUTHERNMOST POINT

About 45 minutes' drive south of Falmouth, the British mainland reaches its southernmost tip at **Lizard Point**, historically one of Britain's deadliest headlands. Hundreds of ships have come to grief here over the centuries, from Spanish treasure galleons to naval frigates – which explains the looming presence of the **Lizard Lighthouse**, built in 1751 and now a heritage centre. It's the only lighthouse in Cornwall you can actually climb; book a guided tour to ascend the tower to see the lamp room and foghorn.

Trails lead out to the point from the village, where a steep track winds down to the long-disused lifeboat station and shingly cove. It's one of the most dramatic patches of coast in Cornwall. Numerous other paths lead around the headland: popular targets include **Housel Bay**, the **Devil's Frying Pan** and **Predannack Wollas**, whose blustery clifftops memorably featured in a BBC adaptation of *Poldark*.

A mile north of Lizard Point, the National Trust–owned inlet of **Kynance Cove** is a showstopper, studded with craggy offshore islands rising out of searingly blue seas that seem almost tropical in colour. The cliffs around the cove are rich in serpentine, a red-green rock popular with Victorian trinket makers. They're also a great place for spotting choughs – look out for their distinctive red bills and feet. When the seas aren't too rough, and the cove offers an exhilarating swim – but it gets busy in summer, so aim to arrive before 10am. The beach cafe offers pasties, drinks, ice creams and an absolutely cracking crab sandwich.

HELSTON'S STREET PARADE

The biggest day of the year in Helston, Flora Day is believed to derive from a pagan celebration marking the coming of spring. It's a mix of street dance, musical parade and floral pageant: the town is always packed, so arrive as early as possible. The two main events are the Hal-An-Tow, in which St Michael and the devil do battle; and the Furry Dance, which kicks off at noon and proceeds around the town's streets (participants take part by invitation only, and the dance is always led by a local couple).

Shipwrecks & Legends

STROLL THE LOE BAR

Located 3 miles southwest of the Lizard's main town of Helston, and a half-hour drive from Falmouth, **Porthleven** (pictured right) is a little harbour set around the massive walls of its stone quay, built to shelter the town from savage winter storms (pictures of gigantic waves smashing over the town steeple went viral in 2014). It's a town with a fast-growing foodie scene and it hosts the three-day **Porthleven Food Festival** every year in April.

 WHERE TO CAMP ON THE LIZARD

Henry's Campsite
Endearingly eccentric campsite dotted with flotsam and jetsam – hand-painted signs, old buoys and fishing tackle. £

Gear Farm
Simple field camping on an organic farm near Mawgan village. Legendary pasties, too. £

Namparra
Back-of-beyond site near Kuggar Sands which makes a virtue of its simplicity – it's what camping should be like. £

143

LOCAL'S LIZARD

The Lizard's villages make for a fun road trip.

Start out in Helston, with a visit to the quirky town museum. Spin along the coast to Mullion in the west, with some attractive beaches nearby.

Mosey on via Lizard village to Cadgwith, a picturesque muddle of lanes and slate-topped cottages. Continue on to Coverack, arguably the most dramatically sited of the fishing villages, overlooking a handsome blue bay.

Further along the coast is the tiny cove of Porthoustock, from where a fine stretch of coast path leads on to Porthallow. Detour via the little creek village of Gillan, a favourite spot for cockle picking; trails wind out from here around Nare Point.

Finish off in Helford village, perhaps with lunch at the Shipwright's Arms.

The surrounding coast is eminently walkable, especially if you combine it with a visit to **Loe Pool**, Cornwall's largest natural freshwater lake (said by some to be the resting place of King Arthur's magical blade, Excalibur). It's actually a lagoon, cut off from the sea by the treacherous sandbank of **Loe Bar**, which was the scene of many a shipwreck down the centuries. Trails wind their way around the lakeshore and the surrounding **Penrose Estate**, but swimming is dangerous due to unpredictable rip currents.

For more adrenaline-heavy activities around the surrounding coast, Helston-based operator **Lizard Adventure** offers coasteering, sea kayaking and surfing lessons.

A Smuggler's Creek

EXPLORE THE HELFORD

The oak-lined banks of the Helford River seem steeped in mystery, so it's little wonder that Daphne du Maurier decided to use it as the setting for her famous smuggling tale, *Frenchman's Creek*. **Koru Kayaking** offers excellent two-hour trips from the Budock Vean Hotel. It also offers riverboat cruises, or you can hire your own vessel from **Helford River Boats** at Helford Passage.

Alternatively, you can park on the edge of Helford village (a 45-minute drive from Falmouth) and walk; a pleasant walk through the woodland circles round to the creek, but an OS map comes in handy. Lunch at the waterfront **Shipwright's Arms** makes a great way to end the walk.

Seal SOS

THE RESIDENTS ARE BARKING

At any given time, there are hundreds – often thousands – of common and grey seals (pictured left) to be found around the Cornish coast but, sadly, not all of them have the happy life they deserve. The **Cornish Seal Sanctuary** in Gweek, a half-hour drive from Falmouth, rescues sick and orphaned seals, nursing them carefully back to health before releasing them back into the wild. There are some fun exclusive experiences on offer, including the chance to be a keeper for the day, feed the seals their breakfast and take a behind-the-scenes tour of the centre. Excitingly, there are also guided walks to a secret creek nearby to spot wild Cornish beavers, reintroduced here as part of an important conservation study.

 WHERE TO GET A DRINK ON THE LIZARD

Cadgwith Cove Inn
A village pub straight from a Cornish postcard. On Friday nights the singers might treat you to a sea shanty or two.

Halzephron Inn
A classic Cornish clifftop pub, high on the hills above the cove of Gunwalloe, which also does very decent food.

Blue Anchor
A local favourite, Helston's spit-and-sawdust pub brews its own Spingo beer. There's a small skittle alley out the back.

THE GUIDE

SOUTH & EAST CORNWALL: FALMOUTH

Helford River Boats, Helford Passage

High-Wire Act

ADVENTURES IN AN ABANDONED QUARRY

In a disused quarry 15 minutes' drive from Falmouth, near Mabe, **BF Adventure** offers a range of heart-in-the-mouth thrills – including Cornwall's only via ferrata, a system of bridges, fixed cables and zip lines that allows you to experience the rush of rock climbing even if you're a complete novice. You can also have proper climbing lessons if you want to take things a stage further, or spend a few hours stand-up paddleboarding, canoeing or practising your archery.

Another nearby flooded quarry contains **Kernow Adventure Park**, the biggest waterpark in this part of Cornwall, where you can splash, slide and glide your way over an inflatable obstacle course.

BEST PLACES TO EAT AROUND THE LIZARD

Cast Cafe
A sophisticated cafe in Helston's studio and gallery space. ££

New Yard
Fine dining on the Trelowarren Estate – nowhere finer for lunch. £££

Kota and Kota Kai
Half Maori, half Chinese-Malay chef Jude Kereama runs two Porthleven restaurants. ££

Potager Garden
Lovely kitchen garden near Constantine, with a great vegetarian cafe. £

Ann's Pasties
Cornwall's best pasties? Rick Stein reckons so. Near Lizard village. £

Croust House
Hearty grub and award-winning ice cream at Roskilly's Farm, near St Keverne. ££

 WHERE TO STAY ON THE LIZARD

Polurrian Hotel
This clifftop hotel on the edge of Mullion is a haven for families (plus pooches). ££

Mullion Cove Hotel
Mullion's second big hotel offers big views and is a little cheaper than the Polurrian. ££

Housel Bay Hotel
Vintage Victorian hotel built by local architect Silvanus Trevail, overlooking a craggy bay. ££

145

BEST FAMILY-FRIENDLY BEACHES ON THE LIZARD

Gunwalloe and Dollar Cove
Gunwalloe is home to the tiny 15th-century Church of St Winwaloe; Dollar Cove is rumoured to be the site of lost treasure.

Kennack Sands
A low, flat, west-facing beach that's easily accessed and good for sunset.

Poldhu Cove
A family-friendly stretch of sand, easily reached from Mullion. There's a good beach cafe, too.

Mullion Cove
This pretty village has a couple of lovely beaches.

Rinsey Cove
Off the beaten track, and all the better for it, this rocky cove is worth the walk.

IAN WOOLCOCK/SHUTTERSTOCK ©

Stithians Lake Watersports Centre

Catch the Breeze

GET SOME WIND IN YOUR SAILS

In the mining country around Carnmenellis, **Stithians Lake** (a 25-minute drive from Falmouth) is one of the largest – and allegedly the windiest – reservoirs in the southwest, which makes it a brilliant location for watersports like yachting and windsurfing. You can take lessons and hire craft from the **Stithians Lake Watersports Centre**; the lake is also a favourite place for trout fishing, along with nearby **Argal Reservoir**. There's also a popular campsite here – good luck putting the tent up.

GETTING AROUND

You really need a car to get the most out of exploring the Lizard, although there are local buses from Helston and Falmouth to Mullion and Lizard village; consult *firstbus.co.uk/adventures-bus/services/lizard* for details. Cycling can be a fun way to get around.

TRURO

Truro

Dominated by the three soaring spires of its 19th-century cathedral, Truro is Cornwall's capital and its only city. It's the county's main centre for shopping and commerce: the streets here are lined with high-street chains and independent shops, while the twice-weekly farmers market brings field-fresh produce to town.

Traces of Truro's wealthy past remain in the smart Georgian town houses and Victorian villas dotted around the city – especially along Strangways Terrace, Walsingham Place and Lemon St – although a rash of 1960s and 1970s architecture has somewhat marred the city's architectural appeal. Still, it's worth a visit to see the mighty cathedral and perhaps enjoy an evening at the Hall for Cornwall, the county's biggest venue for touring theatre and music, which has recently been revamped in impressive style. Lively weekend markets and other events are held on the piazza outside.

TOP TIP

Truro has some pleasant parks to wander around, perfect for a picnic. Victoria Gardens – planted to commemorate Queen Victoria's Golden Jubilee – is right in the centre, while Boscawen Park extends along the banks of the river en route to Malpas. It's a good spot for a bike ride; consider lunch at the Heron pub.

Lemon Quay

TRAVELLIGHT7/SHUTTERSTOCK ©

FARM FEASTS

Deep in the countryside outside Truro, near the village of Zelah, Nancarrow Farm has made a name for itself thanks to its lavish feasts.

They're usually themed – think Spanish fiesta, or seafood extravaganza – but generally there's a focus on big, bold flavours and cooking over an open fire.

Tickets disappear like lightning, so keep your ears to the ground, and check the farm's website for details.

TRURO

Down the River

TRAMP TRELISSICK'S TRAILS

Grandly located at the head of the Fal estuary, 4 miles south of Truro, **Trelissick** is one of Cornwall's largest country estates – and in a county that's awash with them, that's saying something. A sprawling expanse of fields and parkland, it's criss-crossed by walking trails: the prettiest route is to head to the estate's pebble beach and then wander upriver along the Fal's wooded banks. Often, you'll see huge tankers moored up somewhere along the creek – a reminder of just how deep the river gets at high tide. **Canoe Cornwall** operates from the gardens, and offers half-day trips in Canadian-style canoes, along with archery sessions, axe-throwing and bushcraft.

The estate's neo-Palladian house was built in the 19th century, and was gifted to the National Trust in 1955. The ground floor has recently been reopened to visitors during summer, and has a lovely tearoom that makes a pretty dreamy place for afternoon tea after wandering around the gardens – it's usually open from May to September. Trelissick is signed from the A39 between Falmouth

A BOAT TO THE GARDENS

A superb way to reach Trelissick in summer is aboard the **Enterprise Boats** (p139), which chug between Falmouth and Truro and stop en route at the gardens.

WHERE TO GET A COFFEE IN TRURO

108 Coffee
The coffee aficionados' choice: premium beans, latte art, friendly service.

Old Grammar School
Once the home of Cornwall's grammar-school boys; now good grub and coffee.

Blend 71
A reliable bet for a caffeine fix, next door to the Plaza Cinema.

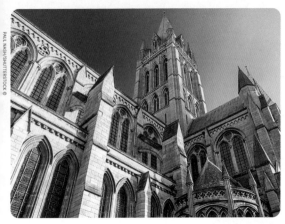

Truro Cathedral

BEST PLACES TO EAT IN TRURO

Heron
Malpas' delightful creek-side pub is worth a visit for its river views. ££

Hooked!
On a side street off Lemon Quay, this is the best place in Truro for seafood. ££

Hub Box
A popular burger joint with several locations; this is the original, in a converted church. £

Sam's in the City
Fowey's long-standing restaurant has a branch in the big city. ££

Cornish Vegan
A little cafe which is well worth seeking out for vegans. £

and Truro. Just beyond the gardens, the minor B3289 road runs down to the river, where the **King Harry Ferry** shuttles across to the Roseland several times an hour.

Neogothic Grandeur

CORNWALL'S ECCLESIASTICAL LANDMARK

Even if you're not in the slightest religious, you simply have to pay your respects at Truro's monumental **cathedral**, which looms like a neogothic supertanker over the city's skyline. Completed in 1910 in Gothic Revival style on the site of a 16th-century parish church, it was the first cathedral to be built in England since St Paul's. Inside, the vast nave contains some fine Victorian stained glass and the impressive Father Willis Organ.

The cathedral was a massive technical undertaking for its architect, John Loughborough Pearson: the foundation stones were laid in 1880 but the building wasn't completed until 30 years later. The copper-topped central tower reaches 76m, while the shorter western spires are 61m, and if you look closely, you might just be able to make out the remains of the old St Mary's Church incorporated into part of the south aisle.

It's not possible for the public to ascend any of the cathedral's three spires, so you'll just have to keep your eyes (and ears) open for forthcoming concerts and recitals. The cathedral's acoustics are amazing, so it's well worth dropping by for evensong.

GETTING AROUND

Truro is on the main London Paddington–Penzance train line, as well as the branch line to Falmouth. It's also a bus hub, with regular services to most main towns in Cornwall. There are several large car parks in the city centre, or you can park at one of the park-and-rides at Threemilestone or on Bodmin Rd, and catch a shuttle into town.

Beyond Truro

The rural Roseland is a peaceful corner of
Cornwall, criss-crossed by hedgerows and lanes,
and dotted with quiet villages and sandy bays.

Truro ● ● Philleigh
St Mawes ● ● Porthcurnick
Beach
St Antony's
Head

Despite what you might hear, the Roseland Peninsula
actually gets its name not from flowers (although there are
plenty of those in summer), but from the Cornish word *ros,*
meaning promontory. The main town on the peninsula is
the harbour of St Mawes, a heart-meltingly pretty spot, with
a curve of whitewashed cottages leading up to a clover-leaf
Tudor castle. Once a fishing port, it's now one of Cornwall's
most cosmopolitan and chi-chi hideaways, with a smattering
of posh hotels. Things feel a lot more rustic along the coast
in villages like Portscatho, Portloe and Veryan.

TOP TIP

The easiest way to get to
the Roseland is via the
King Harry Ferry, which
chugs over the river from
the slipway near Trelissick
several times an hour. It
carries cars, bikes and
foot passengers.

St Mawes

LEFT: ANDY333/SHUTTERSTOCK ©; RIGHT: PAUL NASH/SHUTTERSTOCK ©

Castles & Country Churches

CORNWALL'S ST-TROPEZ?

St Mawes is more millionaire's playground than quaint port these days, but **St Mawes Castle** still dominates the town, just as it has done for nearly five centuries. Along with Pendennis Castle (p137), it's one of the network of 16th-century coastal fortresses built by Henry VIII, and among the best preserved. Clover-leaf shaped, with circular towers around a central keep, it's approached via a drawbridge, and you can wander around the interior chambers and the outside gun decks. Ironically, the castle never saw much action; the threat of Catholic invasion from Spain didn't materialise during Henry VIII's reign.

There are a number of beaches worth seeking out near St Mawes, and the **Percuil River** is a seriously pretty spot. Another essential detour is the creek-side church of **St-Just-in-Roseland** – quite possibly the loveliest chapel in the whole of Cornwall. Lost in a jumble of wildflowers and overhanging yews, the church dates from the 13th century, but there was probably an oratory here as far back as the 6th century.

The best way to explore the waters off St Mawes is by hiring a kayak from **St Mawes Kayaks**.

There are two ways there: a 40-minute drive round the head of the river via Tregony, or a shortcut via the King Harry Ferry, near Trelissick Gardens.

BEST BEACHES ON THE ROSELAND

Carne & Pendower
These side-by-side beaches form one of the Roseland's largest areas of s and at low tide.

Porthcurnick
Popular family beach near Portscatho famed for its cafe, the Hidden Hut. Parking can be devilishly difficult.

Towan
A good hiking target along the coast path from Portscatho.

To the Lighthouse

EXPLORE REAL-LIFE FRAGGLE ROCK

On the opposite side of the Percuil River, a rather roundabout 45-minute drive from Truro, the promontory of **St Antony's Head** makes for wonderful coast walks and bike rides. Its unmissable feature is the 1835-built lighthouse (pictured right), which famously featured in the opening scenes of the 1980s kids' show, *Fraggle Rock*. It's possible to stay inside the lighthouse keeper's old cottage, Sally Port, but most people just explore the remains of the old fortifications and gun batteries around the headland.

 WHERE TO STAY ON THE ROSELAND

Lugger Hotel
A romantic hideaway on the harbour's edge in pretty Portloe, within earshot of the sea. £££

Treloan Farm
This huge campsite occupies spacious fields between Gerrans and Portscatho. £

Roundhouse Barns
Three stone-fronted cottages, plus a B&B suite, on a farm estate 3 miles from St Mawes. ££

CAERHAYS CASTLE

East of the Roseland, on the hills above remote Porthluney Beach, stands the castellated mansion of Caerhays, built for the Trevanion family and later remodelled under the guidance of John Nash (who designed Buckingham Palace and Brighton Pavilion).

The house remains a private residence, but it's open to the public for a few months every spring, when guided tours reveal its secrets.

The real draw here are the gardens, though: they're famous for the fabulous floral displays of camellias, rhododendrons and magnolias. Come in March or April to see them at their best, as they're all but gone by May. Porthluney is worth a paddle, too.

Hidden Hut, Porthcurnick Beach

Cooking the Cornish Way

HONE YOUR KITCHEN SKILLS

At **Philleigh Way**, a half-hour drive from Truro, you get to learn all those culinary skills you've always wanted to learn but have never known who to ask. Filleting fish? Foraging for mushrooms? Creating curries? All covered, and plenty more besides. The 'Cornwall in a Day' course covers pasties, saffron buns, hog's pudding, crab-dressing and clotted cream.

For a different style of cooking altogether, book in a course at **7th Rise** – you get to connect with your wild spirit through foraging, bushcraft and wild brewing, then prepare wild suppers around the campfire. It's in an isolated, off-grid location in a formerly abandoned woodsman's cottage; accommodation is provided in cottage bunks, camping or rustic huts.

Picnic on the Beach

LUNCH AT THE HIDDEN HUT

A coastal-cabin cafe on Porthcurnick Beach, **Hidden Hut** is so tucked away, you might miss it even if you've been here before. The wooden cabin was built as a wartime lookout, but now serves delicious beach food: grilled cheese toasts, hot soups, proper cakes and 'beach salads'. During summer, there are pop-up 'feast nights' once or twice a week, but the tickets are like gold dust – book well ahead if you want to join in the fun.

 GETTING AROUND

Apart from the ferry to St Mawes from Falmouth, public transport on the Roseland is pretty much a non-starter: you'll need a car or a bike to explore the area.

FOWEY

Fowey

In many ways, Fowey feels much like Padstow's south-coast sister – an old working port turned well-heeled holiday town, with a tumble of pastel-coloured houses, port-side pubs and tiered terraces overlooking the wooded banks of the River Fowey. The town's wealth was founded on the export of china clay from St Austell pits, but it's been an important port since Elizabethan times, and later became the adopted home of writer Daphne du Maurier, who lived at the grand house at Menabilly for many years and used it as the model for Manderley in her novel *Rebecca*.

Today it's an attractive and increasingly upmarket town, handy for exploring Cornwall's southeastern corner. Boat trips depart from the town's quays, and the main street is thronged with summer visitors: if it all gets a bit much, a quick kayak trip upriver makes for a wonderfully tranquil escape.

TOP TIP

A passenger ferry shuttles over the river mouth to the village of Polruan, on the east side of the River Fowey, allowing easy access to walks onwards to Polperro and Looe.

153

BEST BEACHES IN FOWEY

Readymoney Cove
From the town centre, the Esplanade leads down to this little cove and the remains of a small Tudor fort.

Polkerris Beach
Three miles west of Fowey, this is the area's largest and busiest beach. Sailing lessons, windsurfing and stand-up paddleboarding available.

Great and Little Lantic
Twin beaches on the coastline between Polruan and Looe. They're remote but worth the effort, with soft sand and good wild swimming.

Lansallos
Small patch of sand and shingle reached by a half-mile trail from Lansallos village.

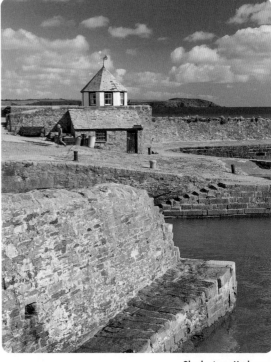

Charlestown Harbour

River Life

KAYAKING, KINGFISHERS AND HERONS

It's said that Kenneth Grahame got the inspiration for his children's classic, *The Wind in the Willows,* while wandering around the quiet creeks of the River Fowey. Like the Fal and the Helford, it's ideal for exploring by kayak, with lots of quiet inlets and plentiful birdlife: several operators run trips and offer kayak hire, including **Encounter Cornwall** and **Fowey River Expeditions**. One of the loveliest sections is the area around Pont Pill Creek, where old oaks dangle their branches into the water, and if you're lucky you might spy herons, cormorants and the odd kingfisher.

LIFE ON THE RIVER

Check out our tips for further river-themed adventures along the **Fal** (p139) and the **Helford** (p144).

WHERE TO EAT AROUND FOWEY

Old Quay House
Serious fine dining with what is, quite probably, the loveliest river view in Fowey. £££

Appletons
Previously at Fifteen and Trevibban Mill near Padstow, Andy Appleton now has a classy bistro on Fore St. ££

North Street Kitchen
Shack-style dining with a chalkboard menu filled with oysters and fresh fish dishes. Also check out Fitzroys. ££

A few miles north along the creek, the riverside hamlet of **Golant** makes a pleasant detour, with a waterfront pub (the Fisherman's Arms) for lunch and excellent kayaking opportunities, while **Lerryn** has a picturesque riverside church.

Avast Me Hearties

EXPLORE A TIME-TRAVEL PORT

Set around its massive granite quay and backed by Georgian buildings, the port of **Charlestown** is the kind of place that almost looks like Long John Silver might stumble out from a pub at any moment. In previous centuries most of the china clay from St Austell quarries was shipped out from here, but it's now a favourite location for film crews; numerous blockbusters and costume dramas have used its quayside as a backdrop, including Tim Burton's *Alice in Wonderland* and the BBC's crackerjack adaptation of *Poldark*. You can now wander around the Georgian quays, and with a bit of luck, see a tall ship docked right alongside the harbour.

While you're here, don't miss a visit to the endearingly quirky **Shipwreck Treasure Museum** to learn about Charlestown's seagoing heritage. The museum houses a massive collection of objects and ephemera recovered from more than 100 shipwrecks – ranging from telescopes, muskets, scrimshaw and coins to howitzer cannons. The layout is a bit of a jumble, but there are fascinating stories to uncover here.

For lunch, **Longstore** serves delicious steaks and seafood in a light, vaulted space beside the harbour, or you could tuck into seafood chowder or crab burgers at **Springtide**. Charlestown is about 8 miles from Fowey, just south (and well signposted) from St Austell.

Lantic Loop

FOLLOW THE HALL WALK

The 3.5-mile circular **Hall Walk** starts across the river from Fowey in Bodinnick, winding along the wooded shores of Pont Pill Creek before following the coastline to the harbour of Polruan, from where you can catch a ferry back to Fowey. You can download a route guide from the National Trust website. It's a gorgeous walk, and you can loop round via Lantic Bay if you fancy a longer hike, factoring in a dip en route.

WHERE TO STAY AROUND FOWEY

Fowey Hall
A hilltop Victorian manor that's well geared for families. ££

Coriander Cottages
Rural cottages on the outskirts of Fowey, with ecofriendly, open-plan barns. ££

Old Quay House
This chic quayside hotel is all natural fabrics, rattan chairs and river views. £££

Fowey Harbour Hotel
Boutique-style sleeps with dreamy views over the river. £££

Hormond House
Cosy B&B across the water from Fowey in Polruan. ££

Havener's
Smart sleeps above the namesake bistro; it's the Estuary Rooms you want. ££

GETTING AROUND

Bus services to Fowey are limited: the only really useful service runs to St Austell, Heligan and Mevagissey via Par train station, where you can catch trains on the main London–Penzance line.

There are two ferry services from Fowey: the Bodinnick Ferry, which carries cars over the river to Bodinnick en route to Polruan, and the pedestrian-only Polruan Ferry.

Eden Project • Fowey • Menheniot
St Austell • St George's Island • Rame Peninsula

Beyond Fowey

Cornwall's southeastern corner is neither as blustery and beachy as the north coast nor as wild and craggy as the west.

Southeast Cornwall is closer in character to the area around the River Fal, a landscape of gentle bays and clifftop fields, but it has its fair share of quaint old fishing ports too, of which Mevagissey and Polperro are the prettiest examples. The area also has two river estuaries to explore, the Fowey and the Tamar – prime territory for kayaking and country walks. The often-overlooked Rame Peninsula is home to a trio of ostentatious country houses. And, of course, there are two sights here that no one should miss – the sci-fi biomes of the fabulous Eden Project, raised from the dust of a disused Cornish clay pit, and the utterly magical Lost Gardens of Heligan.

TOP TIP

Queues at Eden and Heligan can be hellish in summer, so it's worth buying tickets online in advance – or visiting outside peak holiday periods.

Lost Gardens of Heligan

Gardens (Past & Future)

FROM VICTORIAN GREENHOUSES TO SPACE-AGE BIOMES

If Cornwall has a don't-miss attraction, it's surely the **Eden Project**. Built at the bottom of a china clay pit, the giant biomes have become both an iconic landmark and a beacon of Cornish regeneration. Looking rather like a lunar landing station, Eden's bubble-shaped domes recreate a variety of habitats around the globe – from dry savannah to steamy rainforest. It's quite an amazing experience: as you walk through the biomes, you'll see everything from tropical palms to banana trees, coffee plants and stinking rafflesia flowers, and learn loads about Eden's ecological mission. But it's not all education: Eden also offers adrenaline-driven activities, including England's longest zip line, a giant gravity swing, a 12m-high bungee drop and a heart-stopping 25m 'free fall' jump onto an airbag. The site is 3 miles northeast of St Austell (which is a 45-minute bus ride from Fowey); a bike trail runs close by.

Entrepreneur Tim Smit is the brains behind Eden, but his first Cornish labour of love was the restoration of the **Lost Gardens of Heligan**, Cornwall's real-life secret garden (7 miles from St Austell). Formerly the family estate of the Tremaynes, Heligan's magnificent 19th-century gardens fell into disrepair following WWI, when many of its gardeners were killed. Since then, they've been splendidly restored by a huge army of gardeners and volunteers. It's a horticultural wonderland: as you explore the maze of trails, you'll see working kitchen gardens, fruit-filled greenhouses, a secret grotto and a lost-world Jungle Valley of ferns, palms and tropical blooms – complete with its own rope bridge.

Cornwall's Island Eden

CATCH A BOAT TO LOOE ISLAND

A mile offshore from the touristy town of Looe, a 45-minute drive from Fowey, is **Looe Island** (officially named **St George's Island**). In 1965 it was occupied by Surrey sisters Babs and Evelyn Atkins, who established a nature reserve and lived there for most of their lives, restoring habitats and monitoring wildlife populations. The island is now managed by Cornwall Wildlife Trust, which runs boat trips over to the island from Looe. Guided walks are run by the island ranger, who can help you spot grey seals, cormorants (pictured right), shags and oystercatchers.

 WHERE TO STAY IN EAST CORNWALL

Westcroft
Gorgeous guesthouse in charming Kingsand, offering three suites plastered in posh wallpaper and trendy fixtures. ££

Penvith Barns
Escape the Looe crowds at this rural barn conversion in the nearby hamlet of St-Martin-by-Looe. ££

Bosinver Farm
A cottage to suit all tastes, from modern eco-bungalows to traditional stone farmhouses. £££

WHOSE SIDE ARE YOU ON?

The mighty River Tamar has marked the dividing line between Devon and Cornwall for over a thousand years. Since 1859, the two counties have been linked by the great span of the Royal Albert Bridge, a Victorian masterpiece designed by the great railway engineer Isambard Kingdom Brunel. A second crossing, rather unimaginatively named the Tamar Bridge, was built to carry cars and opened in 1962.

Tourists seldom take the time to explore the Tamar, and that's a massive oversight. Paddle pioneer-style in a Canadian canoe with Canoe Tamar, or hit the Tamar Trails, a network of 25km of hiking and biking trails between Gunnislake and Tavistock.

Eden Project (p157)

Clay Country

CYCLE A POST-INDUSTRIAL MOONSCAPE

A web of trails weaves about the clay country around St Austell. Collectively known as the **Clay Trails**, the routes are suitable for pedestrians, horse riders and cyclists; one directly passes the Eden Project, others pass through the **Pentewan Valley** and **Wheal Martyn Country Park**. Nature has reclaimed many areas, and you'll probably spot lots of wildflowers and birdlife flitting around the gorse. The most interesting route weaves through the post-industrial landscape left behind by china clay mining, with spoil heaps, mica dams and vivid turquoise pools.

100% Adrenaline

JUMPING OFF CLIFFS FOR FUN

With the genius tagline 'Throwing people off clifftops since 2009', the octane-fuelled activity centre known as **Adrenalin Quarry** is based at a flooded quarry near Menheniot. If you love the idea of hurtling down a zip line at 40mph, or struggling not to lose your lunch on a giant swing that simulates free fall, this place will be right up your street.

WHERE TO EAT IN EAST CORNWALL

The Bay
A smart seaside bistro-bar on the edge of the beach in Cawsand. ££

The View
The name says it all: incredible clifftop vistas overlooking Whitsand Bay. ££

Finnygook Inn
As cosy as they come, this Crafthole pub is a classic Cornish kiddywink. ££

You can also coasteer around the quarry, then chuck axes at tree stumps. Or just hang out by the lake, have a picnic and go for a wild swim, for free. Handily, it's right next to Menheniot train station, which is a 40-minute drive from Fowey and has direct connections to Liskeard and Plymouth.

Great Estates

TOUR A COUNTRY HOUSE TRIO

If you want to give the crowds the slip, the **Rame Peninsula** (an hour's drive from Fowey) is a good bet. It's overlooked by many visitors, who speed west in search of big surf and better-known beaches. But they're missing a treat: this is one of the most bucolic patches of countryside in Cornwall, rolling down to the River Tamar in a soothing swathe of woods and fields. The three country estates here can be combined into a road trip over a couple of days.

Travelling from Liskeard via the A38, **Port Eliot** is the first estate you'll encounter. It's the family seat of the Earl of St Germans: guided tours take in the kitchen, basements, library, wine cellars and the famous Round Room (with an original mural by the Plymouth painter Robert Lenkiewicz). The estate also has fabulous walks, and for many years ran a popular arts festival, sadly staged for the last time in 2019.

Next comes National Trust–owned **Antony House**, best-known for its decorative gardens designed by the 18th-century landscape architect Humphry Repton and filled with outlandish topiary, some of which featured in Tim Burton's *Alice in Wonderland*. It also has a woodland garden that leads down to the River Lynher, with huge rhododendrons, magnolias and azaleas – look out for an 18th-century bathhouse hidden in the trees.

Final stop is Grade I-listed **Mount Edgcumbe** (pictured right), liberally sprinkled with follies, chapels, grottoes, pavilions and formal gardens. The house was built between 1547 and 1553, but was practically destroyed by German bombing in 1941. It's since been restored in lavish 18th-century style, and the vistas of the Tamar are something to behold.

CHAPEL ON A ROCK

A great bulk of rock topped by a picturesque clifftop chapel, Rame Head is one of Cornwall's most majestic coastal viewpoints, with a jaw-dropping 360-degree panorama stretching east towards Plymouth Sound and the South Hams, and west to Dodman Point, the Roseland and even the Lizard on a really clear day. It was home to an Iron Age hillfort and an early Christian oratory, but the present chapel dedicated to St Michael was built in the late 14th century.

GETTING AROUND

A branch line spurs off from the main railway line at Liskeard and chugs down to Looe. Local buses connect the main towns and villages along the coast, including Mevagissey, Looe and Polperro. Some mainline trains also stop at the tiny station at St Germans (handy for Port Eliot), but you'll need wheels to reach most of the rest of the Rame Peninsula.

Most visitors cross the Tamar into Cornwall via the Tamar Bridge, which is open 24 hours: you only pay the toll when heading back to Devon. A slower way to cross the river is the Torpoint Ferry, which also runs 24 hours. If you're staying in Plymouth, a fun way to get to the Mount Edgcumbe estate is aboard the quaint Cremyll Ferry, which leaves from Royal William Yard.

Engine house ruins, St Agnes (p168)

NORTH CORNWALL & BODMIN MOOR

COAST AND CLIFFTOPS

If it's the quintessential Cornish combination of crags, bays and white-horse surf you're after, the north coast delivers – and then some.

Battered by breakers, whipped by winds and scoured by the ceaseless Atlantic tides, north Cornwall is where you feel the full force of Mother Nature's handiwork. With its stark cliffs, tidal pools, sea caves and golden beaches, the north coast presents the image of Cornwall most people hold in their imaginations, and this is where you'll find many of the county's most popular visitor spots – from well-heeled enclaves like Padstow, Port Isaac and Rock to busy holiday towns like Newquay, Portreath and Perranporth. It's the centre of Cornwall's surfing scene; if you're keen to catch a wave, this is the place to do it. And if you're after dramatic scenery, it doesn't get much more impressive than the area around Tintagel and its famous clifftop castle – there are some spectacular coastal walks to discover here.

Unsurprisingly, north Cornwall's beaches and seaside towns get hectic in season. If you're looking for somewhere quieter, the stretch of coastline around Bude is worth exploring, especially the under-visited Culm Coast, the line of cliffs, bays and beaches that runs northwards to the Hartland Peninsula, just over the Devon border.

And don't overlook the seam of granite that runs down the county's middle: from the wild expanse of Bodmin Moor to the old mining country around Camborne and Redruth, Cornwall's spine offers a compelling insight into its rugged, elemental past.

THE MAIN AREAS

NEWQUAY & THE NORTH COAST	PADSTOW	BODMIN MOOR
Postcard Cornwall: cliffs, beaches, surf.	Foodie central.	Cornwall's roof: wild, weird and windswept.
p166	p172	p181

161

Find Your Way

The north coast has some of Cornwall's most stunning stretches of road. The B3285 between Portreath and Perranporth, and the Atlantic Highway (B3263) between Tintagel and Bude, are standouts; hardcore cyclists could tackle them, but it's punishingly hilly in places.

Padstow, p172

Beloved by poet John Betjeman, the area around Padstow is now famous for its foodie scene, award-winning vineyards and upscale restaurants.

Newquay & the North Coast, p166

Take a road-trip around Cornwall's finest beaches: rocky coves, white-sand bays, secret snorkelling spots and tidal pools.

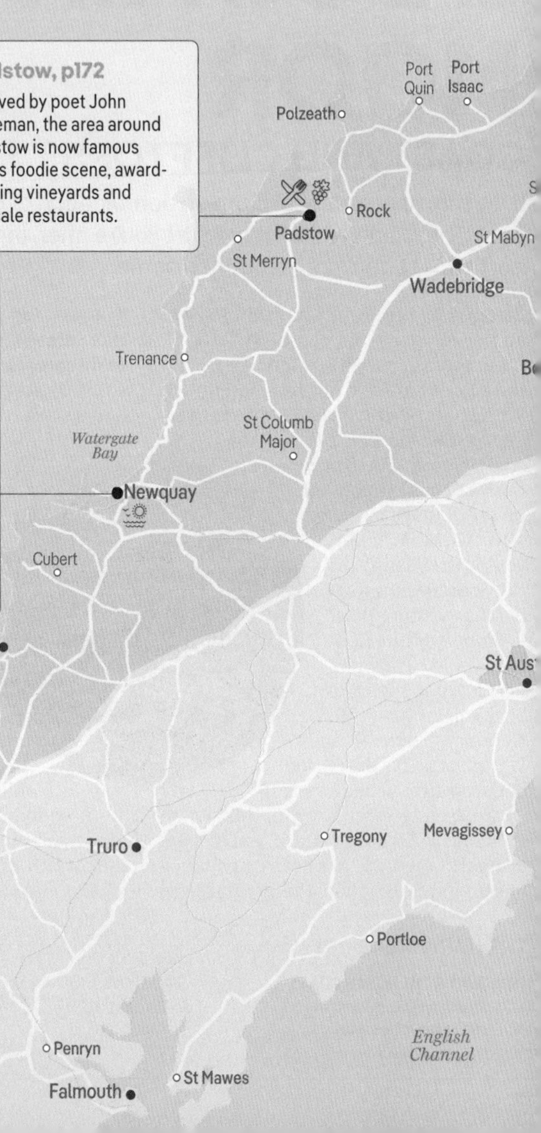

ATLANTIC OCEAN

Tin●

Port Quin
Port Isaac
Polzeath
Rock
St Mabyn
Padstow
St Merryn
Wadebridge
Be
Trenance
St Columb Major
Watergate Bay
Newquay
Cubert
Perranporth
St Aus●
St Agnes
Tregony
Mevagissey
Portreath
Truro
Redruth
Portloe
Camborne
Penmarth
Penryn
English Channel
St Mawes
Falmouth

Millook

Crackington Haven

St Juliot

Boscastle

Davidstow

Camelford

Rough Tor △

Brown Willy △

St Breward

Bolventor

Blisland

Colliford Lake

St Neot

hydrock

Lostwithiel

Fowey

Polruan

Polperro

Looe

Launceston

Trewen

Altarnun

Bodmin Moor

Minions

Siblyback Lake

Liskeard

Saltash

Milton Abbot

Tavistock

Gunnislake

Calstock

Callington

Lopwell

Plymouth

Devonport

0   10 km
0   5 miles

Bodmin Moor, p181

Take a walk on Cornwall's wild side: hike to the summit of Brown Willy, discover pre-historic monuments and hunker down in cosy moorland pubs.

CAR

Having a car enables maximum freedom to explore the more remote beaches. National Trust membership allows free parking at NT car parks such as Wheal Coates and St Agnes Head. The main beach towns like Perranporth and Porthtowan can be a parking nightmare in high summer.

BUS

Bus services are fairly good, with most major towns served by at least one regular bus route, most of which are provided by First Kernow. Newquay is a hub; services are a bit more limited east of Padstow. The open-top Atlantic Coaster between Newquay and Padstow is a fine ride.

TRAIN

Newquay is on the branch railway line from Par, which connects up with the main Paddington–Penzance line. Otherwise there are no rail services, much to poet John Betjeman's dismay.

Plan Your Time

The distances between towns aren't huge along the north coast, but the winding, twisting coast road means that you're best off taking things easy and not trying to pack too much into one day.

Boscastle (p180)

A Day on the Coast

Pay a visit to the evocative ruins of **Tintagel Castle** (p178). This centuries-old fortress is undoubtedly one of the most dramatic sights anywhere on the north coast, and echoes with Arthurian connections; it also has a striking new footbridge that is guaranteed to give vertigo-sufferers the heebie jeebies.

There are fine walks along the cliftops, and if you have wheels, you could also factor in a visit to the pretty village of **Boscastle** (p180), the beach at **Trebarwith Strand** (p180) and ideally a meal at one of Nathan Outlaw's stellar seafood restaurants in **Port Isaac** (p179).

Seasonal Highlights

From a vast summer country show to a clifftop rock festival, there's plenty to keep you busy on the north coast, no matter what time of year you visit.

JANUARY

Britain's biggest wave, the **Cribbar** (aka 'the Widowmaker') often strikes the waters off Newquay in midwinter, attracting some of the world's top big-wave surfers.

MARCH

Crowds accompanied by pipers parade through Perranporth's dunes on 5 March to mark **St Piran's Day**, dedicated to Cornwall's patron saint.

APRIL

Camborne celebrates its native son, inventor and engineer Richard Trevithick, at the end of April on **Trevithick Day**. Expect puffing steam engines aplenty.

A Wild Weekend

Three days allows more beach time: perhaps a surfing lesson or two at one of the beaches around **Newquay** (p166) or **Padstow** (p172), a stroll along the epic sands of **Perranporth** (p169), a dip in the sea pools at **Portreath** (p168) or **Porthtowan** (p171), and some serious rock-pooling and cliff-walking around **St Agnes** (p168). No matter where you go, you're pretty much guaranteed to find a beach nearby: Padstow's **Seven Bays** (p175) are safe bets, but the more remote beaches along the Atlantic coast around Bude are likely to be quieter.

With a Bit More Time

A few more days means you should have time to explore inner Cornwall, away from the beaches and coast, where many visitors never really venture.

The area around **Camborne** (p166) and **Redruth** (p166) is the heartland of Cornish mining: a cycle along the **Great Flat Lode Trail** (p167) is a great way to get orientated, followed by a hike up to the top of **Carn Brea** (p171). Even more impressive is the summit of **Brown Willy** (p183), the craggy peak that looms ominously up from the centre of Bodmin Moor, while archaeology buffs will enjoy pondering the many **ancient sites** (p182) nearby.

MAY

Padstow's **May Day**, said to have its roots in an ancient pagan fertility rite, sees two coloured 'osses twirl through the streets to meet up beneath the maypole.

JUNE

Scorrier House near Redruth hosts the **Great Estate** music festival, while the county's largest agricultural event, the **Royal Cornwall Show**, is held near Wadebridge.

JULY

World and roots music comes to the **Mount Pleasant Eco Park** near Porthtowan during the Tropical Pressure festival.

AUGUST

Big-name bands strut the stage above Watergate Bay in early August for **Boardmasters**, Cornwall's largest music festival (50,000-plus people).

NEWQUAY & THE NORTH COAST

● Newquay

Beaches and cliffs: that's what the this stretch of coast is all about, but it's surprising just how dramatically different the scenery can be as you round yet another stunning curve in the road. Love it or loathe it, Newquay remains the hub of the action here. It's long been Cornwall's premier party town, and the capital of the county's surf scene, but its brash, boozy culture certainly isn't to all tastes (still, the beaches are undeniably spectacular). If you prefer your sands (a little) quieter, head west towards the coastal village of St Agnes to explore the dramatic cliffs, or get in some beach time around Portreath, Porthtowan and Perranporth. It's really worth exploring inland, too: the area around Redruth and Camborne – part of the Unesco-designated Cornwall and West Devon Mining Landscape – is rich in mining heritage, and rewards the curious.

TOP TIP

Sadly, pollution is a problem that still plagues England's beaches. The campaigning Cornish charity Surfers Against Sewage (sas.org.uk) offers a free Safer Seas & Rivers app that reports real-time pollution incidents around the UK.

Hard Rock Country

DELVE INTO CORNWALL'S MINING HERITAGE

Though rarely on the visitors' radar, in many ways the gritty twin towns of **Redruth** (pictured left) and **Camborne** represent the essence of Cornwall's tin-seamed soul. A century and a half ago, they were the beating heart of the county's mining industry, and their hilltops would have thrummed with the sound of mine wheels and engine stacks. Back then, this was the richest patch of real estate in Cornwall, but the loss of the mining industry has been mirrored in the towns' declining fortunes.

TIM WOOLCOCK PHOTOGRAPHY/SHUTTERSTOCK ©

 WHERE TO GET A COFFEE ON THE NORTH COAST

Beach Hut
Wonderful views over Water-gate Bay, great cocktails and darn decent food. ££

Sorting Office
Artisan coffee and smoothies on St Agnes' main street. Gingerbread latte, anyone? £

Chapel Porth Cafe
Local institution, serving bag-uettes, butties and the house special: hedgehog ice cream. £

SIGHTS

1 Beacon
2 Bedruthan Steps
3 Blue Hills Tin
4 Carn Brea
5 Chapel Porth Beach
6 Crantock
7 East Pool Mine
8 Fistral Beach
9 Holywell Bay
10 King Edward Mine
11 Perranporth Beach
12 Portreath
13 Trevaunance Cove
14 Watergate Bay
15 Wheal Coates

ACTIVITIES

16 Camborne
17 Redruth

WOODLAND WALKS

Just south of Portreath, Tehidy Woods is a 102-hectare country park that formerly belonged to the Bassets, one of Cornwall's four richest tin-mining families, who made their fortune from extensive mineral rights across west and central Cornwall.

The estate is now an attractive public woodland, crosshatched by trails, lakes and picnic areas; there's also a pleasant cafe. Local theatre company Rogue Theatre stages outdoor shows in the woods several times a year.

Still, they're fascinating places if you want to understand the region's history. Since 2006, the towns have formed a Unesco World Heritage Site: the Cornwall and West Devon Mining Landscape, a huge area of open moors and clifftops plus historic mine workings and engine houses like **East Pool Mine** and **King Edward Mine**, both near Camborne.

A brilliant way to explore is along the **Great Flat Lode Trail** – a 7.5-mile bike trail that runs along a famously rich seam of tin ore. It's part of the wider Mineral Tramways network.

Pedal Power

BIKE THROUGH A MINING VALLEY

A couple of miles west from St Agnes is the harbour town of **Portreath**, from where vast quantities of Cornwall's mineral ore were shipped out to Swansea for smelting. In its heyday in the mid-19th century, around 100,000 tonnes of ore were passing out of Portreath's harbour; in order to streamline the process, a mineral tramway was built from Portreath to connect the harbour with the productive Gwennap copper mines around Camborne, Redruth and the Gwennap area.

The tramway has long since closed down, but has been resurrected as the **Coast to Coast Cycle Trail**, which runs for 11 miles to the village of Bissoe through the rugged mining country around Scorrier, Chacewater and the Poldice Valley. It's mostly flat and easy, although there are a few uphill and off-road sections, and at several points the trail crosses a minor road. Bikes and maps can be hired at the Devoran end from **Bissoe Bike Hire**, which also has a good cafe. There's car parking at both ends if you want to bring your own bike.

Cliffs & Chimney Stacks

STALK THE ST AGNES COAST

Abandoned engine houses litter the hilltops around **St Agnes**, which once resounded to the thump and clang of mine pumps and steam engines, but now echoes only to the strains of crashing surf and calling gulls. During the 18th and 19th centuries, this was one of Cornwall's tin-mining boom towns, and the rugged clifftops are littered with the remains of former mine workings.

IN SEARCH OF CLIFFS

If you like your cliffs lofty and wild, a visit to **High Cliff** (p180) near Bude is a must.

For many people, this is the quintessential part of the coast path, and it makes for a glorious day's walk. You can either walk up from **Trevaunance Cove** in St Agnes, or park somewhere up on the cliffs. There are National Trust car parks at **St Agnes Head** and **Wheal Coates**, a much-photographed clifftop engine house which still boasts its original brick chimney. If you make it this far, it's well worth heading on to the cove of **Chapel Porth**, an improbably photogenic beach (with a popular cafe) at the bottom of a rock-strewn valley. The views really are something; on a wintry day, the sound of booming surf is deafening, and there's the sting of salt on the breeze. If you're feeling energetic, combine the walk with a loop over the top of the **Beacon**, from where the views stretch across most of Cornwall on a clear day.

 WHERE TO EAT ON THE NORTH COAST

Emily Scott Food
The renowned chef's new base at the Watergate Bay Hotel, in what was formerly Jamie Oliver's Fifteen. **£££**

Canteen at the Eco Park
Farm-driven, plant-based grub at the Mount Pleasant Eco Park near Porthtowan. **££**

Fish House Fistral
The best place for seafood on the coast around Newquay. **££**

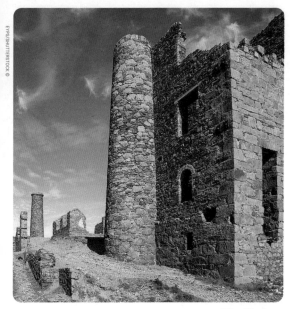

Wheal Coates

Another worthwhile detour lies a mile or so east of St Agnes (signed to Wheal Kitty): the rocky valley of **Trevellas Porth**, home to one of Cornwall's last tin manufacturers, **Blue Hills Tin**. You can watch the whole tinning process, from mining and smelting through to casting and finishing. It sells handmade jewellery, too.

St Piran's Beach

MILES OF WHITE SAND

East of Newquay, the coast road tracks craggy scenery to **Perranporth**, another breezy beach town blessed with a fabulous 3-mile stretch of sand. Its name derives from Cornwall's patron saint, St Piran, who supposedly brought Christianity to the county – the remains of an ancient chapel dedicated to him are hidden in the dunes, and mark the start of a procession on St Piran's Day (5 March).

The town isn't much to look at – an untidy sprawl of chalets, holiday villas and clifftop bungalows – but the beach itself is a stunner, sweeping in a magnificent, multi-mile arc all the

I LIVE HERE

Andy Cameron, MD of Wavehunters at the Extreme Academy (watergatebay.co.uk/ extreme-academy), names his favourite north coast surf spots.

Polzeath
My all-time favourite spot which works on all stages of the tide. The paddle can be tough on a big swell, but that keeps the crowds down.

Watergate Bay
A huge, friendly surfers' beach. Even in summer you can find a wave to yourself. The far end has a super-fun right-hander. Mid to high tide and back is best.

Lunday Bay
A proper winter spot. Not for beginners, but when everywhere else is blown out, Lundy is the spot: catch the right peak and you could be in for a head tuck or even get barrelled.

 WHERE TO GET A DRINK ON THE NORTH COAST

Blue Bar
Porthtowan's beach bar is a favourite for a seaside sundowner.

Watering Hole
Generations of Cornish youngsters have enjoyed this venerable bar right on Perranporth's sands.

Driftwood Spars
Cosy whitewashed pub down beside Trevaunance Cove. Food's not bad either.

BEST PLACES TO EAT IN NEWQUAY

Fish House
Newquay's top place for seafood, beside Fistral's sands. ££

Sprout Health Foods
Superb wholefoods shop serving veggie meals and delicious gluten-free cakes. £

Box & Barber
Everyone's top spot for a flat white in town – and they do a cracking brunch, too. ££

Pavilion Bakery
Newquay's boutique bakery: stunning sourdoughs, artisan breads and melt-in-the-mouth croissants. £

El Hulchol
Delicious Mexican food served from a pop-up truck down by the old harbour. £

LEFT: PJ PHOTOGRAPHY/SHUTTERSTOCK ©. RIGHT: DAVID W BIRD/SHUTTERSTOCK ©

Holywell Bay

way to the grassy dunes of **Penhale Sands**. Breezy swells make Perranporth popular with surfers and bodyboarders, and the level sands make it ideal for wind-powered sports such as kite buggying, power kiting and landboarding. It's also a brilliant spot for a sunset walk, especially once you get away from the crowds and head up towards the dunes.

Surf's Up

CATCH A NEWQUAY WAVE

MORE POOL FUN

For another top tidal pool to wallow in, don't miss **Bude Sea Pool** (p179) on Summerleaze Beach.

Like many Cornish towns, **Newquay** started life as a harbour and pilchard port. (The old 14th-century **Huer's House**, a lookout used for spotting approaching shoals, is perched on the headland between Towan and Fistral.) These days, though, it's surf central. The north coast swells are the most consistent in the UK, and every year they attract thousands of boarders. There are scores of schools to choose from; some are based mainly at one beach, while others travel around in search of the best waves. It's a good idea to check that your

WHERE TO STAY IN LUXURY ON THE NORTH COAST

Watergate Bay Hotel
Cornwall's 'ski resort on a beach': activities, plush rooms and the restaurant of top chef Emily Scott. £££

Scarlet
Striking clifftop architecture, a sexy spa and infinity pool, outdoor hot tubs and widescreen beach views. £££

Bedruthan Hotel
Family-focused hotel with designer style (despite the boxy architecture). Kids' activities and spa for the grown-ups. £££

chosen school is accredited by Surfing England: **Escape Surf School**, **Fistral Beach Surf School** and **SSS Surf School** all have good reputations.

The beach that everyone immediately heads for is **Fistral**, a glorious curve of golden sands that's legendary for its waves. But it's not always the best option, especially for beginners – it gets beyond busy in season. Other options within easy reach of Newquay include **Crantock**, **Holywell Bay** and **Watergate Bay**, where another of the area's best surf schools is based: **Wavehunters** at the Extreme Academy. Many outdoor operators offer other water-based activities, including coasteering, SUP and kayaking; **Newquay Watersports Centre** is a good place to start.

King of the Carn
THE HIGHEST POINT OF CENTRAL CORNWALL

An essential experience in this part of Cornwall is the hike up to the top of **Carn Brea**, the rocky hill brooding over the gorse-thatched landscape between Redruth and Camborne. Standing at 224m, the hill is said to have once been the home of a giant, John of Gaunt. It's now topped by a Celtic cross dedicated to Frances Basset, who owned many of the richest mines in the area. At the top, you'll also find the forbidding bulk of Carn Brea Castle, where the Bassets once hosted lavish feasts (it's now, rather bizarrely, a Middle Eastern restaurant). The view is really something, with both of Cornwall's coasts visible as well as distant Penwith and Bodmin Moor. Come for sunset, and bring a picnic.

Geological Jenga
WATCH THE SUNSET OVER BEDRUTHAN STEPS

The stately rock towers of **Bedruthan Steps** (pictured right; properly known as Carnewas) loom out of the sea like giant stone sentinels between Newquay and Padstow. These great granite pillars have been carved out by countless millennia of wind and waves, and are evidence of both the power of the sea and the instability of Cornwall's clifftops – rockfalls here are commonplace. The area is owned by the National Trust, which runs the car park and cafe; clifftop paths radiate out along the coast. Bedruthan is a sunset spot par excellence: pack a picnic and a blanket, and settle down to watch the show.

BEST TIDAL POOLS

Porthtowan Tidal Pool
Hidden along the coast from the main beach and encircled by rocks.

Portreath Rock Pool
Sheltered by the stout harbour wall, this is a good bet when the seas are rough.

Chapel Rock Tidal Pool
An easy-to-reach pool smack bang on Perranporth Beach.

Whipsiderry Mermaid Pools
Little-known pools on the rocks near Whipsiderry Beach, around the headland from Porth.

Treyarnon Rock Pool
A big, natural sea pool beside Treyarnon Beach, on the south side of Trevose Head.

GETTING AROUND

First Kernow runs buses connecting the main north coast towns between Portreath and Newquay, and also operates links to inland towns, including Truro, Redruth and Camborne. Trains run at least hourly to Newquay from Par. Parking anywhere on the coast in summer can be tricky, so plan to arrive early at popular locations like Perranporth and the Newquay beaches.

PADSTOW

Padstow ●

If anywhere symbolises Cornwall's increasingly chic cachet, it's Padstow. This old fishing port has become the county's most cosmopolitan corner, thanks largely to the celeb chef Rick Stein and others who have followed in his wake: glitzy restaurants and posh boutiques now sit a little incongruously alongside the old pubs and pasty shops, making it quite hard to know where the real Padstow ends and the postcard version begins. Whether the town has managed to hold onto its soul during the gentrification process is debatable, but it's hard not to be charmed by the seaside setting.

Padstow's main asset is its location beside the lovely Camel Estuary, a lifelong favourite of poet John Betjeman, who holidayed here for many years. The sandy sweep of Daymer Bay and the treacherous sandbank known as the Doom Bar unfurl along the estuary, and the small fishing village turned fancy resort town of Rock can be reached by ferry.

TOP TIP

Padstow and the surrounding area is packed in July and August: it's much more pleasant to visit in spring or autumn, when the big crowds have left and you can appreciate the scenery in (relative) peace and quiet. Book accommodation well ahead, or base yourself in nearby Wade.

Padstow

CLARE LOUISE JACKSON/SHUTTERSTOCK ©

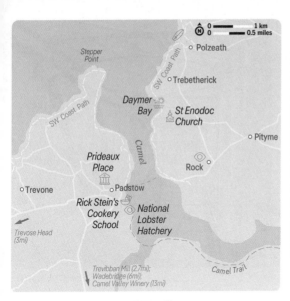

CRAFTY BREWS

The craft-brew company Padstow Brewing has taken off like a bottle rocket over the last couple of years, and has recently opened a tasting room and retail shop in town.

Tutored beer tastings are available, and you can buy individual bottles and gift packs to take home. Its range runs from light and hoppy Kor' Degel to nut-brown, malty Stormrunner. It also brews a special seasonal beer to celebrate May Day.

Cycling the Camel Trail

CORNWALL'S BEST-KNOWN BIKE ROUTE

In his autobiography *Summoned By Bells,* John Betjeman fondly remembers the train ride from Waterloo to Cornwall along the banks of the Camel Estuary. The original line closed in the late 1960s, a casualty of Dr Beeching's railway cutbacks, and has since been reinvented as the **Camel Trail**, Cornwall's most popular bike ride.

The trail starts in Padstow and runs east through Wadebridge (5 miles from Padstow) along the Camel Estuary before continuing on through Bodmin (10.8 miles) to Poley's Bridge (18.3 miles) on Bodmin Moor. The Padstow–Wadebridge section makes a lovely half-day excursion, and the scenery is marvellous, but it does get crowded in summer – some 350,000 people tackle the Camel Trail every year. If you want to avoid the crowds, the Wadebridge–Bodmin section is usually much quieter and, in its own rugged way, just as scenic.

Bikes can be readily hired from both ends: in Padstow, try **Padstow Cycle Hire** or **Trail Bike Hire**, or at the Wadebridge end, try **Bridge Bike Hire**.

ON YER BIKE

Other great Cornish bike rides include the **Coast to Coast Cycle Trail** (p168) between Portreath and Devoran, the **Clay Trails** (p158) near St Austell, and the **Great Flat Lode Trail** (p167) near Camborne.

WHERE TO GET A COFFEE AROUND PADSTOW

Strong Adolfo's
On the road to Wadebridge, this sleek Scandi-style cafe serves delicious lunches and sumptuous cakes. ££

Relish
Wadebridge locals make a beeline for this super little cafe-deli when they're after their morning coffee. £

Surfside
Everyone's favourite Polzeath hang-out: rum cocktails, DJs, seafood and a good Sunday roast. ££

BEST CORNISH PASTIES

Gear Farm
Reckoned by many
Cornish folk to be
practically the perfect
pasty: small-batch,
homemade, delicious. £

Ann's Pasties
Lizard-based Ann
Muller has built a big
reputation on her
traditional pasties,
which come in meat,
cheese and vegan
versions. £

Philps
A classic locals' choice
in Hayle, always packed
at lunchtime. Steak,
cheese-and-onion,
vegetarian. £

Over the Top Pasties
Traditional, delivered-
to-your-door pasties –
perfect for a picnic. £

Chough Bakery
Family-run Padstow
bakery that often does
well at the World Pasty
Championships. £

Camel Trail (p173)

For sustenance en route, stop by the **Camel Trail Tea Garden** halfway along the trail between Wadebridge and Bodmin, or if you're pedalling all the way to Bodmin Moor, the homely **Snails Pace Cafe** near St Breward.

Chef Lessons

LEARN TO COOK THE STEIN WAY

Masterclasses in everything from French fish to perfect sushi are on offer at **Rick Stein's Cookery School**. As you might expect, seafood is central here – from filleting techniques to Asian street food; you can even learn how to cook signature dishes from Stein's own Seafood Restaurant. Popular courses are often booked out months in advance, but it's always worth checking the website for late availability.

Into the Estuary

BOAT TRIPS UP THE CAMEL

The treacheruos sandbank known as the Doom Bar, which has claimed many ships over the years (and also gave its name to a popular local ale), runs in the middle of the Camel Estuary. It's a unique habitat, with important bird and marine life populations. Between Easter and October, the **Jubilee Queen** runs scenic trips along the coastline, while **Padstow Sealife**

 WHERE TO STAY AROUND PADSTOW

The Pig at Harlyn Bay
A new addition to the litter of
these rustic-chic hotels, with
inventive rooms and a super
bistro. £££

Padstow Townhouse
Owned by the town's top chef,
Paul Ainsworth, this six-suite
B&B pulls out all the luxury
stops. £££

Padstow Harbour Hotel
Formerly the Metropole, this
period beauty commands
a panoramic view over the
estuary. £££

Safaris offers visits to local seal and seabird colonies. For listings of local operators, check out *padstowboattrips.com*.

If you're wondering about the peculiar name, it derives from the Cornish 'Dowr Kammel', meaning 'crooked river'.

Upstairs, Downstairs
VISIT A STATELY MANOR

Much favoured by directors of costume dramas and period films, the stately Grade I–listed **Prideaux Place** was built by the Prideaux-Brune family, purportedly descendants of William the Conqueror. Guided tours of the manor last around an hour and take in staterooms, staircases and Prideaux-Brune heirlooms, as well as the house's extensive collection of teddy bears.

Rock On
LIVE THE MILLIONAIRE'S HIGH LIFE

The exclusive enclave of **Rock**, across the Camel Estuary from Padstow, is now one of Cornwall's priciest postcodes – earning the area a whole bevy of disparaging nicknames (Cornwall's St-Tropez, Kensington-on-Sea etc). It's certainly a far cry from the sleepy seaside backwater recalled fondly by John Betjeman. Betjeman's Rock hasn't disappeared entirely, though. The dune-backed white sands of **Daymer Bay** remain as glorious as ever, and if you're a poetry fan, you'll want to stroll up to the **St Enodoc Church**, where the poet was buried on a typically drizzly Cornish day in May 1984. It doesn't take long to find his ornate headstone.

Along the coast is **Polzeath**, the area's main surfing beach: contact **Surf's Up** and **Era Adventures** if you want some watery action.

Beaches & Beacons
HIKE OR BIKE TO TREVOSE HEAD

Four miles west of Padstow town looms the distinctive outcrop of **Trevose Head**, a notorious shipping hazard that was once used as a quarry, and has been topped by a lighthouse since the mid-19th century. It's accessed via a private toll road; the wonderful coastal views are just about worth it, but even better, hike or bike here to drink in the scenery for free.

En route to the headland, you'll pass four of Padstow's so-called **Seven Bays**: Trevone, Harlyn, Mother Ivey's and Booby's Bay. On the opposite side are the more dramatic sands of Constantine and Treyarnon, backed by rugged rocks and a fine tidal pool. Furthest of all is Porthcothan, a 5-mile drive from Padstow.

'OSS ANTICS

Padstow is famous for its raucous 'Obby 'Oss Festival, a May Day celebration that marks the beginning of spring.

The ritual begins just before midnight on 30 April, when revellers announce to the Golden Lion's innkeeper that summer is 'a-come'.

At 10am, the Blue Ribbon (or Peace) 'Oss – a man garbed in a hooped sailcloth dress and snapping horse headdress – dances around town, accompanied by a baton-wielding 'teazer' and a retinue of musicians, dancers, singers and drummers, all singing the traditional May Day Song. An hour later he's followed by the Old (or Red) 'Oss, and after a day of revelling, singing and carousing, the 'osses are 'stabled' for another year.

Foreshore
Staying in Padstow doesn't have to break the bank, thanks to this tents-only campsite beside the estuary. **£**

Treyarnon Bay YHA
A 1930s beach hostel on the bluffs above Treyarnon Bay. Pleasant rooms, plus camping space and bell tents. **£**

Trewornan Manor
Posh B&B in a 17th-century, Grade II–listed manor house surrounded by 10 glorious hectares. **££**

BEST PLACES TO EAT AROUND PADSTOW

Seafood Restaurant
The restaurant that started the Stein saga, now managed by Rick's son Jack. £££

Paul Ainsworth at No 6
TV chef Ainsworth's Michelin standard food deserves all the plaudits. £££

Prawn on the Lawn
This tiny seafood bar is a fresh addition to Padstow's dining line-up. ££

Mariners
Paul Ainsworth-owned pub that's become Rock's go-to spot for gastronomes. ££.

St Kew Inn
A rustic, country pub with beam-and-flagstone appeal, and a lovely beer garden. ££

Camel Valley vineyard

Fruit of the (Cornish) Vine

TASTE OF THE SEASON

The sheltered valleys around Padstow are home to several renowned vineyards, most notably **Camel Valley**, which was started by ex-RAF pilot Bob Lindo and his wife Annie, and has been producing wines since 1989. The range includes award-winning whites and rosés, and a bubbly that's champagne in all but name. The wines have won a wealth of prestigious international awards; aficionados say Camel Valley wines have a fresh, light quality that comes from the mild climate and pure sea air. Book for a tour and to sip wines by the glass on the sun terrace, or just drop by the shop.

A more recent upstart is **Trevibban Mill**, established in 2008 by Engin and Liz Mumcuoglu. One- and three-hour tours take in the vineyard and winery before finishing with a tutored tasting of either five or seven wines. Allow time to sit on the bewitching patio framed by wildflower meadows and sip a crisp, chilled white.

Crustacean Conservation

LEARN ABOUT LOBSTERS

In an effort to combat falling lobster stocks, Padstow's **National Lobster Hatchery** rears baby lobsters in tanks before returning them to the wild. Take an informative tour to learn all about the crustaceans' life cycle, and look into the tanks where you can watch the small residents up close. Warning: after this, you'll never feel quite the same about eating a lobster roll again.

GETTING AROUND

There are a couple of car parks beside the harbour in Padstow, but they fill up quickly, so it's usually better to park at one of the large car parks at the top of town and walk down. First

Kernow buses connect Newquay and Padstow. The Black Tor Ferry runs to Rock year-round, or you can book a late-night trip via the Rock Water Taxi.

Beyond Padstow

Culm Coast
Bude
Boscastle
Tintagel
Port Issac
Padstow

North of Padstow, the coast road grandly dubbed the Atlantic Highway (aka the A39) runs all the way to the Devon border.

This is a stark, seablown corner of Cornwall, which never gets quite as busy as the more popular areas around Padstow, Newquay and St Ives. The signature sight here is undoubtedly the crumbling clifftop fortress at Tintagel, rife with Arthurian connections, but it's worth exploring beyond too, to the valley village of Boscastle, the dramatic beaches south of Bude and the foodie hub of Port Isaac, now HQ for lauded seafood chef Nathan Outlaw (and the setting for the hit TV series *Doc Martin*). It's a great area for road-tripping and coast walks; away from the tourist honeypots, there's Atlantic grandeur in store if you're prepared to strap on your boots and do some exploring.

TOP TIP

Book tickets online for Tintagel Castle to avoid queues in summer. If you're visiting other English Heritage sites, it may be worth taking out EH membership.

Tintagel Castle (p178)

CHRISDORNEY/SHUTTERSTOCK ©

THE ONCE & FUTURE KING

Cornwall is inextricably bound up with King Arthur, the fabled protector of the British Isles. But despite endless research, it's still a matter of conjecture if Arthur even existed.

Cornwall's Arthurian connections are possibly a remnant of its Celtic past: this was, after all, one of the few corners of Britain never conquered by Rome.

The ghost of Arthur haunts several locations: Slaughterbridge near Camelford is said to be the site of his last battle at Camlann, while Dozmary Pool and Loe Pool both claim to be the home of the Lady of the Lake, who gave Arthur Excalibur. A strange site on Bodmin Moor, known as King Arthur's Hall (p182), is most likely a Neolithic burial chamber – but who knows?

VALEREE2000/SHUTTERSTOCK ©

Waterfall, St Nectan's Glen

Idylls of the King

KING ARTHUR'S FABLED BIRTHPLACE

The spectre of King Arthur looms large over **Tintagel Castle** (a 45-minute drive from Padstow) and its breathtaking clifftop castle. Local legend claims the king was born here. In fact, the castle is largely the 13th-century work of Richard, Earl of Cornwall, although archaeological digs have revealed fragments of an earlier fortress, ensuring the legend lives on.

Legends aside, it's a soul-stirring spot for a stronghold. Much of the castle has crumbled, but it's still possible to make out the Great Hall and other rooms. The most striking modern feature is the controversial new footbridge constructed between the two sides of the medieval castle, recreating a land bridge that existed 500 years ago. It's a hair-raising feeling as you walk across and see the rocks far below your feet (the alternative – a dizzyingly steep staircase cut into the rocks – is almost worse).

CASTLE COUNTRY

If Tintagel has stirred your imagination, seek out the castles of **St Mawes** (p151) and **Pendennis** (p137), the hilltop keeps of **Launceston** (p184) and **Restormel** (p157), and the ancient hillfort of **Chûn Castle** (p198).

Trails lead along the headland to the medieval chapel of **St Materiana**, to the Arthur-themed **Gallos statue**, and downhill to the rocky mouth of **Merlin's Cave**, where the wizard supposedly cast his spells.

🛏 WHERE TO STAY ON THE ATLANTIC COAST

Beach at Bude
Space, style and broad views over Summerleaze make this a tempting choice. **££**

Old School Hotel
A former schoolhouse turned friendly small hotel on the hill above Port Isaac. **££**

Outlaw's Guest House
Book a room at Nathan Outlaw's elegant guesthouse in Port Isaac for the ultimate foodie weekend. **£££**

Bathing on the Beach

SAND, SURF AND SEA POOLS

An hour's drive from Padstow, **Bude** is a blustery beach town which has been reeling in day-trippers and beachgoers since the great Victorian tourist boom in the late 19th century. Like Newquay, it's not the prettiest town, and is mainly visited for its beaches. **Summerleaze** is the closest to town; its main attraction is the **Bude Sea Pool**, a saltwater lido built in the 1930s. It's perfect for kids, and warms up fast on sunny days.

SWIMMING IN STYLE

If you've been bitten by the sea-swimming bug, don't miss a dip in Penzance's magnificent **Jubilee Pool** (p202), an art-deco masterpiece with wondrous views over Mount's Bay.

A Fairy Glen

TREK TO A MYSTICAL WATERFALL

A mile east of Tintagel is the magical wooded valley at **St Nectan's Glen**, where an 18m waterfall tumbles down into a mirror-like *kieve* (plunge pool). It's a mystical spot with more Arthurian connections, supposedly frequented by Cornish *piskies* (pixies) and nature spirits – you'll see ribbons and offerings dangling from the trees. It's also a seriously bracing spot for a dip, if you're brave enough to dunk yourself. The remains of St Nectan's hermitage can be seen above the pool.

The surrounding coastline is great for walks: the craggy coves of **Bossiney**, **Benoath** and **Rocky Valley** are all good targets.

Seafood by the Sea

CORNISH FISH PAR EXCELLENCE

East of Tintagel, a 35-minute drive from Padstow, the teeny fishing harbour of **Port Isaac** is a cluster of cobbled alleyways, slender opes and cob-walled cottages collected around a medieval harbour and slipway. It's also a filming location, most notably for the popular TV series *Doc Martin*.

Port Isaac's main claim to fame these days is culinary. It's the home base of chef Nathan Outlaw, whose two stellar restaurants – fine-dining **Outlaw's New Road** and tiny, tapas-style **Outlaw's Fish Kitchen** beside the harbour – set the standard for Cornish seafood for all to follow: book well in advance to bag a table. For something more modest but equally fresh, pick up a crab sandwich from **Fresh from the Sea**, a homely fish shop run by local fisherman Callum Greenhalgh and his wife Tracey.

BEST ATLANTIC COAST EATERIES

Rocket Store
Tiny seafood diner down beside the harbour at Boscastle; space is tight, so bookings essential. ££

Potters
Oly Clarke and his wife Nikki have created a refined dining experience in Bude. ££

Temple
Local suppliers and producers take centre stage at this classy Bude bistro. Dinner only. ££

Life's a Beach
Relaxed cafe-bar that's mainly worth a stop for the superb sunset view over Summerleaze. ££

WHERE TO CAMP ON THE ATLANTIC COAST

Belle Tents	**Pencuke Farm**	**Cornish Tipi Holidays**
These stripy big-top tents will make you feel like you're camping out with the circus. ££	An organic farm between Boscastle and Bude with nine pitches in a spacious sea-view meadow. £	No worries about forgetting the tent poles here: the tipis are pre-pitched in a delightful wooded valley. ££

Witch's Brew

PICNIC ON BOSCASTLE'S CLIFFTOPS

Cornwall's north shore has its share of pretty harbours, but none can hold a candle to **Boscastle** (a 45-minute drive from Padstow). Nestled in the crook of a river valley, it's wonderfully picturesque: slate-roofed cottages, a stout granite harbour, headlands dusted with thrift, sea campion and gorse. The cliffs around the village provide the perfect backdrop for a blustery picnic; pick up supplies at the excellent **Boscastle Farm Shop**, on the hilly B3263 leading out of the village. If you feel up to the walk, a cliffside cascade, **Pentargon Waterfall**, can be found on the cliff path. It's best after a decent spell of rain.

The village's endearingly weird **Museum of Witchcraft and Magic** was founded by the occult expert and ex-MI6 spy Cecil Williamson in 1960. Exhibits include witch's poppets (a kind of voodoo doll), divination pans, enchanted skulls, pickled beasts and a horrific 'witch's bridle' designed to extract confessions from suspected hags.

Crack On

CLAMBER CORNWALL'S HIGHEST CLIFF

The most dramatic of the beaches around Bude, 11 miles southwest of town, **Crackington Haven** is bordered by black cliffs, which are speckled by a blaze of wildflowers in spring. It's a bit off the main tourist radar, making it a wilder alternative to the sandy family beaches nearer town. There are lifeguards in season, plus a small beach cafe and shop. A mile south of the beach looms the appropriately named **High Cliff**, which boasts the highest drop of any cliff in Cornwall (223m).

Culm Walk with Me

TREK TO QUIET BEACHES

North of Bude, a string of beaches runs up the remote **Culm Coast** all the way to the Devon border. You'll see few tourists this far up the coast, so it's a brilliant place for crowd-free walks. The area's unique geology, consisting of shales and sandstones, gives the coastline a shattered, stratified look; it's also known for deposits of a soft coal known as culm, hence the name. The area's main beach is National Trust–owned **Sandymouth Bay** (pictured left), but there are others further north, including **Duckpool**, **Stanbury Mouth** and **Caunter**, often only accessible at low tide. You can also hike to the twin headlands of **Sharpnose Point**, along with the local landmark known as **Hawker's Hut** – a ramshackle wooden cabin built into the cliff by poet Reverend Robert Hawker as a writing retreat.

GETTING AROUND

First Kernow operates buses up the Atlantic coast, with Bude and Padstow the main hubs. This end of the north coast tends to be a little less hectic than the Newquay side, and if you have a car, it's a brilliant area to explore.

BODMIN MOOR

Hugging the edge of the Devon border, the stark, barren expanse of Bodmin Moor dominates east Cornwall and is the county's wildest and weirdest landscape. Pockmarked by bogs and treeless heaths, Cornwall's 'roof' is well worth taking the time to explore – lofty peaks loom on the horizon, stone circles are scattered across the hills, and ancient churches nestle at the foot of granite tors.

It's also home to Cornwall's highest peak, Brown Willy, as well as the infamous Beast of Bodmin Moor, a black catlike creature that's been seen for many years but has still not been conclusively captured on camera. You're unlikely to spy the legendary cat, but on the upside you most likely won't spot many other tourists either: Bodmin Moor is an under-explored corner of Cornwall that's unjustly skipped by most visitors.

TOP TIP

In winter, the area around Brown Willy is one of the best places to watch starling murmurations, which usually happen in November and December. These swirling, balletic formations normally happen at dusk as the flocks settle down to roost for the night, and are quite a sight to behold.

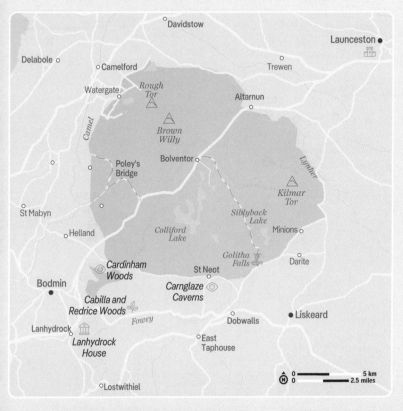

OLD STONES

Like Penwith and Dartmoor, Bodmin Moor is littered with ancient sites that give an insight into Cornwall's past.

Near the little village of Minions, you can see the peculiar rock stack known as the **1 Cheesewring**, which is said to be the work of giants but is actually the result of natural erosion. It's unclear whether it was revered by ancient people, but it may well have been, given its proximity to the triple stone circle called **2 The Hurlers**, along with the pair of standing stones known as **3 The Pipers**. According to legend, both monuments are the frozen remains of folk caught messing about on the Sabbath: the former is allegedly a team of Cornish hurlers, while the latter is said to be a duo of pipe-players.

Near Darite is **4 Trethevy Quoit**, a classic dolmen (Neolithic burial chamber) dating from 3500 BCE to 2500 BCE. How

its builders hoisted the capstone into place is a matter of debate, given that it weighs in excess of 20 tonnes. Further east near Hawk's Tor stand the **5 Stripple Stones**, a circular alignment that is thought to have once enclosed 28 stones (today, only four are still standing).

A good hike from St Breward is **6 King Arthur's Hall**, perhaps the most mysterious of the moor's monuments. This impressive structure consists of 56 stones (originally there would have been more than 140), arranged in a rough rectangle measuring about 20m by 50m. No one is sure of its purpose, but given its size, it must have once been an important site, perhaps used as a meeting place or ceremonial temple. If you feel like extending the walk, the remains of a number of Bronze Age hut enclosures can be seen around **7 Garrow Tor**.

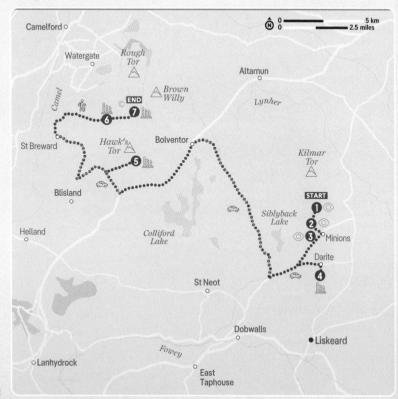

Rough Tor

Cornwall's Rooftop

HIKE TO THE SUMMIT OF BROWN WILLY

Now, now, stop sniggering at the back. A perennial source of amusement for Cornish schoolkids, Cornwall's highest hill, **Brown Willy**, actually gets its name from the Cornish *'bronn wennili'* or 'hill of swallows'. From the car park at Poldue Downs, it's a there-and-back tramp of about 5.5 miles; the ascent is steep but straightforward, winding through heathland, bog, gorse and boulders to the 419m summit. Along the way, you can also bag Cornwall's second-highest summit, **Rough Tor** (pronounced 'row', to rhyme with 'cow'). Keep your eyes peeled for the remains of ancient field systems and several hut circles along the way. The ground can be wet underfoot, even in midsummer, so waterproof hiking boots are a good idea.

A Waterfall Walk

HIKE TO GOLITHA FALLS

With a 90m drop, the crashing cascade of **Golitha Falls** is one of the most renowned beauty spots on the moor. The site is surrounded by the remains of an ancient oak wood that once covered much of the moor. The falls are just over a mile west of St Cleer; they make for a lovely short walk and a memorable place for a picnic. You can swim in the pool if you're up to it, but be warned: it's chilly all year round. There's a car park half a mile's walk from the falls, near Draynes Bridge.

WHY I LOVE
BODMIN MOOR

Oliver Berry
@olivertomberry

'Many visitors race across Bodmin Moor without giving it much of a second glance (the main A38 road cuts right through the middle of it). But the moor is a mysterious place where you still get a sense of a much older, wilder Cornwall than the one you see on most of the postcards.

'It has a wealth of strange ancient sites to visit, not to mention some beautiful woodlands, lakes and waterfalls – and, of course, it's home to Cornwall's grandest view, the rocky, spectacular summit of Bronn Wennili.

'Come summer, I'll take the windswept moor over the busy beaches any day of the month.'

🛏 **WHERE TO STAY ON BODMIN MOOR**

St Tudy Inn
Smart rooms at the best gastropub on the moor, in the small village of St Tudy. £££

Coombeshead Farm
Chic, countrified rooms in an old farm manor house at this epicurean retreat. £££

Spring Park
Stay in a train carriage, a wood-panelled wagon, a potting shed or a pocket-sized chapel at this sweet moorland retreat. ££

BODMIN JAIL

For nearly 150 years, the name of Bodmin Jail struck dread into the hearts of Cornish ne'er-do-wells.

Between 1779 and its closure in 1927, it was Cornwall's main site of incarceration – and execution.

Notorious for the numerous ghosts said to haunt it, it's now been renovated as a 'dark tourism' visitor attraction. You can wander around the old cells, visit the governor's office and – macabre – see the Victorian 'hanging pit', the only one of its kind left in Britain, where 55 souls met their grisly end. You can even stay overnight, if you really want to: half of the jail has now been turned, bizarrely, into a boutique hotel. Spook sightings possible, but not guaranteed...

Cardinham Woods

Into the Woods

BIRDWATCHING AND FOREST BATHING

Two lovely forests can be explored around Bodmin. The largest and best known is **Cardinham Woods**, owned by the Forestry Commission, with mountain-bike trails to tackle if you're feeling more energetic. Handily, the Bodmin & Wenford Railway stops at Coleslogget Halt, from where a 1.5-mile trail leads to Cardinham. The **Woods Cafe** does an excellent afternoon tea.

Cabilla and Redrice Woods, managed by Cornwall Wildlife Trust, is less frequented. Consisting mainly of ancient stands of coppiced oak and hazel, and carpeted with bluebells in spring, it's bird-spotting heaven. It's about a mile east of Bodmin Parkway station on the A38.

Castle in the Sky

A CLASSIC NORMAN KEEP

Way out on the eastern edge of the moor is the old market town of **Launceston** and its 13th-century castle, a circular keep plonked on top of a grassy hillock – resembling a stage set from *Monty Python and the Holy Grail*. A spiral staircase leads up to the battlements for 360-degree views.

 WHERE TO EAT ON BODMIN MOOR

Coombeshead Farm
A working farm, bakery and upmarket restaurant run by chefs Tom Adams and April Bloomfield. £££

St Tudy Inn
The best spot for Sunday lunch on the moor – or pretty much any night of the week, come to think of it. £££

Crocadon Farm
This organic farm has a garden-to-plate restaurant that's only open a few nights a week; book ahead. ££

Going Deeper Underground

HEAD DOWN SPOOKY SLATE CAVERNS

Slate was once an important export on Bodmin Moor, and the complex of deep chambers known as **Carnglaze Caverns** were – almost incredibly – cut out almost entirely by hand by miners, leaving behind an atmospheric network of caves and a glittering underground pool. It's an atmospheric place to visit (just outside St Neot), and concerts and plays are sometimes held inside the caves in summer.

A Very Big House in the Country

HOW THE OTHER HALF LIVED

About 2.5 miles southeast of Bodmin, **Lanhydrock House** offers a fascinating insight into *Upstairs, Downstairs* life in Victorian England. The house was rebuilt after a devastating fire in 1881 as a home for the Agar-Robartes family who, like many wealthy Cornish families, made their fortune predominantly from mineral mining, particularly tin and china clay. No expense was spared in the refurbishment: the house was equipped with mod cons such as radiators, roasting ovens, warming cupboards and flushing loos, as well as a pioneering cold room beside the vast kitchens (pictured below). The ornate Long Gallery, famous for its plaster ceiling, somehow survived the fire.

It's one of those rare country houses which still feels like a family home: wandering around the kitchens, drawing room and children's nursery, it feels like the family have all just popped out for the afternoon and might return at any moment.

The Lanhydrock story proved to be a sad one: the family's beloved eldest son and heir, Tommy Agar-Robartes, was killed in WWI while trying to save a comrade from no-man's land. The family never recovered from the loss; the estate dwindled in both size and fortune over the following decades, and the house was gifted to the National Trust in 1951, along with 160 hectares of parkland offering a wealth of gorgeous walks.

ALL ABOARD

Train buffs won't want to miss a trip on the Bodmin & Wenford Railway, the only 'standard gauge' line of its type left in Cornwall.

The route chuffs and clatters for 6.5 miles between Bodmin and Boscarne Junction, and many trains are still decked out in original 1950s livery.

At the Boscarne end, the line links up with the Camel Trail (p173); you can carry your bike on the train if there's space.

Look out for special trips in summer, including Pullman-style dining trains with a silver-service supper, plus murder-mystery and pub-quiz trains.

GETTING AROUND

Bus services are very limited on most of the moor, so you'll really need a car to explore. The nearest train stations are at Bodmin Parkway and Liskeard, both on the main railway line between Penzance, Plymouth and London Paddington. If you're feeling fit, an extension of the Camel Trail runs from Poley's Bridge (near Boscarne Junction) all the way to Wadebridge.

St Ives (p192)

WEST CORNWALL & THE ISLES OF SCILLY

LAST-STOP BRITAIN

Stark moorland, mysterious monuments, hidden beaches: Cornwall's western corner has a wild edge other areas of the county lack.

Rugged and rocky, west Cornwall is a place that still feels ruled by the elements. This is a land of heath, cliff, gorse and granite, where stone monuments rise up from the hilltops, ancient moorland butts against gorse-topped cliffs and forgotten mine stacks stand out in relief against the skyline. Of course, it has its share of tourist honeypots – especially the artistic hub of St Ives – but the rest of this sparsely populated region feels largely untamed, governed by the whims of weather, wind and tide.

It's not hard to see why so many artists have been drawn here over the decades, finding inspiration in the wide-open landscapes and moody skies. If you're searching for big coastal vistas, they really don't come much grander than on the cliffs of West Penwith, not least around the sea-smashed point of Land's End, where the British mainland runs out of road and drops into the foamy Atlantic (just try to ignore the tacky theme park someone decided to plonk there in the 1980s). Popular areas such as St Ives, Porthcurno, Gwithian, Mousehole, and St Michael's Mount and can feel uncomfortably busy between July and September; visit in early spring or autumn and you'll find things are quieter, and you can usually reach less crowded coves via the coast path.

For real Robinson Crusoes, the Isles of Scilly await 28 miles out to sea – Cornwall's own island getaway.

THE MAIN AREAS

Find Your Way

The main sights and towns are quite widely spread out across west Cornwall, but a decent bus network allows you to reach most areas without having to drive. Our coverage is centred around the area's two main towns, St Ives and Penzance.

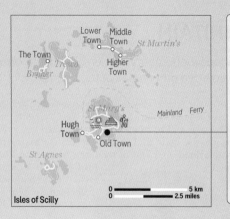

Lower Town
Middle Town
St Martin's
The Town
Tresco
Bryher
Higher Town
St Mary's
Mainland Ferry
Hugh Town
St Agnes
Old Town

0   5 km
0   2.5 miles

Isles of Scilly

Isles of Scilly, p207

With over a hundred islands to explore, the archipelago offers some of the most beautiful beaches and wildest seaside scenery anywhere in Britain.

Isles of Scilly

Hugh Town

See Isles of Scilly Enlargement

ATLANTIC OCEAN

0   10 km
0   5 miles

St Ives, p192

Famous for its artistic heritage, St Ives is a place to wander galleries, paddle on the beach and soak up the seaside sights – it gets packed in summer.

Penzance, p201

This salty old port town has fast-growing art and food scenes, and is handy for visits to Mousehole, Newlyn and the island abbey of St Michael's Mount.

Map labels: Newquay, Cubert, Perranporth, St Agnes, Blackwater, Truro, Portreath, Redruth, Camborne, Devoran, St Ives Bay, St Ives, Carbis Bay, Zennor, Hayle, Four Lanes, Morvah, Mulfra, Penmarth, Penryn, St Mawes, Canonstown, Leedstown, Hernis, Trewellard, Crowlas, Falmouth, Newbridge, Penzance, Marazion, Nancegollan, ust-with, Sancreed, Newlyn, St Michael's Mount, Breage, en, St Buryan, Helston, Lamorna, Porthleven, Helford, Treen, Gunwalloe, Garras, St Keverne, Porthcurno, Mullion, Coverack, Cadgwith, Kennack Sands, Lizard, Housel Cove, English Channel

CAR

Having your own car certainly makes life easier in this far-western end of the county, but it's not essential. Be prepared for traffic jams and problematic parking in popular areas (St Ives and Porthcurno are a driver's nightmare in peak season, so consider public transport if you can).

BUS

There are regular bus services linking Penzance and St Ives with most of the villages around Penwith, including several open-top services that run in summer and allow you to make the most of the views.

TRAIN

Penzance and Hayle are both on the main train line through Cornwall, with regular connections from Exeter, Bristol and London Paddington. A scenic branch line also runs to St Ives from St Erth.

Plan Your Time

You can cover the Penwith basics in a few days, but you'll need at least a week to get under the peninsula's skin – especially if you want to explore the wonderful Isles of Scilly.

Mousehole (p206)

An Arty Day

Base yourself in **St Ives** (p192) and soak up the town's art and culture.

In a day you could visit the **Tate St Ives** (p192) and **Barbara Hepworth Museum and Sculpture Garden** (p194), see the ceramics at the renowned **Leach Pottery** (p194), paddle on the beaches of **Porthminster** and **Porthmeor** (p194), and finish with a slap-up supper at one of the town's excellent restaurants.

With another day to spare, you could book an art lesson at the **St Ives School of Painting** (p194), take a road trip over to **Gwithian** and **Godrevy** (p196), or hop on a wildlife tour around **Seal Island** (p199).

Seasonal Highlights

Town fairs and summer celebrations are the highlight of the calendar in west Cornwall, but there are fun events scattered throughout the year – including a seriously peculiar Christmas parade in Penzance.

APRIL

Teams from all over the world head for the Isles of Scilly for the **World Pilot Gig Championships**; book well ahead.

MAY

The **Scilly Folk Festival** takes over the islands for a week, with traditional songs, concerts and barn dances.

JUNE

Ten days of music, art and Cornish culture in Penzance during the **Golowan Festival**, centring around a street parade on Mazey Day.

Three Days

A few extra days gives you time to cross over the peninsula to Penzance. Visit the town's art galleries, including the **Exchange** and **Penlee House Gallery & Museum** (p204), then take a dip in the glorious **Jubilee Pool** (p201), Cornwall's most beautiful lido.

Walk or cycle along Penzance's promenade to nearby **Newlyn** (p202), one of the southwest's busiest fishing ports, with a fast-growing foodie scene. Nearby **Mousehole** (p206) is one of the prettiest of all Cornwall's villages, while in the opposite direction, across from **Marazion** (p204), the unmistakeable silhouette of **St Michael's Mount** (p205) rises from the blue waters of Mount's Bay.

A Week in the West

A week or so will enable you to delve into Penwith's prehistory by visiting some of the area's many **ancient monuments** (p198): quoits, stone circles, menhirs, hillforts and Bronze Age villages are dotted across the moors.

You'll also have time to take a trip around the peninsula via **Zennor** (p196) and **Sennen** (p200) to **Land's End** (p200), and ideally catch a performance at the amazing **Minack Theatre** (p206).

Hopefully, you'll also be able to spend a few days out on the **Isles of Scilly** (p207), accessible by boat or seaplane – or arrange a day trip if you're really pushed for time.

JULY

St Just hosts its big town fair, **Lafrowda Day**, featuring music, art, stalls and food trucks, with a strong input from the local community.

AUGUST

The **Cornwall Design Fair** brings top designers, makers and craftspeople to showcase their wares in the grounds of Trereife House.

SEPTEMBER

The **St Ives September Festival** features music, exhibitions and events at various venues around town.

DECEMBER

Penzance's chaotic **Montol Festival** honours the season's pagan origins. Mousehole puts up its Christmas lights and celebrates **Tom Bawcock's Eve** on 23 December.

ST IVES

If there was a prize for the prettiest of Cornish ports, St Ives would surely take the top spot. It's a dazzling sight: a tightly packed cluster of slate roofs, old fishers' cottages and church towers spread around a brilliant turquoise bay. Once a busy pilchard harbour, St Ives became the centre of Cornwall's art scene in the 1920s and 1930s, when luminary figures such as Barbara Hepworth, Terry Frost, Ben Nicholson and Naum Gabo migrated here in search of artistic freedom and escape.

St Ives remains an artistic centre, with numerous galleries lining its cobbled streets – including the renowned Tate St Ives, a westerly outpost of the London original. But it's also one of the towns that's been most changed by Cornwall's tourism boom: an infamous hotspot for second homes and sky-high house prices, it's packed to the gunwales in summer. Visit in early spring or autumn if you can.

St Ives

TOP TIP

Parking in St Ives is hellish for much of the year; thankfully, there's an alternative. A scenic branch line trundles along the coast to St Ives from the mainline station of St Erth, so you can let the train take the strain. There's plenty of parking next to St Erth station.

Art on the Beach

CORNWALL'S PREMIER GALLERY

St Ives has no shortage of art galleries, but the **Tate St Ives** is the undisputed centrepiece. Hovering like a spiral conch shell above Porthmeor Beach (pictured below), constructed from white concrete and gleaming glass, the gallery's architecture makes striking use of its seaside setting. It's an essential stop for art lovers. Focusing on the coterie of experimental artists who congregated at St Ives after WWII and turned the little seaside town into a magnet for modern artists, the museum showcases the work of luminaries like Barbara Hepworth, Terry Frost, Peter Lanyon, Patrick Heron and Naum Gabo in luminous, white-walled surroundings. It offers a compelling insight into the St Ives story, and its role in the wider development of modern art; while a new exhibition space hosts a seasonal exhibition devoted to a contemporary artist, providing a contextual counterpoint to the main collection. Whatever you make of the work on show, the gallery itself certainly makes a statement. And while you're here, don't miss a coffee or a bite to eat at the rooftop cafe, which offers widescreen views over Porthmeor Beach.

There are many more artistic sights to investigate around town. Visit the gallery of the **St Ives Society of Artists**, one of the town's oldest and most influential art collectives (founded in 1929), in a converted church on Norway Sq, then wander down to the harbourside **Sloop Craft Market**, where a little mews of shops offers everything from driftwood furniture to handmade jewellery. For more contemporary work, seek out the **New Craftsman Gallery**: Peter Lanyon and Patrick Heron once exhibited here.

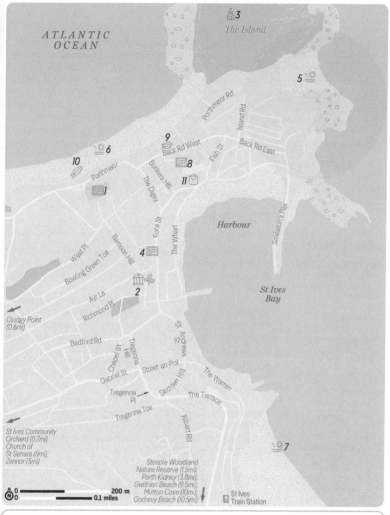

HIGHLIGHTS
1 Tate St Ives

SIGHTS
2 Barbara Hepworth Museum
3 Chapel of St Nicholas

4 New Craftsman Gallery
5 Porthgwidden Beach
6 Porthmeor Beach
7 Porthminster Beach
8 St Ives Society of Artists

ACTIVITIES & COURSES
9 St Ives School of Painting
10 St Ives Surf School

SHOPPING
11 Sloop Craft Market

WHERE TO DRINK IN ST IVES

Sloop Inn
The classic St Ives boozer, in a prime quayside spot. Arrive early to bag an outside table.

Brewhouse
Smart taproom run by the Padstow Brewing Company – sip premium craft beer with views over town.

Hub St Ives
A harbourfront bar near the lifeboat station that does a good line in burgers, beers and late-night cocktails.

Art Lessons

PAINT LIKE THE PROS

SETTING THE SCENE

Learn about the history of Cornwall's art scene in our essay **Cornwall & the Arts** (p244).

If St Ives has inspired you to pick up a brush, book a course at the **St Ives School of Painting**. It has been tutoring budding painters from its studios near Porthmeor Beach since it was opened by artists Borlase Smart and Leonard Fuller in 1938. It now runs courses focusing on painting in watercolour, gouache, oils and other media, covering everything from landscapes to life drawing. You can choose from short two-hour workshops, or book longer courses lasting from two to six days covering everything from mark making to experimental landscapes. It's a wonderful way to see St Ives in a new light: not as a tourist, but as an artist.

Shapes in Stone

VISIT BARBARA HEPWORTH'S FORMER STUDIO

KURT JACKSON

Way out west of St Ives, the old mining town of St Just has been given a boost thanks to the arrival of the Jackson Foundation Gallery.

This ambitious, environmentally themed gallery space was founded by the well-known local landscape artist Kurt Jackson and his wife Caroline. Housed in a former industrial building on North Row, the gallery is super ecofriendly (solar panels, heat pumps) and features annual exhibitions exploring issues around the natural world.

If you buy something, they'll even deliver it in an e-van. The gallery is usually open Tuesday to Saturday, with an hour for cleaning from 1pm to 2pm.

Barbara Hepworth was one of the leading abstract sculptors of the 20th century, and a key figure in the St Ives art scene, so it seems fitting that her former studio is now a moving **museum**. The studio has remained practically untouched since her death in a fire in 1975, and the adjoining **sculpture garden** contains some of her most famous artworks, many of which were inspired by the elemental forces she discovered in her adopted Cornish home: rock, sea, sand, wind, sky. You can wander freely around the garden and spot the sculptures, which were placed according to Hepworth's instructions: among the subtropical shrubs, look out for the harplike *Garden Sculpture (Model for Meridian)* and *Four Square,* the largest work Hepworth created. Her art is also liberally sprinkled around town; there's a Hepworth outside the Guildhall, and her moving *Madonna and Child* inside St Ia Church commemorates her son Paul Skeaping, who was killed in an air crash in 1953.

Seaside St Ives

SUNBATHE, SWIM, SUP

The largest town beaches are **Porthmeor** and **Porthminster**, both of which have sand and space aplenty. Between them juts the grassy promontory known as the Island, topped by the tiny pre-14th-century **Chapel of St Nicholas**, the patron saint of children and sailors. It's allegedly the oldest church in St Ives – and certainly the smallest. On the headland's east

WHERE TO STAY AROUND ST IVES

Primrose House
Scandi chic and proximity to Porthminster are the draws – and it has parking, too. £££

Trevose Harbour House
Posh, six-room B&B decked out in a sea-themed combo of fresh whites and stripy blues. £££

Boskerris
A stylish hotel in the neighbouring town of Carbis Bay, pleasantly removed from the St Ives bustle. £££

Barbara Hepworth Sculpture Garden

POT LUCK

While other St Ives artists broke new ground in sculpture and abstract art, potter Bernard Leach was hard at work reinventing British ceramics in his studio in Higher Stennack.

Drawing inspiration from Japanese and oriental sculpture, and using a hand-built 'climbing' kiln based on ones he had seen in Japan, Leach's pottery created a unique fusion of Asian and European ideas. His former studio, Leach Pottery, displays examples of his work, and has been enhanced by a new museum and working pottery studio, as well as a shop selling Leach ceramics alongside other contemporary potters.

If you'd like to learn how to throw a pot or perfect a glaze, book one of the excellent pottery courses.

side is the little cove of **Porthgwidden**, which can be a good place to escape the crowds. Even better, hike out to **Clodgy Point**, west of town, to see a view of St Ives most visitors miss.

You can hire paddleboards and kayaks from **St Ives Surf School**, which also runs coasteering sessions along the rocky coastline – a combination of rock climbing, scrambling and swimming, combined with cold-water plunges into the deep blue sea.

Woodlands & Wild Food

ORCHARDS AND EDIBLES

For a local side of St Ives that's well off the usual tourist track, head to the **St Ives Community Orchard**, a patch of land on the edge of Penbeagle Hill where volunteers have set up a delightful, diverse orchard complete with beehives, perennial veg plots, a living willow dome and even a pizza oven. They hold events throughout the year (including a wassailing day near Christmas) and often have volunteer days, so check the website for what's on. Paths lead around the orchard to a small nature reserve. It's also worth walking up Steeple Lane to **Steeple Woodland Nature Reserve**, a 16-hectare woodland topped by the landmark of **Knill's Monument**.

For a deeper dive into St Ives' natural history, local forager Josh Quick of **Wild St Ives** offers guided walks in search of wild edibles.

Pedn-Olva
Despite the boxy exterior, this town hotel is a surprise: bright and beachy, with panoramic views over the bay. **££**

Saltwater
It's driftwood-chic all the way at Saltwater, where bright blue and yellow bedrooms echo the landscape. **££**

11 Sea View Terrace
Good-value B&B in an Edwardian villa offering elevated views over the harbour. **££**

Out on the Towans

GOLDEN SAND, GRASSY DUNES

On the east side of St Ives Bay, the dune-backed flats of **Gwithian** and **Godrevy** unfurl in a sea-fringed curve and join together at low tide to form Hayle's much-lauded '3 miles of golden sand'. At the southwestern end is the Hayle Estuary, once a busy industrial harbour, while at the opposite end, the **Godrevy Lighthouse** perches on a rocky island – it famously inspired Virginia Woolf's classic *To the Lighthouse*.

The twin beaches are brilliant for a blustery walk. You can usually see a colony of seals at **Mutton Cove**, a pebbly beach at the base of a steep cliff to the east of Godrevy Point. The cliffs are also good for spotting cormorants, guillemots and several gull species; the grassy dunes (towans in Cornish) provide an important coastal habitat.Gwithian and Godrevy get busy in summer, and parking can be tough. An alternative is to head for the opposite side of the Hayle Estuary, where the broad, flat beach of **Porth Kidney** is usually much less crowded, if a little less picturesque.

Coast On

DRIVE PENWITH'S MOST DRAMATIC ROAD

The twisting B3306 coast road makes for a roller-coaster trip, winding through granite-strewn moorland and patchwork fields, some of which date back to medieval times. Craggy tors and auburn heaths dominate the horizon, and broken cliffs tumble down into booming surf. The stretch between St Ives and Sennen is awe-inspiring, and also offers access to spectacular coast walks. **Gurnard's Head** (pictured left), **Pendour Cove** and **Porthmeor Cove** are all classic coast path targets here, with a stop in the quaint village of **Zennor** to see its little **Church of St Senara**. Inside, look out for a carved bench end that depicts a mermaid holding a mirror and comb – a reference to the folk tale of the Mermaid of Zennor, who fell in love with the singing voice of a local lad. It's said you can still sometimes hear them singing down at Pendour Cove.

While you're here, don't miss an ice-cream from the **Moomaid of Zennor**, which has their main shop in the village: unusual flavours include expresso martini, orange and mascarpone, and creme fraiche and lemon curd.

GETTING AROUND

Attempting to drive through the town centre is a recipe for holiday nightmares. If you're driving, the largest car park by far is Trenwith, a brisk uphill walk from town, and usually the likeliest to have spaces. Otherwise, consider leaving your car at St Erth or Lelant stations, and then catching the scenic St Ives train line into town. First Kernow runs buses to Penzance, Marazion and along the Zennor coast road via Sennen and Land's End.

Beyond St Ives

Venture west of St Ives to experience coast roads, secluded coves and Cornwall's prehistoric past.

West and south of St Ives sprawls the wild expanse of the Penwith Peninsula, a crooked finger of land edging out into the Atlantic like a toe testing the water. Stark and remote, spotted with mine stacks, ancient farmland and windswept moor, this is an untamed corner of Cornwall, a long way from the county's cosy harbour towns and neatly kept beaches. The peninsula takes its name from two Cornish words – *penn* (headland) and *wydh* (end). It's scarcely populated now, but during Neolithic times this empty landscape was home to a string of ancient settlements and sacred sites, the remains of which can still be seen scattered among the granite rocks.

TOP TIP

Get a good map if you're searching for the ancient sites: the *Ordnance Survey Explorer Map 102: Land's End Map, Penzance & St Ives* is the one to go for.

Levant Mine & Beam Engine ruins (p199)

PENWITH'S PREHISTORY

There are many archaeological remains, in Penwith, dating from Neolithic times to the Bronze Age. Take the coastal B3306 from Zennor. Continue past Carn Galver Engine House and then take the left turn (signed 'Penzance 5/Madron 4') and continue until you reach a junction with a sign for Great Bosullow/Chûn Castle. Just past here, there is a small layby where you can park and walk up to the ring-shaped **1 Mên-an-tol** (holed stone). According to lore, crawling through it you'll either fall pregnant or get cured of rickets! A trail leads to the **2 Nine Maidens** stone circle and the carved stone of **3 Mên Scryfa** (writing stone).

Back in the car, backtrack to the turning to Great Bosullow and drive to the tiny Boswens car park. From here, it's a muddy hike to **4 Chûn Castle**, an Iron Age hillfort. You can still make out the enclosing ditch and interior walls, and the view is incredible. **5 Chûn Quoit** is nearby. Return to the Mên-an-tol layby and continue past **6 Lanyon Quoit** on your left – it's one of the best examples of a dolmen. Near Madron is an ancient **7 holy well**, one of many in Penwith – the water is said to have curative

properties. On the outskirts of Penzance turn at Heamoor on to Joseph's Ln and continue to Polmennor Rd before turning left up the unmarked Gear Hill. Drive through New Mill and turn right at the sign for **8 Chysauster**, Cornwall's most important Iron Age village.

Retrace your route to Heamoor and turn left on to Madron Rd. After 500m join the A30, heading west for Land's End. Continue through Drift and Catchall, then look out for a small layby just before Lower Leha. Park and walk to the great stone circle of **9 Boscawen-un**, consisting of 19 upright stones and a leaning stone near the centre. It dates from the Bronze Age; the name derives from the Cornish words *bos* (farmstead), *scawen* (elder tree) and *un* (pasture).

Back in the car continue on about 1km and take a left turn towards St Buryan. At the church in St Buryan take Rectory Rd towards Lamorna. At the B3315 turn left and travel 500m to a layby to see the **10 Merry Maidens**, supposedly the petrified remains of 19 girls turned to stone for dancing on the Sabbath. Nearby are **11 The Pipers**, who presumably earned the same fate for tootling the tune to which the girls danced.

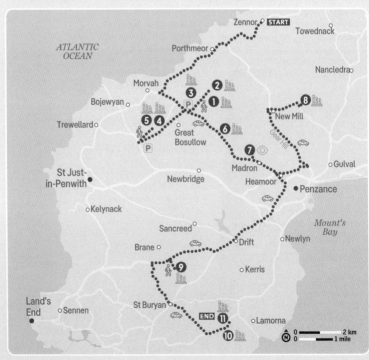

PETER TITMUSS/SHUTTERSTOCK ©

Geevor Tin Mine

SEALS & SHIPWRECKS

St Ives Bay is a great place to spot marine life, especially seals, dolphins, porpoises and all kinds of seabirds, as well as the chance to see basking sharks in summer.

St Ives Boats runs daily trips to see the seal colonies on Seal Island and Godrevy Island; there's also the opportunity to book a trip on St Ives' century-old lifeboat, James Steven No 10, which was built in 1899 and served from 1900 to 1933. En route you'll learn about historic shipwrecks and daring rescues before skirting round Godrevy Island.

Into the Dark

TOUR A REAL-LIFE TIN MINE

Tin mining was west Cornwall's staple industry, and deserted engine houses punctuate the crag-backed coastline. To experience what life was like for Cornwall's 'hard rock men' and 'bal maidens', you can venture underground at **Geevor Tin Mine**, the last working mine in west Cornwall to close in 1990. Above ground you can wander around the old machinery where the tin ore was extracted, while below ground you can take a guided tour into the mine itself – a maze of dank shafts and tunnels where miners worked for hours at a stretch, enduring ever-present dangers of rockfalls, air pollution and underground explosions. Insight is provided by former miners who paint an evocative picture of mining conditions. The mine is near Pendeen (a 25-minute drive from St Ives).

Nearby is the National Trust–owned **Levant Mine & Beam Engine**, which once ran lifts, powered trains and pumped floodwater from the deep underground shafts. The pioneering engine design was later exported across the world, but Levant is one of the only working examples. Closed in 1930, it has since been restored by a team of enthusiasts, and is a sight to behold when it's in full steam.

 WHERE TO EAT IN PENWITH

Gurnard's Head
One of west Cornwall's top dining pubs, on the Zennor coast road: best of British dishes, inspired by Cornish produce. £££

Tinner's Arms
Zennor's pub may well be Cornwall's most venerable boozer; it's believed to have been built around 1271. ££

Trevaskis Farm
Farm-grown produce, pick-your-own fruit and a legendary Sunday roast (reservations essential). Near Gwithian. ££

WILD EDIBLES

Fancy yourself as a budding Ray Mears? Then a weekend of delving through the undergrowth in search of berries, edible roots and samphire in the company of Fat Hen will be right up your boulevard.

Head forager-ecologist Caroline Davey leads guided trips in search of wild goodies, before retiring to the headquarters at Boscawen-noon Farm to see the raw materials transformed into something tasty by the Fat Hen chefs. Hedgerow cocktails, anyone?

It's also worth making a detour via **Cape Cornwall**, Cornwall's only cape, and the nearby lighthouse at **Pendeen**, built in 1900 and automated since 1995. A remote beach, **Portheras Cove**, can be reached via the coast path.

Surf & Turf

PIT STOP IN SENNEN

Tucked into the arc of Whitesand Bay, **Sennen** (a 35-minute drive from St Ives) boasts one of west Penwith's most impressive sands. With vivid blue waters and a mile of beach backed by dunes and marram grass, it's a great place to learn to surf: contact the **Sennen Surfing Centre** for lessons. For quieter sands, **Gwenver** just up the coast is normally a good bet.

Sennen is also a good base for coast walks. You can also follow the coast round to Land's End; en route you'll pass the remains of the Iron Age hillfort of **Maen Castle**. It's about a 1.5-mile walk, although it can feel a good deal longer on a blazing hot day.

Last Stop Kernow

MAINLAND BRITAIN'S WESTERNMOST POINT

The clue's in the name. The rugged headland of **Land's End** (a 40-minute drive from St Ives) is where Cornwall comes to a screeching halt, and the black granite cliffs fall away into a maelstrom of white surf. Famous as the last port of call for charity walkers on the 874-mile slog from John O'Groats in Scotland, the views are epic: the restless Atlantic seems to wrap itself around the horizon, shimmering in the late-afternoon light, and on a clear evening, the sunsets are out of this world. Look out for the **Longships Lighthouse**, 1.25 miles offshore, and the faint outlines of the Isles of Scilly, 28 miles out to sea. The photo-op beside the famous signpost (New York 3147; John O' Groats 874) is a cliché, but essential nonetheless.

Unfortunately, the site has been blighted by the addition of a spectacularly tacky theme park in the 1980s. Thankfully, you can bypass the tat entirely and just pay for the car park. The coast path south of Land's End remains as wild and beautiful as any in Cornwall; the rocky beach at **Nanjizal Bay** (pictured) has impressive sea caves to explore.

GETTING AROUND

Having a car comes in handy for exploring the Penwith Peninsula, but First Kernow (firstbus. co.uk/adventures-bus/services) runs local buses from St Ives and Penzance to the various villages – including the open-top Land's End Coaster in summer, which also stops at Zennor, Geevor, St Just and Sennen. The Tin Coaster is another option, looping from Penzance via St Just, Botallack, Geevor and Pendeen.

PENZANCE

Overlooking the majestic sweep of Mount's Bay, the old harbour of Penzance has a salty, sea-blown charm that feels altogether more authentic than many of Cornwall's polished-up ports. Its streets and shopping arcades still feel real and just a touch ramshackle, and there's nowhere better for a windy-day walk than the town's seafront Victorian promenade. Penzance also has a decent array of places to eat, as well as an interesting art scene, with several galleries dotted around town.

Along the seafront promenade, near Battery Rocks, is Penzance's premier attraction: the elegant curves of Jubilee Pool. Further along the prom lies the working fishing port of Newlyn, and beyond it the improbably pretty seaside village of Mousehole. Penzance also makes an ideal base for a walk over to St Michael's Mount, the iconic island abbey that's visible from every seafront angle.

Penzance

TOP TIP

Penzance's promenade makes for a fine stroll or bike ride. You can follow the seafront on foot all the way to Newlyn and Mousehole – much less stressful than attempting to find parking in summer. Along the way, you'll find a few swimming spots and a natural sea pool revealed by the receding tide.

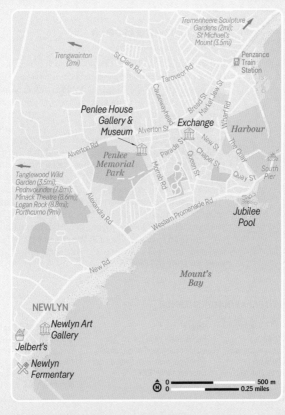

CORNWALL CALLING

The quirky PK Porthcurno charts the unlikely tale of Porthcurno's role in transatlantic tele-communications.

In 1870 an underwater cable was laid here, which enabled telegraph messages to be sent as far as Bombay in less than a minute. Over the next century, 14 cables ran into Porthcurno, carrying a good chunk of Britain's global telecommunications.

The telegraph station was decommissioned in 1970. The museum explores the story in imaginative ways, with interactive morse-code kits, vintage equipment, archive footage and so on. You can explore a network of underground tunnels that were built here during WWII.

There's also a good cafe for lunch.

Jubilee Pool

Fresh off the Boats

TRY THE CATCH OF THE DAY

Fish, fish and shellfish – that's what you should be eating here. For fresh crab and lobster, the wharfside warehouses in Newlyn are the place to go. At **W Harvey & Sons**, you can buy unpicked whole hens and cocks or, if you'd rather avoid the hard work, there are prepackaged sachets of dressed white and dark meat, too. Depending on the season, you can also pick up mussels, anchovies, crevettes and more.

PJ Tonkin & Co is a reliable all-round fish merchant, with stocks of whatever happens to have been landed off the boats that day – dover sole, lemon sole, hake, pollack and more besides. It also offers fish selection boxes if you can't choose.

For something tasty to go alongside, **Newlyn Fermentary** sells sauerkrauts, pickles and kimchis, and runs workshops so you can learn how to make your own. Hipster rating: high. And don't miss an ice cream from **Jelbert's**: it's a local institution, and sells only one flavour – vanilla, with optional chocolate flake and clotted cream on top.

 WHERE TO EAT AROUND PENZANCE

Argoe
Local boy Rich Adams is making waves with his stylish Newlyn seafood place, specialising in local fish and shellfish. £££

Shore
Penzance's best bistro, big on local seafood and Cornish produce, overseen by top chef Bruce Rennie. £££

Mackerel Sky Seafood Bar
Cute cafe beside Newlyn's bridge, great for a fishy lunch, from mackerel pâté on hot toast to a crab ciabatta sandwich. ££

Getting into Hot Water

SWIM IN A LISTED LIDO

The glorious **Jubilee Pool** is Penzance's most beautiful landmark. Built in the 1930s during Britain's lido-building boom, this art deco marvel has had a chequered history: it lay derelict for many years, but has been beautifully restored and now makes for one of Cornwall's most memorable swims. A £1.8-million investment has also brought a very 21st-century addition: one section of the open-air pool is now geothermally heated to a toasty 35°C, powered by hot rocks deep underground. It's without a doubt Cornwall's most stylish swimming pool – but demand for the geothermal section is high, so book well in advance. The cafe is excellent, too.

Snorkel for Sea Life

TAKE AN UNDERWATER TOUR

More spectacular swims can be experienced out in Mount's Bay courtesy of **Tonic of the Sea**, run by open-water swimmer and snorkel instructor Katie Maggs. She offers one-hour guided swims in search of marine wildlife, from colourful crabs and jellyfish to nudibranches, starfish and anemones – along with the occasional inquisitive seal swimming by to say hello.

Western Wines

VINTAGES AT PZ'S VINEYARD

Located just outside town, **Polgoon** is earning a sparkling reputation for its rosés and whites, which come in both still and bubbly varieties, and also makes cider and juices from its own orchard. Informative tours are offered year-round, and of course you get to taste the latest vintages.

Galleries Old & New

FROM NEWLYN MASTERS TO CONTEMPORARY ARTISTS

Penzance has long been a focus for west Cornwall's art scene, and there are several galleries which are well worth visiting. The **Exchange** is housed in Penzance's former telecoms building, and hosts regular exhibitions of contemporary art (recent shows have included Grayson Perry). Its sister institution, **Newlyn Art Gallery**, is a mile west along Penzance's prom. Though it was founded in 1895, since

I LIVE HERE

Katie Maggs (@tonic ofthesea) runs guided snorkelling tours around Penzance.

Battery Rocks
Locals swim or snorkel here year-round, even on Christmas and New Year's Day! Come in early spring to see seaweeds, shoals of sand eels, spiny starfish and even inquisitive seals.

Long Rock & Marazion Beach
St Michael's Mount makes a stunning backdrop here. You'll often spot scuttling spider crabs in July and blooms of colourful jellyfish like the blue, moon and compass.

Newlyn Beach
The sheltered coves between Newlyn and Mousehole are good for kelp forests and seagrass meadows, and also larger fish, starfish and sometimes bull seals. Stay close to the rocks, as fishing boats pull their lobster pots here!

Tolcarne Inn
Ben Tunnicliffe's much-lauded gastropub in Newlyn consistently wins awards for its superior seafood. £££

Honey Pot
A homely cafe along a Penzance back street, serving delicious homemade cakes and hearty lunches. £

2 Fore St
This laid-back harbourside bistro majors in Gallic-inspired classics; the head chef trained under Raymond Blanc. ££

2007 its focus has been firmly on contemporary art. The upstairs cafe has wonderful bay views, too.

For a historic overview of the area's art scene, swing by **Penlee House Gallery & Museum**, which owns a fine collection of paintings by artists of the Newlyn and Lamorna Schools, the group of late-19th-century artists who moved to the area and drew inspiration from scenes of rustic Cornish life. Their collection encompasses major names like Stanhope Forbes, Norman Garstin and Walter Langley, but what you see is a bit down to pot luck.

Green Spaces

PENZANCE'S GARDENS AND NATURE RESERVES

Three gardens lie within easy driving distance of Penzance.

For views, head for National Trust–owned **Trengwainton**, a walled garden near Madron which has a renowned collection of ferns, shrubs, magnolias and rhododendrons.

For art and sculpture, make a beeline for **Tremenheere Sculpture Gardens**, a plant-filled valley where site-specific artworks hide among the foliage.

And for wildlife, visit **Tanglewood Wild Garden**, a 3.5-hectare nature garden rescued and restored by owners Tony and Kerry Marr, or take a wander around **Marazion Marsh**, an RSPB (Royal Society for the Protection of Birds) reserve where you could spy everything from mallards and ducks to kingfishers and herons.

Bargain-Hunting

DIG FOR SECONDHAND TREASURE

Every Sunday, one of Cornwall's biggest car-boot sales takes over the main sports ground in the village of **Rosudgeon** (rosudgeoncarboot.co.uk). It's a vast affair, covering several fields, and there are normally a couple of food trucks catering to peckish punters. It tends to be bric-a-brac rather than antique, but then again, one person's tat is another's treasure.

ICE CREAM, ANYONE?

If you're an ice-cream connoisseur, you'll also want to taste-test **Moomaid of Zennor** (p196) and **Roskilly's** (p145) on the Lizard. All in the name of research, of course.

Dedicated delvers might also want to take a detour to **Shiver Me Timbers** (shivermetimberscornwall.co.uk), near Crowlas, a chaotic junkyard piled high with vintage furniture, reclaimed floorboards, vintage signs, old bathtubs and heaven knows what else. Happy hunting.

WHERE TO SLEEP AROUND PENZANCE

Artist Residence Penzance
This converted town house on Chapel St combines period architecture with a quirky modern style. £££

Old Coastguard Hotel
One of Cornwall's top shoreside hotels, offering gardens and sea views on the edge of Mousehole. £££

Venton Vean
A modern B&B in Penzance, finished in stylish greys and blues, with stripped wood floors and bay windows. ££

TONY MILLS/SHUTTERSTOCK ©

Common teal, Marazion Marsh

THE KING OF PRUSSIA

East of Marazion, the A394 road rolls through a string of nondescript villages on its way to the Lizard, but it's worth a detour to visit Prussia Cove. Named after a notorious smuggler and local hero, John Carter (who was nicknamed the King of Prussia because of his alleged resemblance to Frederick the Great), the cove now forms part of the private Porth-en-Alls Estate.

There are several other coves to explore nearby, including Bessy's Cove, King's Cove, Coule's Cove and Piskies Cove. Further up the coast is rocky Rinsey, surrounded by old mine-workings: it's usually a good spot for swimming as it's quite sheltered from prevailing winds.

Holy Island

WALK TO AN ISLAND ABBEY

Looming up in the middle of Mount's Bay and connected to the mainland by a cobbled tidal causeway, the iconic abbey-crowned island of **St Michael's Mount** is Cornwall's very own fairy-tale castle. There's been a monastery here since at least the 5th century, but the present abbey was mostly built by Benedictine monks (the same religious order that also constructed the island's sister abbey at Mont St-Michel in France) during the 12th century. Highlights of the main house include the rococo drawing room, the armoury and the 14th-century church, but it's the amazing clifftop gardens that really steal the show. Thanks to the local subclimate, many exotic flowers and shrubs flourish here, and it's all a riot of colour in summer.

The most atmospheric way to reach the Mount is via the cobbled causeway from Marazion, which can be crossed for around four hours around low tide, just as the pilgrims of old would have done. It's also the only way to get to the island in winter. The online booking system allows you to plan your crossing times; check out the website. From April to October, ferryboats run when the causeway is covered.

 WHERE TO GET A DRINK IN PENZANCE

Admiral Benbow
The salty old Benbow has nautical decor mostly reclaimed from shipwrecks: anchors, lanterns, figure-heads and all.

Turk's Head
Purportedly the town's oldest pub and once a smugglers' hang-out; it's said a secret tunnel leads to the harbour from the cellar.

Dolphin Inn
Maritime artefacts aplenty at this harbourside pub. It's claimed Walter Raleigh smoked England's first pipe of tobacco here.

MOUSEHOLE

A picturesque muddle of cottages and alleyways gathered behind a granite breakwater, Mousehole looks like something from a children's storybook (Antonia Barber set her fairy-tale *The Mousehole Cat* here).

This was once Cornwall's busiest pilchard port, but the fish dried up in the late 19th century, and the village now survives mostly on tourism.

Packed in summer and all but deserted in winter, it's ripe for a wander, with a maze of slips, old net lofts and courtyards to explore.

Don't miss a pint at the Ship Inn, which dates to the 1700s. On 23 December, it serves stargazey pie, a pilchard pie honouring local hero Tom Bawcock, who braved stormy seas to save the village from famine.

The Play's the Thing

THEATRE ON THE EDGE

Forget the West End: for Britain's most unforgettable night at the theatre, visit **Minack Theatre**. Carved into the crags overlooking Porthcurno and the azure Atlantic, this amazing clifftop amphitheatre was the lifelong passion of theatre lover Rowena Cade, who dreamt up the idea in the 1930s. It's now a hugely popular place for alfresco theatre, with plays staged from mid-May to mid-September. You can pre-book daytime visits to explore the terraces and take in the ocean views. Experienced theatregoers bring wine, picnic supplies, wet-weather gear and – most importantly, as the seats are carved out of granite – a comfy cushion.

On the Beach

SUNBATHE ON POSTCARD-PERFECT SANDS

Beneath the Minack lies the sandy wedge of **Porthcurno**, a hugely popular beach with excellent swimming and sunbathing (it gets very busy in season). Just around the headland, but only accessible by a perilously steep coastal trail, is **Pednvounder** (also known as Treen to locals) – spectacularly framed by towering cliffs – that attracts folks who prefer to sunbathe au naturel. Once a local secret, thanks to social media it's now overrun for much of summer, but off-season it's gloriously quiet. The walk down is not for the faint-hearted.

The Rocking Rock That Doesn't

WATCH THE SUNSET OVER A CORNISH LANDMARK

If the beach is too busy, follow the coast path along the headland to the craggy promontory of **Logan Rock** (pictured). Once, the eponymous boulder rocked back and forth on its own natural pivot (its name supposedly derives from the Cornish verb *log,* meaning 'to rock', often used to describe a drunken man). The rock was knocked off its perch in 1871 by a young naval lieutenant by the name of Hugh Goldsmith. It was later restored at great expense, but never rocked again. The surrounding sheer cliffs are now popular with climbers; take care if you're walking out to it, as the drops are very real. It's a stunning spot for sunset; the nearby **Logan Rock Inn** is ideal for supper.

GETTING AROUND

Penzance is the last stop on the line from London Paddington. It's a handy bus hub, with regular services to St Ives and Land's End, including open-top double-deckers in summer. Penzance is also the home dock for the *Scillonian III,* which sails to the Isles of Scilly between April and September.

ISLES OF SCILLY

While only 28 miles west of the mainland, in many ways the Isles of Scilly feels like a different world altogether. Life on this little archipelago seems hardly to have changed in decades: there are no traffic jams, no supermarkets, no multinational hotels, and the only noise pollution comes from breaking waves and cawing gulls. Life ticks along at its own island pace; after a few days here, stepping off the boat at Penzance Dock comes as a real culture shock.

Only five of the islands are inhabited: St Mary's is the largest, followed by Tresco, while a handful of hardy souls live on Bryher, St Martin's and St Agnes. Regular ferry boats run between all five islands. The archipelago is renowned for its beaches, and there are few places better to escape – but, unsurprisingly, summer is by far the busiest time. Many Scilly businesses shut down completely in winter.

Isles of Scilly

TOP TIP

Bad weather and fog often play havoc with the islands' travel schedules, so it's worth checking on the latest status before you set out – the IOS Travel (@IOSTravel) Twitter account is very useful.

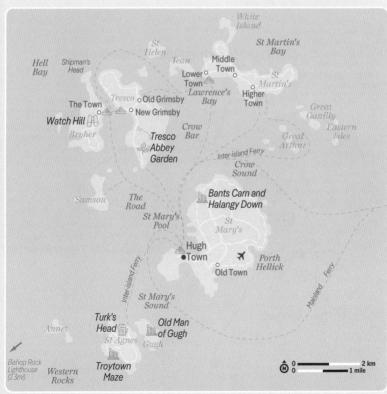

White Island

Hell Bay

Shipman's Head

St Helen

Tean

St Martin's Bay

Middle Town

Lower Town

St Martin's

Old Grimsby

Lawrence's Bay

Higher Town

Tresco

New Grimsby

The Town

Watch Hill

Bryher

Crow Bar

Great Gunilly

Eastern Isles

Tresco Abbey Garden

Great Arthur

Inter-island Ferry

Crow Sound

Samson

The Road

St Mary's Pool

Bants Carn and Halangy Down

St Mary's

Hugh Town

Inter-island Ferry

Old Town

Porth Hellick

Mainland Ferry

St Mary's Sound

Annet

Turk's Head

St Agnes

Old Man of Gugh

Gugh

Bishop Rock Lighthouse (2.3mi)

Western Rocks

Troytown Maze

0 — 2 km
0 — 1 mile

CYCLING AROUND ST MARY'S

First stop for every visitor to the Isles of Scilly is St Mary's, the largest and busiest of the islands – but at just over 3 miles at its widest point and covering an area of roughly 6 sq miles, it's hardly huge. It can be easily circumnavigated in a half-day bike ride, or a full day via the coast path. Bikes can be hired from St Mary's Bike Hire in **1 Hugh Town**, the island's main settlement and the docking point for the *Scillonian III* ferry. Alternatively, less able visitors could hire a motorised buggy from Scilly Carts.

First off, make a circuit of the headland southwest of town to see the **2 Garrison**, the imposing fort that guards the approaches to Hugh Town. Have a paddle on **3 Porthcressa Beach**, then head back through Hugh Town and up the island's west coast past **4 Porthmellon Beach** and **5 Porthloo Beach** for a coffee and some cake at **6 Juliet's Garden**, a long-standing restaurant with fantastic views. Continue onwards around **7 Halangy Down** (p210) to see the area's many prehistoric remains.

After that, loop round for a tipple at the **8 Holy Vale Winery** (p213) in Maypole, St Mary's own boutique vineyard. Have a swim at **9 Pelistry Bay**, then spin along the south coast past the island's airport to Old Town Bay, where the **10 Old Town Cafe** and **11 Bondy's Cafe** both make good spots for lunch. Take a detour along King Edward's Rd to see the lighthouse at **12 Peninnis Head**, then ride downhill back into Hugh Town, for a coffee at **13 Dibble and Grub** and a cooling dip at Porthcressa, or perhaps a refreshing pint at the **14 Mermaid Inn**.

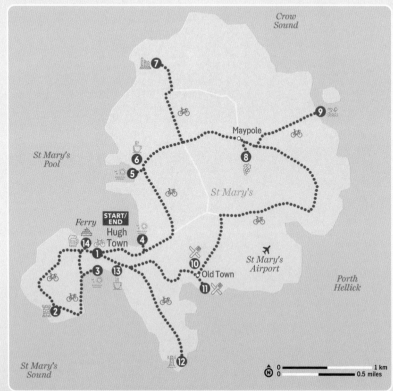

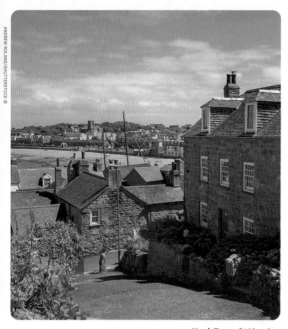

ANDREW ROLAND/SHUTTERSTOCK ©

Hugh Town, St Mary's

Island Insights

EXPLORE ST MARY'S WILDLIFE AND HISTORY

Scilly local and resident ornithologist Will Wagstaff is the undisputed authority on the islands' natural history. He runs fascinating walks in search of birdlife, insects and other creatures across various islands through his company **Island Wildlife Tours**. For a different side of the archipelago, book a spot with **Scilly Walks**, three-hour historical tours exploring the islands' past, conducted by local historian and archaeologist Katherine Sawyer. And to understand Scilly's coastal habitats, take a guided walk with **Scilly Rockpool Safaris**, whose guides know all the best spots to turn up starfish, sea anemones, brittlestars and Cornish clingfish.

All tours run regularly on St Mary's, with occasional walks on other islands too. Book ahead to be sure of a spot, and remember to add on the cost of the boat transfer if you're transferring to other islands.

GIG ROWING

The six-oared wooden boats, or 'pilot gigs', were once a common sight around Cornwall's shores, and were mostly used for transporting goods and passengers from tall ships too large to moor in the shallow coastal harbours.

These days the boats are used for gig racing, a highly competitive and physically demanding sport. Every April or May, St Mary's hosts the World Pilot Gig Championships, which attracts teams from as far afield as the Netherlands, Canada and Australia. There's not a bed to be found during the event, so book well ahead if you want to attend.

Even if you're not here for the gig-racing regatta, you'll often spot local teams practising in the waters around St Mary's. Organised races are held most weekends.

WHERE TO STAY ON THE ISLES OF SCILLY

Star Castle
This former fort on Garrison Point is St Mary's top hotel. Heritage-style rooms, incredible island views. **£££**

New Inn
Tresco's pub offers smart rooms and a cosy beamed atmosphere; sea-view rooms command a premium. **£££**

Hell Bay Hotel
This Bryher getaway has the feel of a luxurious beach villa, lovingly tended gardens and an excellent restaurant. **£££**

THE BOATMEN OF SCILLY

For more than five decades, St Mary's Boatmen's Association (scillyboating.co.uk) has provided the vital transport links between the islands, operating year-round ferries between St Mary's and the smaller islands surrounding it.

Services usually run at least daily between April and October, leaving St Mary's in the morning and usually returning in the afternoon. There's a reduced service in winter.

The boatmen also offer wildlife-watching trips, a cruise out to see the lighthouse at Bishop Rock and a drop-off at Samson, as well as an evening supper boat to St Agnes.

Prehistoric Scilly

TRAVEL BACK IN ISLAND TIME

Astonishing as it may seem, this far-flung archipelago was being visited long before Christianity came to the British Isles. Dolmens, burial tombs and settlements are scattered over many of the islands, especially St Mary's. On **Halangy Down** in the island's northwest, the remains of an Iron Age village can be visited, consisting of one large courtyard house and several smaller roundhouses dating from around 200 BCE, complete with hearths and exterior walls. They clearly liked a good sea view, even back in the Iron Age.

On the edge of Halangy Down is **Bant's Carn**, a well-preserved Neolithic chamber tomb. It dates from between 4500 BCE and 3000 BCE, and was probably the burial site of an important chieftain or notable family.

Tresco Treasures

AN ISLAND PARADISE BY BIKE

A short boat trip across the channel from St Mary's brings you to **Tresco**, the second largest of the Scilly islands. Its key attraction – and one of Scilly's must-see gems – is **Tresco Abbey Garden**, laid out in 1834 on the site of a 12th-century Benedictine priory by the horticultural visionary Augustus Smith. The 7-hectare gardens are now home to more than 20,000 exotic species, from towering palms to desert cacti and crimson flame trees, all nurtured by the temperate Gulf Stream. Admission also covers the Valhalla Collection, an outdoor museum made up of figureheads and nameplates salvaged from the many ships wrecked off Tresco. Wandering around the gardens feels like discovering your very own secret garden; look out for red squirrels as you explore.

Two-wheeled transport is pretty much the only option on Tresco. Bikes can be hired from the bike shack next to Tresco Stores.

Exploring the Coastline

PADDLE AROUND TRESCO'S COAST

Tresco looks even lovelier when you explore it from the water. The **Raven's Porth Sailing Base**, linked with the sailing centre on St Mary's, hires out sit-on kayaks and paddleboards that enable you to explore the island's crumpled coastline with freedom, and seek out beaches you'd otherwise miss from the land.

 WHERE TO EAT ON THE ISLES OF SCILLY ─────────

Juliet's Garden
St Mary's top bistro has been in business for three decades and is still the best place on the island to eat. ££

New Inn
Tresco's pub serves tasty soul food and a good range of local ales from Cornish breweries. ££

Hell Bay Hotel
Fine dining at Bryher's luxe hotel. For something simpler, try the homely Crab Shack in the garden. £££

Hell Bay, Bryher

WHY I LOVE THE ISLES OF SCILLY

Oliver Berry
@olivertomberry

'It's barely a couple of hours away by sea (and 20 minutes by plane), but every time I visit Scilly I feel like I'm travelling into another country.

Life feels different here: time seems to pass more slowly, you feel closer to the elements and more connected with the forces of nature.

I've been to the islands in all weathers (even stuck for a week or two during a wild winter storm), but no matter when I go, they never fail to fascinate me. And they're home to two of my favourite pubs in the world: the Turk's Head on St Agnes and the Seven Stones on St Martin's. I can't think of anywhere more perfect for a pint.'

Around Bryher on Foot

CIRCUMNAVIGATE BRYHER'S COAST PATH

Only around 80 people live on **Bryher**, Scilly's smallest and wildest inhabited island. Covered by rough bracken and heather, and fringed by white sand, this slender chunk of rock takes a fearsome battering from the Atlantic – the grand sandy beach at **Hell Bay** hasn't earned its ominous name for nothing. But on a bright sunny day, it's an island idyll, ideal for exploring on foot. A coast path runs right around the island's perimeter, and takes you past little island studios, pop-up tearooms and little stalls selling freshly cut flowers, homegrown veg, jams and packets of fudge.

It's worth climbing up to the summit of **Watch Hill**, from where you can get a panorama right across the archipelago. It's a superb spot to sit and watch the sunset, but – in the words of the locals – it can be hellish windy up top. The hill gets its name from the days of the tall ships, when watchers would sit on the summit and look out for masts, then signal down to pilots who would row out to meet the ships.

Adam's Fish & Chips
Fish as fresh as can be on St Martin's – what's caught on the day makes it into your batter. **£**

Island Bakery
Gorgeous organic breads, Cornish pasties, pies and takeaway pizzas on St Martin's. **£**

Troytown Farm Ice Cream
Small-batch ice cream from the dairy herd on St Agnes' farm – seriously good. **£**

Turk's Head, St Agnes

THE UNINHABITED ISLANDS

There are over 100 islands in the Scilly archipelago, most of which are only frequented by seals and seabirds – although a few once had human populations.

The largest of these is Samson, south of Bryher, which has been abandoned since 1855. The only signs that anyone ever lived here are a few crumbling cottages, all but swallowed up by the bracken and gorse. It feels fantastically isolated, and is great for bird-spotting. At low tide the remains of fields swamped during the last ice age become visible at Samson Flats.

Day trips can be arranged with local boatmen on St Mary's and Bryher; you might also be able to visit other uninhabited islands including St Helen's, Teän and Annet.

Into the Briny Blue

SEALS AND WILD SWIMS

Living on these far-flung islands certainly has its challenges, but there's one thing that Scilly isn't short of – and that's finding somewhere to go for a swim.

All the islands offer fantastic swimming and snorkelling. Based on St Mary's, **Wild and Scilly Mermaids** knows all the best spots, and will happily share them on one of its Adventure Swims, which combine a wild-swimming session with an alfresco picnic. You're in very safe hands: Ruth is a chef and Anna is a paramedic.

Over on St Martin's, **Scilly Seal Snorkelling** offers the chance to swim with wild grey seals in the clear waters off the island. The more inquisitive ones come right up close – and the boldest have even been known to nibble your fins. Trips last about three hours, and you can get collected from your accommodation on St Martin's, or catch a morning transfer from Tresco or St Mary's.

For deeper water, contact **St Martin's Dive School**, which rents out gear to qualified divers and also gives tips on the top dive spots.

 WHERE TO CAMP ON THE ISLES OF SCILLY

Bryher Campsite
Bare-bones but beautiful, the island's campsite sits in a secluded spot just steps from the sea. £

St Martin's Campsite
Scilly's second-largest campsite, at the western end of Lawrence's Bay, spread across three fields. £

Troytown Farm
Located on St Agnes' sunset coast, surrounded by drystone walls and a sea-blue, big-sky horizon. £

St Agnes Stroll

GET LOST ON ST AGNES

Scilly's southernmost island, **St Agnes**, feels really remote, with a string of empty coves and a scattering of intriguing prehistoric sites. You'll be dropped off at Porth Conger, near the old lighthouse, from where you wander along the coast path around the whole island.

At low tide, a narrow sandbar appears and provides a land bridge to the neighbouring island of Gugh, where many ancient burial sites and a few chamber tombs can be found, along with the slanting 3m-high menhir known as the **Old Man of Gugh**. Make sure you check the tides to avoid being cut off. The St Agnes coast path also leads to the **Troytown Maze**, a concentric maze of stones that's thought to be around two centuries old, but might be based on a prehistoric original.

Finish the day with a pint at St Agnes' wonderful pub, the **Turk's Head**, which also happens to be Britain's most southerly alehouse. It's covered in maritime memorabilia – model ships in glass cabinets, vintage maps of the islands, black-and-white photos of seafarers.

Escape to the Outer Isles

FARAWAY SCILLY

Still not quite managed to leave the outside world behind? Then you'll want to arrange a boat trip to the most remote corners of Scilly, including the wild **Eastern Isles**, the many shipwreck spots around the **Western Rocks**, and the famous **Bishop Rock Lighthouse** (pictured right), a marvel of 19th-century engineering raised on a narrow sliver of rock barely 46m long by 16m wide. Regular and bespoke boat trips are run by local boat companies: contact St Mary's Boatmen's Association (p210) to see what's on offer, or join **St Agnes Boating** for one of its weekly wildlife trips.

SCILLY VINTAGES

Strange as it may seem, Scilly's climate is actually ideal for grape growing.

The island has two working vineyards: Holy Vale Winery on St Mary's and the longer established St Martin's Vineyard, which has been producing its own range of organic white, rosé and red wines since 1996.

Tastings are available most days at Holy Vale, while at St Martin's you can also follow a self-guided tour around the vines, or book in for a tasting flight.

GETTING AROUND

Bookings for flights and ferries are handled by the Isles of Scilly Travel Centre in Penzance. There's a small enquiries office in Hugh Town on St Mary's.

The cheapest (and slowest) route to the islands is aboard the *Scillonian III* passenger ferry from Penzance to St Mary's. The crossing takes about three hours; the ferry only runs between April and October. Much faster (just over 20 minutes), but prone to bad-weather cancellation, is to fly. Regular flights run to St

Mary's from Land's End Airport, near Zennor, as well as Newquay and Exeter, or you can catch a chopper with Penzance Helicopters.

The ferry generally goes in all but the worst weather. On the islands, if your return flight is grounded, you'll usually be transferred to the next departing ferry. Note that the last ferry of the day usually departs at 4.30pm. Special day-trip fares allow you to catch an early flight, and either the ferry or an afternoon flight home.

TOOLKIT

The chapters in this section cover the most important topics you'll need to know about in Devon & Cornwall. They're full of nuts-and-bolts information and valuable insights to help you understand and navigate Devon & Cornwall and get the most out of your trip.

Arriving
p216

Getting Around
p217

Money
p218

Accommodation
p219

Health & Safe Travel
p220

Safety on Moors & Beaches
p221

Food, Drink & Nightlife
p222

Responsible Travel
p224

LGBTiQ+ Travellers
p226

Accessible Travel
p227

Family Travel
p228

Nuts & Bolts
p229

Sloop Inn (p193), St Ives

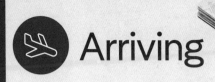

Arriving

Most visitors to Devon and Cornwall come by car, but public transport is improving. Exeter and Plymouth are major transport hubs with direct rail connections to London and Bristol. Exeter Airport and Cornwall Airport Newquay provide air links with the rest of the UK and some international destinations, though for most overseas visitors the closest major airports are in London.

Sleeper train

An overnight train runs from London to Cornwall; it's one of just two in the UK. The Night Riviera Sleeper departs London Paddington at 11.45pm, arriving in Penzance at 8am.

Ferries

Overseas visitors wishing to bring their own car can take the Roscoff–Plymouth ferry from France (between six and eight hours). On the Devon–Cornwall border, Plymouth provides easy access to both.

Congestion

The vast majority of visitors come by car. During peak seasons this can lead to serious traffic jams – in summer, delays of over two hours on the drive from London are not uncommon.

SIM cards

International visitors to the UK can pick up local 'pay as you go' SIM cards in newsagents and supermarkets and top up with a prepaid data package.

Public Transport from Airport to City Centre

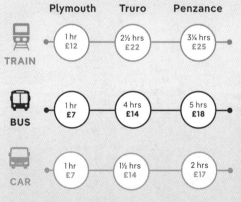

	Plymouth	Truro	Penzance
TRAIN	1 hr £12	2½ hrs £22	3¼ hrs £25
BUS	1 hr £7	4 hrs £14	5 hrs £18
CAR	1 hr £7	1½ hrs £14	2 hrs £17

ATLANTIC HIGHWAY

For most arrivals to the southwest, the central A30 is the more direct driving route through Devon and Cornwall, forging a 284-mile straight line from West London to Land's End.

A longer, but more scenic, option is to detour onto the north-coast-hugging A39, grandly nicknamed the Atlantic Highway. Running southwest from Bath to Falmouth, the road follows the north coast most of the way, after a short stint through the Somerset countryside. It's a popular road-trip route, with sea views, good driving conditions and plentiful stop-offs along the way.

Getting Around

Driving offers more freedom and the ability to reach remote areas not served by bus. However, decent public transport networks exist; using them helps ease the southwest's seasonal congestion.

TRAVEL COSTS

Car rental
Approx. £43/day

Petrol
Approx. £1.61/litre

Bike rental
£17/day

Advance train ticket from Exeter to Truro
from £16.20

Renting a Car

Cars can be hired in most major towns and cities and at airports. Opting for a smaller car may help with parking in busy beach towns and navigating narrow country lanes. Most cars in the UK are manual; renting an automatic can drive costs up.

Road Conditions

Driving conditions are generally good, especially on main A-roads. However, serious congestion is common at peak times, such as British school holidays and public holidays. In rural areas, roads are often winding and single-lane; be ready to reverse if you meet oncoming vehicles.

TIP

Phone signals can be non-existent in rural areas. Download offline maps to your phone or satnav in advance.

RURAL ETIQUETTE

The speed limit on country roads is usually 60mph, but it's rarely safe to drive that fast. Exercise caution, especially if the area is unfamiliar. When meeting someone coming the other way on a single-lane road, the general etiquette is for the driver nearest a passing place to reverse, but try to give way to vehicles coming uphill. Horse riders will usually stop for cars to pass; slow down and give them as much room as you can.

DRIVING ESSENTIALS

Drive on the left

National speed limit on single carriageway is 60pmh

35mg

Breath-alcohol limit per 100mL of blood

Public Transport

Most towns and villages are served by fairly decent bus networks, although in rural areas these can be frustratingly slow and infrequent. In popular areas, seasonal hop-on/hop-off tourist buses are common; these are convenient but usually more costly than public buses.

Train Tickets

Travel costs vary wildly on trains. Travelling off-peak can dramatically reduce costs, and advance tickets are usually cheaper (often by around 50%), so book early if possible. If you plan on travelling by train frequently, purchasing an annual railcard from National Rail can help reduce costs.

Car Parking

Several parking apps allow for easy, cash-free payments in car parks across the UK. Devon's car parks tend to use RingGo, Cornwall's JustPark. Download both in advance of your trip. It's still a good idea to carry some small change for the smaller, rural car parks.

£ Money

CURRENCY: **POUND STERLING (GBP) £**

Card Payments

Most businesses are able to accept contactless card and smartphone payments, including buses, most car parks and small businesses such as food stalls.

However, it's wise to carry some cash just in case. Visa and MasterCard are widely accepted, but other credit cards less so.

Free Admission

Devon and Cornwall have plentiful free attractions. National parks have free admission, as do almost all beaches and many museums.

Tipping

Restaurants Tip 10% to 15% in restaurants with table service. Some add tips to the bill automatically as a discretionary 'service charge'.

Pubs & bars Tipping is not expected if you order and pay at the bar.

Taxis Round the fare up to the nearest pound, or add 10% for good service.

Discounts

Occasionally, several attractions offer discounted joint tickets. A student card gets you reduced admission to most attractions; many also give discounts to seniors.

HOW MUCH FOR A...

Adult day pass for a hop-on hop-off bus
£5–10

Historic property visit
£12

Surfboard rental
£17

Train ticket Truro to Falmouth
£5

HOW TO... SAVE MONEY ON HERITAGE

Many of Devon and Cornwall's heritage properties are owned by either the **National Trust** or **English Heritage**. Both offer annual memberships allowing entry to all attractions, as well as temporary memberships for overseas visitors. These can be well worth purchasing if you plan on visiting several attractions. National Trust membership includes free car parking at a number of beauty spots throughout the southwest.

Scan this QR code for the National Trust guide to Devon

Scan this QR code for the National Trust guide to Cornwall

SEASONAL SPIKES

The time of year you visit can have a big impact on how much a trip to Devon and Cornwall will cost. Summertime is peak season, with the region getting particularly busy during the British school holidays and bank holidays. Travel costs, especially accommodation, can rise significantly at peak times. The shoulder seasons of May and September are often quieter and cheaper times to visit (with the exception of the Easter holidays) and can still have good weather. Midweek prices are also, in general, lower than weekends.

LOCAL TIP

Local newspapers can be a good source for money-off vouchers, as can social media. Many businesses announce upcoming special offers on their own channels and in local Facebook groups.

Accommodation

Camp Out

Devon and Cornwall's outdoorsy vibes and wide swathes of countryside are perfect for camping and caravanning adventures, with pitches starting from around £12. Campsites range from the ultra-basic (think field with a Portaloo) to holiday parks with swimming pools. The trend for glamping has swept through the region; many sites offer bell tents with wood burners, wooden shepherds' huts and retro caravans.

Home Away from Home

Self-catering accommodation is one of the most popular options for visitors to the southwest, especially families and large groups. There's a wide range of properties available to suit all budgets and tastes, ranging from historic cottages to luxurious barn conversions and chic city-centre flats.

Budget Sleeps

For budget travellers, hikers and cyclists there are many good options. In rural areas and national parks, bunkhouses and camping barns provide basic, dorm-style accommodation – but you'll still need to bring a sleeping bag and camping gear. There are 16 YHA hostels and several independent hostels across Devon and Cornwall, with dorm beds starting from around £25.

HOW MUCH FOR A NIGHT IN...

a campsite
£20

a seaside B&B
£120

a luxurious country manor
£210

A touch of luxury

The southwest is scattered with historic countryside manors turned luxury hotels. Expect to pay upwards of £200 a night for the chance to sleep like royalty in one of these lavish country piles. Many smaller boutique hotels and independent B&Bs are similarly luxurious – although plenty of midrange and cheaper options also exist in all tourist areas.

Cosy Pubs

Across the southwest, ancient inns and cosy county pubs offer hearty British meals, local ales and comfy places to spend the night – usually right at the heart of a community. The range is vast, from stylishly renovated spaces to poky rooms bordering on seedy. Prices vary massively, too, from around £50/70 for a single/double to £100/160 and above.

NEGATIVE IMPACT

Airbnb and similar holiday-home rental sites have long been a point of contention for locals in Devon and Cornwall (p238). On the one hand, these sites offer property-owning locals the opportunity to make additional income from their homes. On the other, there's a rise in people buying up properties solely to lease as holiday homes. This has had an impact on the housing market, creating scarcity and driving up property and rental prices, and generally making it harder for locals to find a place to live.

Health & Safe Travel

HEALTH & SAFE TRAVEL

Insurance is not compulsory for travelling to the UK, but it's good to have – even for British citizens. At the time of writing, those visiting the UK from an EU country or Switzerland can use the European Health Insurance Card (EHIC) to obtain free emergency medical treatment, including pre-existing medical conditions and routine maternity care.

Fires

Droughts and extreme summer temperatures are increasingly common. In the rural southwest, this brings a risk of wildfires, often caused by negligence. Disposable barbecues are among the worst offenders; many people are calling for a total ban. During hot, dry weather, don't have any barbecues or campfires on grassland, take extreme care with cigarettes and take all litter home.

Sunburn & Heatstroke

Sunburn is a common issue in southwest England during summer and can increase the risk of skin cancer. Avoid the sun between 11am and 3pm, cover up with suitable clothing and use water-resistant suncream. Very high temperatures can also cause heat exhaustion and heatstroke: stay hydrated, avoid intense exercise and avoid excess alcohol.

WATER

Tap water is safe to drink and of good quality throughout Devon and Cornwall.

RURAL ROAD SIGNS

Narrow or single-track road flag
Be prepared to use passing places.

Hump bridge
These can be narrow; approach slowly.

River crossing
These may be impassable after heavy rain. Test your brakes after crossing.

Accompanied horses or ponies
Slow down to pass. Similar signs warn of other animals, eg cattle or deer.

Slippery road
Slow down as road surface may be wet or slippery.

Wildlife

Adders Britain's only venomous snake, common in the region's heaths, moors and coast paths. They attack if threatened. The poison is usually of little danger to healthy adults, but bites are painful and require medical attention.

Ticks Common in grassy and wooded areas. Generally harmless but some carry Lyme disease. Use insect repellent and wear long trousers when hiking.

CRIME

According to official statistics, Devon and Cornwall have the lowest crime rates in England and Wales. But don't let that lull you into being less vigilant than you would anywhere else. Local police advise tourists not to leave valuables unattended on the beach or in cars, and to keep anything left in vehicles out of sight.

Safety on Moors & Beaches

Red and yellow flag
Lifeguarded area and the safest area to swim.

Red flag
Danger: do not go in the water under any circumstances.

Black and white flag
Area for surfboards, kayaks and other non-powered craft. Never swim or bodyboard here.

Orange windsock
Offshore wind or unsafe conditions – don't use inflatables.

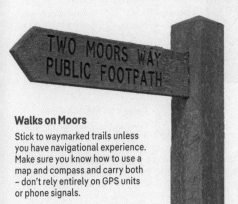

Walks on Moors

Stick to waymarked trails unless you have navigational experience. Make sure you know how to use a map and compass and carry both – don't rely entirely on GPS units or phone signals.

MILITARY TRAINING RANGES

The Ministry of Defence (MOD) has several training areas in Dartmoor and on the coast. Most allow public access or have a permissive path, except when in use for live firing – announced by red flags or red lamps at night. Check firing times at *gov.uk*. Always stick to footpaths in these areas, and if you come across any unidentified metal objects, don't touch them. Mark the location and inform the police or MOD.

Bogs & Rivers

Moors are wet places and bogs are common. Stick to firmer ground, even if it means going the long way around. If unsure of a patch of ground, use a walking pole or stick to test the depth before stepping.

Heavy rainfall can cause rivers to rise very fast. Always have an alternative route planned.

Tides & Currents

Always check tide times when exploring areas affected by tidal water and know when the incoming tide is due to avoid being cut off.

When swimming, be wary of rip currents. If caught in one, call for help, keep hold of any buoyancy aids and swim parallel to the shore – *not* against the current.

Mist is a frequent hazard on higher moors. Check the weather before setting out and make sure you know exactly where you are at all times.

Food, Drink & Nightlife

When to Eat

Breakfast From 8am to 10am, though brunch is served until midday in many places. The 'Full English' is a classic when dining out.

Lunch Noon to 3pm. Many places offer a cheaper lunch menu or two-course fixed-price special.

Dinner From 6pm to 9pm or 10pm. Most Brits eat around 6pm to 9pm at home; dining out very late is uncommon.

Where to Eat & Drink

Cafe Casual eatery that usually serves breakfasts and light lunches. Often called a 'caff' locally.

Tearoom Serves cakes, teas and light lunches.

Pub Drinking establishment which often serves food. Gastropubs place more emphasis on food.

Bar Serves drinks but isn't a pub. Bars tend to be more contemporary, open later and don't serve food.

Fish and chip shop ('Chippy') Classic seaside takeaway establishment.

Restaurant Anywhere with table service and sit-down dining that isn't a pub or cafe.

MENU DECODER

Nibbles Very small dishes, such as a bowl of olives, ordered before a meal.

Courses Three is standard – starter, main and dessert.

Supper Another name for the evening meal. Confusingly, 'tea' is also a common term for dinner in southern England.

Set menu Dishes that can be ordered together for a fixed price (two or three courses).

Pudding Dessert

Tasting menu Fixed-price menu with multiple courses of smaller dishes.

Cream tea Scones served with clotted cream, jam and a pot of tea.

Afternoon tea A meal composed of small finger sandwiches, scones and a selection of cakes.

Pub classics Dishes traditionally found in British pubs. Includes fish and chips, pie and mash, sausage and mash, and ham with egg and chips.

HOW TO... forage on the coastline

Foraging is undergoing a revival in the UK and can be a fun way to add local flavour to your cooking. Devon and Cornwall's coastlines provide particularly rich foraging grounds – below are some of the top things to look for. Only eat something if you're 100% sure what it is.

Rock samphire (May to September) Popular wild herb with an intense flavour, often partnered with fish. Find it on coastal cliffs.

Sea kale (June to August) Grows on shingle beaches. Can be eaten raw or cooked and shredded like cabbage.

Purple laver (all year) Edible seaweed, particularly common on the north Devon coast. Used to make the Welsh dish laverbread.

Cockles (all year) Shellfish found on estuary beaches. Boil them for a couple of minutes until the shells open.

Mussels (don't collect between May and August) Pick them straight from the rocks at low tide.

HOW MUCH FOR A...

Pasty
£4

Takeaway
fish and chips
£10

Ice cream
£2.50

Cream tea
£7

Pub lunch
£12

Pint of cider
£3.50

Dinner at a high-
end restaurant
from £50

Glass of wine
(175mL)
£6

HOW TO...

eat a cream tea

Few baked goods are as hotly debated as the humble scone – and few debates are as quaintly British! From how to eat it to how to say it, the arguments are endless, impassioned and (mostly) good-humoured.

How to say it? There's about a 50/50 split in England between pronouncing scone to rhyme with 'gone' and with 'bone' – in the southwest, the former is more common. It also happens to be how Queen Elizabeth pronounced the word, which for many is an end to the argument.

Jam or cream first? A cream tea is common in southwest England, involving a pot of tea, a scone (or two), jam and cream. And this is the basis of the next debate: does one apply the jam first or the cream? In Devon, it's cream then jam while, west of the Tamar, the Cornish say it should be jam first, then cream. There are, however, dissenters in both counties. Asking a local their preference is always a good ice-breaker.

When to eat it? Traditionally, cream tea is eaten around 3pm or 4pm as a smaller version of afternoon tea. But you can order it at any time of day. Cream tea makes a good light lunch; some places offer savoury versions with cheese scones and cream cheese.

Who started it?

Both Devon and Cornwall claim the cream tea as their own, but local historians suggest the southwest's favourite dish was created by Benedictine monks at Tavistock Abbey as long ago as the 11th century!

GOING OUT

A night out in the southwest can mean a lot of different things. British comedian Micky Flanagan coined the popular phrase 'going out-out' to explain the difference between a casual evening having some drinks in a pub (going out) and a night out drinking, dancing and staying out late ('out-out').

Going 'out-out' often starts with dinner or some 'pre-drinks' at a quieter spot like a cosy pub or swanky cocktail bar, before moving onto a nightclub. Clubs usually start picking up around 11pm or later, closing around 2am or as late as 4am on weekends. In Devon and Cornwall, bars and pubs are much more common than nightclubs, which have been declining across the UK over the last 15 years – and more so since the COVID-19 pandemic – with more and more people favouring smaller venues.

There's also an increasing trend towards activity-based nights out in the UK, and the southwest is no exception. Live music and quiz nights have always been popular, but more unique offerings like retro arcades, board-game cafes and games bars are on the rise. In Exeter and Plymouth, Boom Battle Bar combines drinks with things like shuffleboard and augmented-reality axe throwing, and similar venues are popping up across Devon and Cornwall.

If you're looking for lively nightlife, the three cities of Plymouth, Exeter and Truro have the best options, along with the university town of Falmouth and the (sometimes rowdy) surfer hub of Newquay.

Responsible Travel

Climate Change & Travel

It's impossible to ignore the impact we have when travelling, and the importance of making changes where we can. Lonely Planet urges all travellers to engage with their travel carbon footprint. There are many carbon calculators online that enable travellers to estimate the carbon emissions generated by their journey; try resurgence. org/resources/carbon-calculator.html. Many airlines and booking sites offer travellers the option of offsetting the impact of greenhouse gas emissions by contributing to climate-friendly initiatives around the world. We continue to offset the carbon footprint of all Lonely Planet staff travel, while recognising this is a mitigation more than a solution.

Stargazing

Stargaze at the **International Dark Sky Reserve** in Exmoor, where the National Park Authority actively works with local councils, businesses and communities to reduce light pollution.

Help with a Survey

Support local conservation initiatives by helping **East Devon Conservation Volunteers** (eastdevon.gov.uk) with things like scrub clearance and wildlife surveys, or volunteer with **Shoresearch** (cornwall wildlifetrust.org.uk) to survey marine environments while you're at the beach.

Surf & Protect

Approved in 2022, the **North Devon Surfing Reserve** is the UK's only World Surfing Reserve, protecting around 18 miles of coastline. Download the **Save the Waves** (savethewaves.org) app to report and track coastal threats.

Regional Rankings

The 2022 Thriving Places Index ranked Devon as one of the most sustainable counties in England. Cornwall's sustainability score was lower, but both counties scored highly for equality and community.

Take a wild-food foraging course with **Wild Walks South West** (wildwalks-southwest.co.uk) to learn how to enjoy this fun foodie trend in a low-impact, sustainable way.

Visit animal sanctuaries for a fun day out where your ticket fee helps support rescue and conservation work; don't miss the **Cornish Seal Sanctuary** (p144), **Exmoor Owl and Hawk Centre** (p115) and **Donkey Sanctuary Sidmouth** (p59).

Grab a litter picker and plastic bag from one of the **#2MinuteBeach Clean** stations found on beaches across the region and spend two minutes clearing litter. Find your nearest station at *2minute.org*.

Grab a coffee at **No Limits Cafe**, a training cafe in Newton Abbot that helps young people with additional needs learn new skills and gain work experience – aiding the transition into paid work.

Shop for local arts and crafts at **MAKE Southwest** (crafts.org.uk) in Bovey Tracey.

Sip a cocktail made with **Two Drifters Rum** – small-batch, carbon-negative rum made in Exeter.

Buy Local
Pick up fresh, local ingredients directly from suppliers at farmers markets like the ones at Helston (Cornwall's biggest), Truro, Totnes and Tavistock, the latter voted the best in the southwest.

Take the Bus
Summertime congestion around coastal towns is a huge problem for both local communities and the environment. Ditch the car and stick to public transport, or hike the coastal trails (southwestcoastpath.org.uk).

Transition Town
Take a Transition Walk with **Transition Town Totnes** (transitiontowntotnes.org) to learn more about Devon's most ethical town (p85). See what other events they're running to join in with a volunteer day or communal gardening session.

Public transport is generally more ecofriendly than driving, especially in Plymouth, where a new fleet of low-carbon emission-certified buses have been introduced on routes in low-air-quality areas.

---

nationalparks.uk
Find out more about the area's parks.

wildlifetrusts.org
Information on protected nature reserves and volunteering opportunities.

countryside-jobs.com
To find volunteering opportunities.

LGBTIQ+ Travellers

Like in the rest of the UK, the attitude towards LGBTIQ+ travellers in the southwest is generally tolerant and welcoming. Pride events are on the rise, as are LGBTIQ-friendly accommodation options and bars/clubs – although there's not always a big selection. That said, issues sadly still exist throughout the UK, ranging from mild hostility and ignorance to outright homophobia.

Nightlife

You'll find a scattering of LGBTIQ+ clubs and bars across the southwest – especially in larger towns such as Exeter and Truro – though they aren't always specifically advertised as such. For the best party scene, head to Plymouth. The largest city in the region and a lively university town, Plymouth has a small but growing 'Gay Village' with three popular LGBTIQ+ bars.

Rainbow Riviera

The English Riviera has long been popular with the LGBTIQ+ community, and Torquay in particular is emerging as one of the region's more gay-friendly destinations. Soho Bar is a popular LGBTIQ+ nightlife spot, and there are some fabulous events throughout the year, from Pride celebrations to drag acts.

SMALLTOWN MINDSETS

Though outright hostility is generally uncommon, you may encounter minor hostilities such as misjudged jokes or funny looks. In smaller towns and rural areas, LGBTIQ+ communities are sometimes less visible, and most issues arise from a lack of understanding rather than from any malice or hostility.

NEGATIVE ATTITUDES

Sadly, intolerance can be an issue in the southwest. In 2022, Newquay Pride was targeted by a homophobic leafletting campaign, and later that year the Drag Queen Story Hour tour met protests throughout the region (and worldwide). Recent statistics suggest sexual-orientation-based hate crimes are rising, though local authorities believe this is at least partly because more people are actually reporting crimes.

RESOURCES

Intercom Trust (intercomtrust.org.uk) is a local charity providing resources and support for the southwest's LGBTIQ+ communities; its website lists local LGBTIQ+ groups. Search for LGBTIQ+ accommodation on **Purple Roofs** (purpleroofs.com), which has several listings in the southwest.

Celebrations

Exeter Pride The queer calendar kicks off in May with one of the biggest free Pride events in the country.

Cornwall Pride A local charity runs Pride events across Cornwall throughout the year; Truro's is huge.

Totnes Pride Organised by grassroots social enterprise Proud2Be, this creative Pride event in Devon's most ethical town (p85) is held on the first Saturday of September.

The Rainbow Ball Torquay's 'most outrageous night of the year'; an annual LGBTIQ+ fundraising ball that takes place on or near World AIDS Day (1 December).

Accessible Travel

Rural areas and historic towns can present some accessibility issues, but the southwest is continually improving. Service providers in the UK are required by law to make 'reasonable adjustments' to allow persons with disabilities to use their services, and almost all do so.

RESOURCES

Tourism for All (tourismforall.org.uk) is a national charity working to improve accessibility in tourism, with a wealth of information, resources and advice on its website. Its Travel Planner has a search function to find accessible accommodation, things to do and places to eat across the UK.

Disability Rights UK (disabilityrightsuk.org) has useful factsheets and guides on its website.

MILES WITHOUT STILES

Dartmoor's **Miles Without Stiles** routes are stile-free and accessible; find a full list at *dartmoor.gov.uk*. The Cornwall tourism board (visitcornwall.com) and Exmoor National Park (exmoor-nationalpark.gov.uk) list accessible walks on their websites.

Scan this QR code for a list of accessible walks in Cornwall

Trains

Mainline trains in the UK have space for wheelchairs. **National Rail** (nationalrail.co.uk) lists accessibility information for all UK stations. Its Passenger Assist service enables you to pre-book assistance for rail journeys by phone or app.

Scan this QR code for details of National Rail's services and facilities

Railcard

The Disabled Person's Railcard (£20 per year) allows those with a disability that meets the eligibility criteria a third off rail travel for themselves and an adult companion.

Accommodation

Most hotels have at least one adapted room, although not always fully accessible. Historic buildings are harder to adapt and may have narrow hallways, uneven floors or a lack of step-free access.

Airports

Exeter airport offers Special Travel Assistance to travellers with access needs; arrange this with your airline or travel company at least 48 hours before departure. Those with hidden disabilities can obtain a lanyard from the Special Assistance Desk.

Hire a Tramper

Countryside Mobility is a nonprofit scheme in the southwest through which visitors can hire a 'tramper' (off-road mobility scooter) at an ever-growing number of locations.

BEACH DAYS

Many of the region's beaches are accessible; some have sand chairs available for hire – local tourist boards can provide details. The Wave Project offers adaptive surfing for young people with disabilities at its base in Croyde.

ADVENTURES FOR ALL

Those with accessibility issues needn't miss out on the southwest's spirit of adventure. **Calvert Trust Exmoor** is an accessible adventure centre for people with physical, learning, behavioural and sensory disabilities. Activities include climbing, canoeing and horse riding.

👨‍👩‍👧 Family Travel

Devon and Cornwall have long been firm family favourites, particularly the classic coastal resorts. There are bucketloads of safe, sandy beaches, free national parks and fun attractions to keep kids of all ages entertained. Accommodation offerings are very good for families too; there's a huge range of self-catering options, plenty of child-friendly hotels and several excellent holiday parks.

Facilities

Most tourist-focused businesses cater well for kids, especially in larger destinations, with cots and highchairs readily available. However, it pays to check before booking. Changing facilities are common but in some establishments are only in the women's toilets. Breastfeeding is allowed (by law) in all public places; a small minority may react but most will barely notice. Some pubs don't allow children in the evening.

Best Spots for Families

- **The English Riviera** Holiday parks and plenty of family-friendly attractions around a sheltered bay.
- **Newquay** An aquarium, steam trains, watersports and lifeguarded beaches. Nearby Bude, Perranporth and St Agnes are also good spots.
- **Falmouth** Safe swimming, ferry rides, the National Maritime Museum and plenty to do nearby.
- **Westward Ho!** Sandy beaches, arcades, retro vibes and a rocky pool for safe bathing.

Getting Around

On buses and trains, children under five travel free of charge, while those aged five to 15 pay a reduced fare. Purchasing National Rail's Family & Friends Railcard could save you money if you plan on frequent train travel.

Prams

In historic towns and villages, pavements can be narrow, uneven or cobbled. Similarly, older buildings may not have step-free access. Dartmoor's Miles Without Stiles and the South West Coast Path's easy-access walks provide pram-friendly hiking for families.

ROCK-POOLING

One of the best child-friendly activities in Devon and Cornwall only requires a plastic bucket! Rock-pooling is a great way to experience nature, especially for kids who don't live near a coast. Low tide is best, as more rock pools are exposed, but take care on slippery rocks and check when the tide will return. Approach slowly and avoid casting a shadow onto the pool. Carefully turn over stones to see what's hiding underneath, or gently lower a bucket into the water and bring it up for a closer look. Crabs, starfish, beadlet anemones, shrimp and small fish are all common in British rock-pools.

TOP PICKS FOR CHILDREN

- **Crealy Theme Park** (p59)
  Popular, family-friendly theme park near Exeter.
- **Paignton Zoo** (p90)
  Innovative zoo that is run by a conservation charity.
- **Dartmouth Steam Railway** (p81)
  Travel from Paignton to Dartmouth on a historic steam train.

- **Eden Project** (p157)
  Cornwall's famous indoor garden has plenty of fun, thought-provoking things for kids to enjoy.
- **National Marine Aquarium** (p72)
  Vast tanks showcasing local and exotic marine life near Plymouth's waterfront.

Nuts & Bolts

OPENING HOURS

Opening hours vary throughout the year. Many tourist-oriented businesses only operate from Easter to October.

Banks 9.30am to 4pm Monday to Friday (some also open Saturday mornings)

Shops 9am to 5.30pm Monday to Saturday, 11am to 5pm Sunday

Pubs Noon to 11pm (some till midnight or 1am on weekends)

Restaurants Lunch noon to 3pm, dinner 6pm to 9pm or 10pm

Electricity
230V/50Hz

Type G
230V/50Hz

GOOD TO KNOW

Time zone
GMT/UTC in winter; BST (British Summer Time: GMT/UTC plus 1 hour) April to October

Country code
44

Emergency number
999

Population
1,788,000

PUBLIC HOLIDAYS

There are eight bank holidays in England. Many businesses close or operate shorter Sunday hours on these days. Additional bank holidays are included for national events, such as royal weddings and funerals.

New Year's Day* 1 January

Good Friday March/April

Easter Monday March/April

Early May Bank Holiday First Monday in May

Spring Bank Holiday Last Monday in May

Summer Bank Holiday Last Monday in August

Christmas Day* 25 December

Boxing Day* 26 December

*When these bank holidays fall on a weekend, a 'substitute' weekday becomes a bank holiday, normally the following Monday.

Weights & Measures
Officially, the UK uses the metric system, though many people use imperial and metric interchangeably. Road speeds and distances are measured in miles.

Smoking
Smoking isn't allowed in any enclosed public place or on public transport.

Toilets
Public toilets are available in most tourist areas. Some charge a fee (around 20p).

STORYBOOK

Our writers delve deep into different
aspects of Devon & Cornwall's life

History

A history of Devon and
Cornwall in 15 places

Oliver Berry

p232

People

Meet the people of
Devon and Cornwall

Oliver Berry

p236

Feeling the Squeeze

Poverty, Overtourism &
Second Homes

Emily Luxton

p238

The Great Gardens
of Devon & Cornwall

Oliver Berry

p241

Cornwall & the Arts

Oliver Berry

p244

A Literary Inspiration

Emily Luxton

p246

Lanyon Quoit (p198), Penwith Moor
IAN WOOLCOCK/SHUTTERSTOCK ©

A HISTORY OF DEVON & CORNWALL IN
15 PLACES

If you've got a penchant for the past, you're in luck – the southwest of England packs an astonishing amount of history into a tiny space. Celts, Vikings, Romans, Saxons, Normans, Tudors, Victorians and many others have all left their mark on the region's architectural landscape.

AS YOU'RE WALKING along the cliffs or exploring the moors, it's worth remembering that you're also standing on some of the oldest land in the British Isles. The rocky spine that runs down the centre of Devon and Cornwall is part of the great Cornubian batholith, a seam of granite formed around 280 million years ago – long before the first dinosaurs walked the earth. Millions of years later, this very same granite mass is also what made this corner of Britain a centre of mining: alongside the granite, huge deposits of tin, copper and other metals were also formed, which for a period of about 150 years made Cornwall and Devon pretty much the wealthiest patch of real estate in the Western world. However, the mining boom collapsed in the mid-1800s, and thousands of miners from Devon and Cornwall emigrated overseas. But mining is far from the only reminder of the past here: you'll also encounter medieval abbeys, Methodist churches and mighty cathedrals, not to mention countless castles, stately homes, statues, monuments, stone circles and menhirs. In fact, the far west of Britain has borne witness to pretty much every period of Britain's history. Time travel is possible, after all.

1. Boscawen-un Stone Circle
TIME OF STONES

Nowhere in Britain has a collection of ancient monuments quite as concentrated as Cornwall. There are scores of them, scattered from the Isles of Scilly all the way to Bodmin Moor – and this is just a fraction of the original number. Boscawen-un, also known as the Nine Maidens, is perhaps the grandest of all: a great ring of 19 upright stones, with another menhir at its centre. Was it a meeting place? A temple? A site of sacrifice? We will probably never know, but there was clearly something of huge spiritual or magical significance to this corner of Cornwall.

For more on Cornwall's ancient sites, see page 182

2. Chysauster
BACK TO THE IRON AGE

The ancient past can feel impossibly distant sometimes, but at Chysauster, you really get a glimpse of how our ancestors might have lived. This 2000-year-old village dates from the Iron Age. You can see the stone foundations of several circular huts (which originally would have been thatched). These are known as 'courtyard houses', and are found only on the Land's End peninsula and the Isles of Scilly. Each has a central courtyard, with adjoining rooms for sleeping and cooking, and the huts are arranged along a village 'street'. You can almost imagine the villagers meeting for a morning gossip.

For more on Chysauster, see page 198

3. Exeter's Roman Walls
THEY CAME, THEY SAW, THEY BUILT

Roman remains are rare in Devon, and all but nonexistent in Cornwall – a reminder that the far west was a Celtic stronghold, and one of the few areas of Britain the legions never fully conquered. Exeter is an exception: in the 1st century CE, this was Isca Dumnoniorum, the site of an important Roman fort and the home base for around 5500 men of the Second Augustan Legion. Sections of the fort's original walls can still be seen, but the rest of the Roman remains have long since been buried – including a grand bathhouse, which was revealed during excavations in the 1970s under Cathedral Green.

For more on Exeter's Roman walls, see page 55

4. St Michael's Mount
HOLY ISLAND

This rocky island in Mount's Bay has been a landmark since ancient times. It's believed to have been a trading post for locally mined copper and tin as far back as the Bronze Age, and may also be the island of Ictis, a tin trading centre mentioned in the 1st century BCE by the historian Diodorus Siculus. A monastery has existed here since at least the 5th century, but the present abbey was built in the 12th century by the Benedictines (who also constructed Mont St-Michel in France). Since then it's been used as a fortress, prison and, most recently, a stately home.

For more on St Michael's Mount, see page 205

5. Tintagel Castle
KING ARTHUR'S BIRTHPLACE?

Mysteries and myths swirl around this clifftop castle, not least the one claiming that King Arthur was either born or possibly conceived, depending on which tale you read. In truth, there's no firm archaeology that links the castle with Arthur at all; there was an important Iron Age hillfort here, but the existing castle was built by Richard, Earl of Cornwall, during the 1230s. Still, it's hard not to see the romantic appeal of the place – and various nearby sites (including the waterfall at St Nectan's Glen) definitely have something of the fairy tale about them. So who knows?

For more on Tintagel, see page 178

6. Restormel Castle
HELLO NORMANS

In the centuries following the Battle of Hastings, the Normans quickly colonised much of Devon and Cornwall. This impressive circular castle (pictured below) is a quintessential example of a Norman

'shell keep', complete with an encircling moat, arrow slits, original battlements and a gatehouse which would once have housed a portcullis. Few internal rooms remain, but you can see fireplaces, garderobes and the outline of the Great Hall. It was occupied by several noble families, and twice visited by Edward the Black Prince (the first Duke of Cornwall).

For more on Restormel, see page 157

7. Exeter Cathedral
MEDIEVAL MARVEL

There's no better example of the religious devotion that defined the Middle Ages than Exeter Cathedral. It's a classic example of Anglo-Norman architecture, with two squat towers built in the Romanesque style, albeit with substantial subsequent additions (including the entire east face). The cathedral's vast, vaulted nave is the longest medieval ceiling of its kind in the world; it must have entailed the labour of scores of highly skilled artisans and been built at quite unimaginable expense – a sign of the religious devotion (and deep pockets) of its builders. Look out also for the misericords, the minstrels' gallery and the unusual astronomical clock.

For more on Exeter Cathedral, see page 53

8. Pendennis Castle
TUDOR TIMES

Perched on a headland above Falmouth, this stout castle was constructed during Henry VIII's great fortress-building endeavour in the mid-1500s. It was designed to work in tandem with its sister castle over the water in St Mawes: any unauthorised vessel entering the important harbour known as the Carrick Roads would have been shredded to matchsticks by cannon crossfire. During the Civil War, the castle was engaged in a six-month siege under the command of Captain John Arundell of Trerice, during which the garrison allegedly ate the castle's dogs, rats and horses to survive.

For more on Pendennis, see page 137

9. Lizard Lighthouse
AGE OF SAILS

Over the centuries, the treacherous rocks and reefs around the coastline of Devon and Cornwall have claimed hundreds – if not thousands – of ships. During the 18th and 19th centuries, a major programme of lighthouse building took place around the region's shores, with beacons strategically placed to serve as a warning to shipping. None was more important than that at Lizard Point: it was one of the first to be built, in 1751. Originally the light would have come from coal-fired braziers; these were later replaced by Argand lamps, and were electrified in 1874. The lighthouse has been automated since 1998.

For more on Lizard Lighthouse, see page 143

10. Royal William Yard
RULE BRITANNIA

During the late 18th and most of the 19th centuries, Britain really did rule the waves. The Royal Navy was the most powerful naval force on the planet, and underpinned the expansion of the entire British Empire. This impressive naval victualling depot in Plymouth (pictured right) was built between 1826 and 1835, and serviced the needs of vessels stationed at the vital naval base at Devonport Dockyard nearby. A massive site covering 6.5 hectares, it once contained mills, bakeries, cooperages and even a slaughterhouse – a physical reminder of the scale and complexity involved in keeping the navy fed, watered and fighting fit.

For more on the Royal William Yard, see page 72

11. Levant Mine & Beam Engine
BOOMTIME

No one travelling around the southwest can fail to notice the many mine stacks that pepper the hilltops, valleys, moors and coastline. During the 18th and 19th centuries, the southwest enjoyed its own version of the gold rush: huge deposits of tin and copper were dug out of the ground by local miners, fuelling the factories and machinery of the Industrial Revolution. The mine at Levant is home to a working Cornish beam engine: a highly efficient, steam-powered engine used to pump water from mines, which was initially developed by the Cornish engineer Richard Trevithick, born near Redruth.

For more on Cornish mining, see page 199

12. PK Porthcurno
COME IN, CORNWALL

A remote cove in the far west of Cornwall might seem like an improbable spot for an epoch-changing moment in the history of telecommunications – but fact is always stranger than fiction. Back in 1870, the first telegraph cable connecting Britain to India came ashore at Porthcurno. For the first time, Britain could send messages at high speed to the far reaches of the Empire – an early step towards our modern interconnected world. The old telegraph station is now a fascinating museum, where you can also find out about the vital role it played in maintaining Allied communications during WWII.

For more on the PK Porthcurno, see page 202

13. Royal Albert Bridge
THE RAILWAY IS COMING

For centuries, the far southwest had effectively been cut off from the rest of Britain by the River Tamar, but the building of this monumental bridge in 1859 made it possible, for the first time, to travel to Cornwall by rail – opening up new markets for the county's farms, fisheries and heavy industries, and laying the foundations for the great tourism boom of the late 19th century and beyond. The bridge was designed by Isambard Kingdom Brunel, the great British engineer and mastermind of the Great Western Railway.

For more on the Tamar Valley, see page 78

14. Castle Drogo
EDWARDIAN ECCENTRICITY

This bizarre architectural fantasy was dreamt up by the wealthy merchant Julius Drewe (owner of the Home and Colonial Stores), who in the early 1900s decided he wanted to build his very own castle on the edge of Dartmoor. He commissioned the renowned architect Edwin Lutyens to turn his dream into reality. The first stone was laid in 1911, but the castle wasn't completed until 1930; Julius died just a year later. Though beset by architectural problems, Drogo has the distinction of being the last castle to be built in England – and serves as a reminder that mega-rich men with madcap ideas are definitely not solely a 21st-century phenomenon.

For more on Castle Drogo, see page 105

15. Eden Project
TO THE FUTURE AND BEYOND

When it comes to marvellous modern architecture, there really is nowhere in the southwest (or anywhere in Britain, for that matter) that makes quite as big an impression as the Eden Project. These gigantic, bubble-shaped biomes were built at the bottom of an old Cornish clay pit around the beginning of the millennium, and house exotic plants collected from all around the world. They've become a sign of Cornwall's post-industrial renaissance, and a beacon of hope in a world facing the threats of deforestation, biodiversity loss and climate change.

For more on the Eden Project, see page 157

MEET THE PEOPLE OF DEVON & CORNWALL

They might share a border, but Devon and Cornwall definitely aren't the same place – and don't make the mistake of thinking they are. OLIVER BERRY introduces his people.

DESPITE THE IMPRESSION you'll get from Instagram and the glossy tourist brochures, the southwest isn't actually a place where everyone pops out for a quick surf on their lunch break before jumping in their camper van for a sea-shanty singalong down the local boozer.

Sure, there's no doubt that life down west is lived at a more leisurely pace than in many other parts of Britain. There's still a strong sense of community, especially in the more rural corners, which are often bound together by a shared tradition and history stretching back centuries. The coast and countryside prompt a more laid-back approach to life, and a love of the outdoors (whether a weekend ramble, a wild swim or a winter surf) is a pretty universal passion.

For many people, Devon and Cornwall are places of escape, and increasingly, that doesn't just mean during the summer holidays. Every year, thousands more people arrive here in search of a new life, and that can be deeply complicated in an area where wages, job prospects and public services languish far below the national average. Like other popular tourist areas, Devon and Cornwall are grappling with issues to which there's no easy answer: spiralling house prices, perennially low wages and a tsunami-like wave of second homes and holiday lets, all of which pose profound problems for local people (and their kids)

POPULATION BOOM

Between 2011 and 2021, the population of Cornwall grew by a bumper 7.1%, but east Devon's has risen by even more: an astonishing 13.8%.

looking to build a life here. Many people now find themselves hopelessly priced out of the places where they grew up, and that's creating a growing sense of unease as it divides families, breaks up communities and causes the occasional friction between 'locals' and 'incomers'.

So it's maybe not surprising to see growing calls for the region to have more control over its own destiny. Cornwall has a political party devoted to promoting the cause, Mebyon Kernow (Sons of Cornwall), and there's now growing momentum behind the campaign for increased devolution to allow Devon and Cornwall to take more control of its own affairs. There's also a growing revival of the Cornish language, Kernewek – an ancient tongue related to other Celtic languages such as Breton and Gaelic. It's now taught in many Cornish schools, and you'll see Kernewek on many street signs these days. You'll probably find many people know at least a few words (even if it's only *Dydh da!*).

There's always been a bit of friendly rivalry between the two sides of the Tamar. You'll gain no friends by blithely assuming they're the same place: think close cousins, not identical twins. Proposals to create a cross-county political constituency a few years back met with howls of protest, and the plans were promptly shelved. And don't even get started on the subject of the proper way to eat a cream tea.

I LOVE CORNWALL, BUT IT'S COMPLICATED

I've lived my whole life in Cornwall, and it's changed a lot since I was small. Growing up, I remember Cornish accents were so common I never really noticed them – but now, hearing one comes as a bit of a surprise. I miss the music of those Cornish voices of my childhood sometimes. When I went away to university 20 years ago, the beaches were empty save for two months in the summer. Now they're pretty packed no matter the time of year. Like many, I have complicated feelings about the changes: we've gained amazing things like the Eden Project and the National Maritime Museum, but I now have no chance of affording a house in the place where I grew up. On this subject, I'd recommend delving into the excellent *Homesick: Why I Live In A Shed* by Catrina Davies, *The Reason Why* podcast by Seamas Carey and the film *Bait* by Mark Jenkin.

FEELING THE SQUEEZE: POVERTY, OVERTOURISM & SECOND HOMES

How Devon and Cornwall get at once too much attention and too little. By Emily Luxton.

VISITING AT THE height of summer, when the beaches are full and hotels rammed to the rafters, it's hard to imagine that Devon and Cornwall are among the UK's poorest counties, with many locals earning below the living wage (a wage rate based on the cost of living in the UK).

In 2018, the European Union found that Cornwall was the second poorest region in northern Europe. Average incomes in Cornwall and large parts of Devon still fall well below UK averages, and some neighbourhoods are among the most deprived in England.

All this may seem surprising. But the southwest's thriving tourism industry is a double-edged sword: it brings an econo mic boost, but also overcrowding, soaring property prices and the struggles of seasonal employment.

Overtourism & Undertourism

There are two Devons and two Cornwalls in the southwest. Tourists see lively beach towns, busy hotels and trendy eateries. In winter, those beach towns are empty; many hotels and other businesses close completely from October to March.

Tourism directly or indirectly accounts for roughly 10% of all employment in Devon and 20% in Cornwall. Many of these workers are only employed for around 60% of the year. This 'gig' economy, along with wages around 18% lower than average (in Cornwall), are often cited as causes for the region's poverty issues.

In peak season, tourism spikes bring other problems. While good for the economy, summer crowds are bad for almost everything else. Price hikes drive up everyday costs like car parking for locals. Traffic congestion is a constant issue, impacting both communities and the environment. Busy beaches, litter and crowded beauty spots are ongoing problems, but many parts of Devon and Cornwall simply wouldn't survive without tourism.

Brexit, Covid-19 & the Cost of Living

Devon and Cornwall voted in favour of leaving the EU by a large margin in 2016. Before the vote, Cornwall had actively campaigned for – and received –

238

considerable funding from the EU. Both counties had received farming subsidies, environmental grants and funding for things like the Eden Project. Cornwall was set to receive £100 million a year in funding for seven years from the EU. In early 2022, the UK government announced a one-off budget of £132 million to replace it, alongside funding for various regions in Devon and other parts of the UK. Local campaigners say Cornwall will be poorer as a result.

Many explanations have been suggested as to why counties that gained most from the EU voted to leave it. The southwest's ongoing poverty, frustration with conventional politics and strong regional identity are all factors, but the Brexit question is a complicated issue throughout the UK.

An interesting side effect of the Covid-19 pandemic has been a dramatic rise in domestic tourism in Britain, with popular spots across the southwest often overrun with visitors. Prices have soared, giving a much-needed boost to businesses that survived the lockdowns, but the environmental and societal issues of overtourism in hotspots like Devon and Cornwall have became more visible than ever.

The uncertainty and economic difficulties created by both Brexit and Covid-19 are at least partly to blame for the 'cost-of-living crisis' that followed. At the time of writing, energy bills and other living costs are still rising, pushing more people than ever before into poverty, particularly in poorer regions like Cornwall. A potential knock-on effect could see less money spent on leisure and tourism over the coming years, further impacting Devon and Cornwall's economies.

FROM TRAVELLING OUTSIDE THE PEAK SEASONS TO FREQUENTING INDEPENDENT, LOCALLY RUN BUSINESSES, RESPONSIBLE TRAVELLERS CAN MAKE A DIFFERENCE.

Second Homes, Holiday Lets & House Prices

In March 2022, the seaside village of St Agnes made the news when a protest group graffitied several pretty, whitewashed and – crucially for this story – empty cottages. 'Second homeowners, give something back', demanded the painted slogans, 'rent or sell your empty houses to local people at a fair price'.

Devon and Cornwall are beautiful places, and many visitors dream of year-round access to that beauty. For years, the demand for second homes – along with wealthy investors buying up properties for short-term holiday lets – has steadily driven property prices up. At the time of writing, the average house price in both counties was over 10 times the average wage in Devon and Cornwall. This is officially one of the UK's least affordable areas for first-time buyers, and it's easy to see why locals are becoming increasingly frustrated.

In Cornwall, where the housing crisis is getting continually worse, there are over 23,000 second homes and holiday lets: almost exactly the same number as are currently on the housing register. In some areas of Devon, almost half of properties are second homes; in Salcombe, the figure is nearly 60%.

Airbnb and similar sites have long been a controversial topic. At their best, they enable local homeowners to supplement their income by renting out a room or two. On the darker side, the popularity of these sites attracts property investors – often at the expense of locals. Anecdotal evidence suggests tenants are being evicted from rental properties because landlords can make more money from short-term holiday lets.

There have been improvements in recent years. Some towns, including St Ives and Salcombe, have banned the selling of new-build properties as second homes. In January 2022, the UK government announced plans to close a legal loophole that had previously allowed second homeowners to avoid paying any business rates or council tax on their properties – the result of a two-year campaign fought by Devon's South Hams District Council.

How Can Tourists Help?

There are no easy solutions to these problems. Tourists continue to love Devon and Cornwall, and the region continues to depend on tourism. On the positive side, there are various ways visitors can help, or at least avoid making things worse.

From travelling outside the peak seasons when possible to frequenting independent, locally run businesses, ensuring their money goes directly into the local economy, responsible travellers can make a difference. Try to seek out holiday rentals that don't take homes away from locals, use public transport instead of driving when possible, and help combat overtourism by visiting places that don't usually see as many visitors. The southwest's less explored areas have much to entice.

THE GREAT GARDENS OF DEVON & CORNWALL

Plucky plant hunters, alien blooms, madcap aristocrats: who said gardens were boring? By Oliver Berry

EVERY SPRING, IN a corner of the Lost Gardens of Heligan known as Flora's Green, one of Britain's biggest shrubs bursts into bloom.

It's a giant rhododendron bush measuring nearly 30m across: a monster, bigger than a couple of double-decker buses parked end to end. Along with 350 others, it forms part of an internationally renowned rhododendron collection that's the envy of botanists and plant experts all around the world.

This is rather peculiar, when you stop and think about it – because the rhododendron isn't a native shrub of the British Isles. Far from it, in fact. Its natural home is more than 7000 miles away, in the foothills of the Himalayas – a very long way from Cornwall, indeed. So just how did this shrub end up so far from home? Who brought it here? And why in the name of Monty Don has it grown to such a Brobdingnagian size?

Mild Climes

To answer that, we first need to think about the weather. The southwest, like the rest of Britain, benefits from a unique meteorological phenomenon known as the Gulf Stream. This invisible ocean current funnels warm, temperate water and air from across the Atlantic, and wafts it around Britain like a planet-sized greenhouse sprinkler. It raises the temperature across the British Isles by around 3.4°C, but its effects are most pronounced in the southwest.

Year-round, Devon and Cornwall stay notably milder, damper and more humid than the rest of Britain. When the Gulf Stream combines with the steep, sheltered valleys that pockmark the southwest's coastline, it creates unique microclimates, allowing exotic plants to flourish here that wouldn't stand a chance of survival elsewhere: tropical palms, jungle-sized gunnera, African lilies, giant sequoias, even the odd banana tree. But that doesn't answer the question of how these outlandish plants ended up here in the first place.

British Adventurers

For that, we need to travel back to the age of exploration. During the 16th and 17th centuries, British adventurers returned from the far corners of the globe, bringing back all kinds of previously unknown plants, fruits, trees, nuts and seeds. They soon discovered that many of these exotic plants grew more vigorously in the sheltered valleys of Devon and Cornwall than pretty much anywhere else. As mining and maritime trade boomed during the 17th and 18th centuries, the southwest's aristocratic families – noble names like the Rashleighs, Vyvyans, Foxes, Boscawens, Edgcumbes, Eliots and St Aubyns – grew fabulously wealthy and developed a taste for showy landscaping, lavishing huge sums on developing their estates as a means to show off their power, taste and prestige. The great garden boom was taking root.

The trend reached its zenith during the Victorian era. As Britain's empire flourished, intrepid plant hunters were commissioned to discover ever more exotic species. This was the heyday of men such as Frank Kingdon-Ward, Sir Joseph Hooker, EH Wilson and the Lobb Brothers (born near Wadebridge), who braved treacherous seas and tropical diseases to discover new species with which to delight their benefactors. There was a touch of Indiana Jones about these plant hunters, but many of them were also serious scientists, natural historians and botanists, with an insatiable passion for scientific discovery and an abiding fascination for the natural world.

> WHEN THE GULF STREAM MEETS THE SOUTHWEST'S COASTLINE, UNIQUE MICRO-CLIMATES ARE CREATED, ALLOWING EXOTIC SPECIES TO FLOURISH HERE THAT WOULDN'T STAND A CHANCE OF SURVIVAL ELSEWHERE.

Exotic Plantings

Ports like Plymouth, Dartmouth and Falmouth, home of the empire-spanning Packet Service, were often the first places to receive these exotic new arrivals, and the region's horticulturalists took full advantage. Azaleas from Japan, rhododendrons, magnolias and camellias from the Himalayas, tree ferns from New Zealand and Australia, North American pines and sequoias, Canadian maples, South American monkey puzzles – all of these found their way into the region's gardens, and were soon growing with abandon. Jungle valleys, arboretums, grottoes, tropical hothouses, lakes and rockeries were created so that wealthy landowners could show off their latest acquisitions.

The great gardens of Devon and Cornwall are, essentially, the end result of all this horticultural exhibitionism. One famous story tells how Charles Fox, the creator of Trebah Garden near Falmouth, instructed his head gardener to construct scaffolds so that he could envision the final height of each tree, triangulating its position using a telescope from an attic window while barking out his orders via megaphone. Now that's perfectionism.

Even the Isles of Scilly weren't immune to the garden mania. When Augustus Smith arrived as Lord Proprietor of the islands in 1834, he set about restoring the ruined abbey and transforming a little corner of the rugged, breezy island of Tresco into his own miniature version of the Garden of Eden. Today, the Tresco Abbey Garden is one of the southwest's great garden wonders: on this tiny island marooned in the Atlantic, you can admire plants from Chile, California, South Africa, Australia, Mexico, New Zealand, Nepal, India, the Canary Islands and goodness knows where else.

You don't even have to visit one of the region's landmark gardens to see the effects of the great plant-hunting craze. Take the humble Monterey pine, a tree so commonplace most people never give it a second glance. Planted liberally as a windbreak or shelter tree, twisted into strange shapes by winter gales, it's such an unremarkable sight that most people simply assume it's native to the UK. In fact, the Monterey pine was brought back from California in 1833 by the famous tree hunter David Douglas, and planted widely across Cornwall due to its hardiness and tolerance of salty climes. The rest is horticultural history – and today the southwest's landscape would look entirely different without it.

Still a Garden Innovator

These days, the region remains a hotbed of horticultural innovation. From the research gardens at RHS Rosemoor to the imaginative sculpture gardens of Broomhill and Tremenheere and the futuristic greenhouses of the Eden Project, Devon and Cornwall are still a paradise for plant lovers. Our advice? Breathe deep, smell the flowers and visit as many gardens as you possibly can.

243

CORNWALL & THE ARTS

Whether it's the wild landscape or the quality of light, there's something special about Cornwall for artists. By Oliver Berry

HERE'S A STAT for you: it's estimated that there's a higher concentration of artists currently working in Cornwall than anywhere else in the UK (excluding London, of course). Painters, potters, sculptors, collagists, filmmakers, photographers, even landscape artists and sand painters: Cornwall is a hotbed of creativity and craft, and has been for well over a century. But what is it that draws artists to the far west?

Cornwall's art scene can trace its roots back to the mid-1800s. Among the earliest artists to make a pilgrimage to Cornwall was JMW Turner, who secured a commission to tour the southwest in 1811 to produce watercolours for a series of engravings entitled *Picturesque Views on the Southern Coast of England*. But it was the extension of the Great Western Railway west of the Tamar in 1877 that really put the region on the artistic map. For the first time, artists enjoyed easy access to Cornwall's scenery and landscapes, and they arrived in ever-increasing numbers as the century wore to its close.

Cornwall's Artist Colonies

A loose group of artists settled around the fishing port of Newlyn in the early 1880s, spearheaded by Birmingham-born Walter Langley, Dubliner Stanhope Forbes and Lincolnshire artist Frank Bramley. Following in the footsteps of French plein-air painters, especially the Barbizon School, the Newlyn artists set out to depict the everyday reality of ordinary lives in a naturalistic way. The Newlyn School, as they became known, was particularly fascinated by Newlyn's fishermen, and documented their lives in closely observed detail. Some depicted everyday tasks as net repair, sail rigging or fish sales on the quayside; others explored the natural drama and pathos of the fishermen's lot: poverty, hardship, storms and the ever-present danger of shipwrecks.

Half a century later, an art movement of a very different kind hit St Ives, kicking powerfully against the figurative concerns and representational style of its predecessors. In the 1940s and 1950s, St Ives became a centre of the avant-garde, with experimental artists and abstract sculptors exploring a very different side of Cornwall: one that was inspired more by shape, light, texture and form than figurative reality.

Among them was Barbara Hepworth, the groundbreaking sculptor who moved to St Ives in 1939 with her husband, painter Ben Nicholson. Over the next 30 years, Hepworth became entranced by her adopted home, using stone, metal and sinuous shapes to echo the rugged Cornish landscape, its many industrial remains and mysterious ancient monuments. St Ives soon welcomed another new wave of young artists – names like Wilhelmina Barns-Graham, Terry Frost, Patrick Heron, Roger Hilton and Peter Lanyon – who helped consolidate the town's position as a hub of artistic risk-taking throughout the 1950s and 1960s.

Kurt Jackson is perhaps Cornwall's best-known contemporary artist. Born in Dorset in 1961, he has been based near St Just since the mid-1980s, and is known for his large-scale, expressive landscapes: big, bold canvases packed with mood and emotion, often driven by a powerfully ecological or environmental theme. He has recently opened his own exhibition space, the Jackson Foundation Gallery, in St Just – the latest in a line-up of interesting galleries and studios dotted around the county, including Kestle Barton on the Lizard, CAST in Helston, Krowji in Redruth and, of course, the award-winning Tate St Ives.

Devon's Experimental Hub

It's curious that Devon never really had its own artistic 'movements' to match those in Cornwall. There are certainly many talented artists based here – some have become well known, including Beryl Cook, whose saucy, larger-than-life figures reflected her life in working-class Plymouth, and Robert Lenkiewicz, whose dramatic portraits have an air of Renaissance Rembrandt about them. The best-known centre for the arts in Devon was Dartington College of Arts,

which became a hub for experimental art, design and theatre between 1961 and 2010. Ilfracombe has a growing art scene thanks to its association with Damien Hirst, whose controversial *Verity* statue stands beside the quayside. Another striking statue, *Messenger,* by Cornish-born Joseph Hillier, appeared outside Theatre Royal Plymouth in 2019; at 7m high, it's the UK's largest cast bronze statue.

Theatre, Film & Creative Arts

It's not just visual arts where the southwest excels. For 30 years, Cornwall's beloved theatre company, Kneehigh, delighted audiences around the world with an anarchic style, mischievous wit and playful imagination that encapsulated much about its Cornish homeland. Sadly, the company announced its final curtain call in 2022, but its spirit lives on in Wildworks, founded by the late Bill Mitchell, who cut his theatrical teeth with Kneehigh and pioneered its reputation for large-scale landscape-based theatre. Theatre Royal Plymouth, Exeter Northcott Theatre and Truro's Hall for Cornwall also stage major productions and commission new theatre work.

More recently, Cornwall's film industry has been boosted by the sleeper success of *Bait*, an experimental, hand-processed, black-and-white film made with a clock-work camera by Newlyn-based filmmaker Mark Jenkin. Its tale of a disenfranchised fisherman living in a small Cornish town blighted by loss, gentrification and the scourge of second homes captured the national zeitgeist upon release in 2019; Jenkin won a BAFTA for it. His follow-up is an 'ecosophical horror' set on an isolated Cornish island: the title, *Enys Men*, means 'stone island' in Cornish.

Meanwhile, educating the next generation of artists is vital for the future. Falmouth University is a leading centre for the creative arts; it now incorporates the Falmouth School of Art, founded in 1902, as well as the renowned Dartington College of Arts. Here, young painters get to rub shoulders with sculptors, designers, animators, filmmakers, graphic artists, theatre-makers and even video-game designers – a bubbling cauldron of creativity which can only bode well for the county's artistic future.

A LITERARY INSPIRATION

Exploring the landscapes and legends that inspired Devon and Cornwall's rich literary heritage. By Emily Luxton

DEVON AND CORNWALL'S landscapes have inspired countless writers and poets. DH Lawrence wrote of Cornwall's 'great, black, jutting cliffs', John Betjeman of its 'golden and unpeopled bays', and Thomas Hardy of 'that wild weird western shore'. Arthur Conan Doyle captured Dartmoor's 'grim charm', and Henry Williamson described Exmoor as the 'high country of the winds'. Virginia Woolf spoke of being 'incredibly and incurably romantic about Cornwall' and Alice Oswald's evocative descriptions of 'a bowl of the moor where echoes can't get out' in *Dart* (2002) speak of her deep love for Devon's nature.

So rich is the region's artistic heritage that it's hard to find a location without some literary connection. South Devon is Agatha Christie country: the Torquay-born crime writer is inescapable there, just as Devon itself is inescapable in her lengthy portfolio. But the rest of the county has also had its share of literary inspiration. Henry Williamson's beloved children's book *Tarka the Otter* (1927) was based

around the Taw and Torridge rivers; his prose is infused with north Devon's nature and landscapes. Dartmoor provided the bleakly beautiful setting for Michael Morpurgo's famous novel *War Horse* (1982), Richard Blackmore's 17th-century epic *Lorna Doone* (1869) is based in Exmoor, and poet laureate Ted Hughes captured north Devon and Dartmoor, his 'land of totems', in numerous poems.

Cornwall is captured in the writings of another poet laureate, John Betjeman, who fell for the county on childhood holidays, and those of Launceston-born Charles Causley. Winston Graham's *Poldark* series (1945–2002), a sprawling family drama set in Georgian Cornwall, was recently repopularised by a 2015 TV adaptation. Fowey-based Daphne du Maurier, best known for dramatic, romantic novels like *Rebecca* (1938), used her beloved Cornwall almost as an additional character. The landscapes around Fowey-inspired Kenneth Grahame's *Wind in the Willows* (1908), while the wild Scilly Isles provided inspiration for many of Morpurgo's novels, including *Why the Whales Came* (1985).

The Impact of Local Legends

The southwest's rich folklore and evocative legends also lend themselves to literary inspiration. Arthur Conan Doyle set his most famous Sherlock Holmes story, *The Hound of the Baskervilles* (1902), on Dartmoor after hearing a local legend of demonic hounds that haunt the moors. Doyle stayed at Princetown while writing the novel, and it's widely believed that Grimpen Mire was based on Fox Tor Mire.

A much older local legend – that of King Arthur – has been passed down through literature so much over the centuries that it's impossible to separate fact from fiction. The famous story of a young boy who pulled a sword from a stone (or a lake, depending which version you read) and became king has become intrinsically tied to the southwest. Never mind that the original version of the legend might have been Welsh, or that many suspect the real Arthur was a 5th-century Romano-British warlord nicknamed Artos (Celtic for 'bear') – when it comes to Arthur, the English refuse to let the truth get in the way of a good story.

Arthur as we know him today, the Arthur of magical swords and Merlin, is largely based on a book written several hundred years after he supposedly lived. Geoffrey of Monmouth's *History of the Kings of Britain* (1136) linked Arthur to several locations in southwest England, most famously Tintagel. Monmouth claimed his work was based on an ancient text he alone could translate; modern historians believe his version of Arthur was an amalgamation of several different stories and folklore. Either way, the Arthurian legend continues to permeate the landscape.

Daphne du Maurier's Cornwall

Cornwall's history, both real and mythical, continues to inspire. Daphne du Maurier holidayed in Cornwall from a young age and later moved to Fowey. The author's love

for her adopted home was fierce, and real-life Cornish locations form a rich backdrop for her fiction.

'Those who desire to understand the Cornish, and their country, must use their imagination and travel back in time', wrote du Maurier in *Vanishing Cornwall* (1967), her part history, part love letter to the county. That is precisely what du Maurier did in her fiction, which was very often period pieces set in Cornwall, like the 17th-century swashbuckling romance of *Frenchman's Creek* (1941). One of her best works, *Jamaica Inn* (1936) – a darkly Gothic tale of 19th-century wreckers – is set in a very real 18th-century inn which still stands on Bodmin, where 'mile upon mile of bleak moorland' create the perfect atmosphere for the novel's drama.

Devon & the Queen of Crime

Around the same time as du Maurier was publishing Cornwall-based romances, across the Tamar Agatha Christie was busy becoming the world's most prolific crime-fiction writer. Christie lived on the south Devon coast for most of her life, peppering her novels with real-life locations.

Brixham's Elberry Cove appears in the *ABC Murders* (1936), and Torquay's Imperial Hotel featured in both *Peril at End House* (1932) and Miss Marple's final case, *Sleeping Murder* (1976). And *Then There Were None* (1939), arguably Christie's best work and the world's best-selling crime novel, is set on tiny, tidal Burgh Island. It is the original version of an oft-copied trope: 10 strangers are invited to the island by an anonymous host, where one by one they meet gruesome deaths.

Walk These Words

Perhaps what makes the literary scene in Devon and Cornwall so special is how tangible the landscapes are. Many of the locations have changed little since these authors first described them. Du Maurier's Bodmin Moor is still as bleak, Doyle's Dartmoor still grimly charming. Burgh Island, Christie's 'Soldier Island', still feels like 'a world of its own'. In the southwest, literature feels alive.

247

INDEX

Map Pages **000**

Map Pages **000**

Tamar Valley Area of Outstanding
  Natural Beauty 76, 77
Tarr Steps 117
Tavistock 77, 113